MW00529074

Once I started reading the book 1 [...] hard to put down. It should be r [...] ment agencies, lawmakers, prosecutors anu every[...] justice, and interested in the history of this state, which in the times of which Juliet has written, was (perhaps deservedly) referred to by some as "The Wild West".

Malcolm McCusker AC CVO QC
Governor of WA 2011-2014

This is a shocking book. As the cover proclaims, it is all about what is alleged to be a "state sanctioned murder". Perhaps we might expect such allegations to involve tales of intrigue or dirty dealings in some obscure part of a foreign country many years ago. Instead, it involves the relatively recent activities of the police and associated agencies in Perth, Western Australia in the 1970s.

The author has provided a valuable service to all of us who live in Australia by having held as it were a mirror up to nature, and allowed us to see an important aspect of our society for what it is. It is a great achievement on her part—and a terrible disgrace on the part of others.

Dr Robert Moles LLB (Honours)
Author and Retired Associate Professor of Law – Adelaide University

Dirty Girl challenges the notion that a justice system can function with the policy of 'containing' certain crimes as opposed to seeking eradication or legalization. The policy of containment leads to inconsistent application of the law, favoritism, corruption, and cover-ups. And, in the case of Shirley Finn, likely resulted in her death.

Corruption can only end when individuals within the law enforcement community stand up against the system when it fails to serve the community.

There is much to learn from *Dirty Girl*. Juliet Wills should be congratulated for spending years researching and writing this important book.

Professor Justin Brooks
Director, California Innocence Project
California Western School of Law, San Diego, CA

Juliet Wills has choppered into crocodile breeding grounds, been chased by rioting armed gangs, and jumped from a civilian plane with the 13th load at 13,000 feet on Friday the 13th. She has also pursued the story of brothel madam Shirley Finn's murder with fearless obstinacy.

Born in Sydney, Juliet has lived and worked throughout Australia. She has been awarded for her Excellence in Television Journalism, written for major newspapers, and lectured in broadcast journalism at two universities.

The mother of three lives in Perth and now works in real estate. Her first book, *The Diamond Dakota*, was published by Allen and Unwin in 2006.

DIRTY
GIRL

· THE · STATE · SANCTIONED · MURDER ·
· OF · BROTHEL · MADAM · SHIRLEY FINN ·

FONTAINE
PRESS

JULIET WILLS

Copyright © Juliet Wills, 2017
www.finnmurder.com

ISBN: 978-0-9924658-3-4

Published by Fontaine Press
P.O. Box 948, Fremantle
Western Australia 6959
www.fontainepress.com

Cataloguing-in-Publication data is available from the National Library of Australia

For Bridget

Contents

The summer's flower is to the summer sweet,

Though to itself it only live and die,

But if that flower with base infection meet,

The basest weed out-braves his dignity;

For sweetest things turn sourest by their deeds;

Lilies that fester smell far worse than weeds.

— William Shakespeare

Foreword

Western Australian writer Dorothy Hewitt once described the palpable sense of corruption she experienced in both Sydney and Perth. Writing in 1982, she said the glitzy materialism and conspicuous consumption linked with vice and organised crime in Sydney was "vulgar, articulate, and unashamed"; whereas in Perth, "the worm in the bud is secretive."

It is this secretiveness that most observant followers of Western Australian cultural life consider the decisive factor behind Shirley Finn's murder in 1975, and which forms the subject of *Dirty Girl*.

I first met Juliet Wills in 2008 while researching Shirley Finn's murder. This project began for me in 1998 when I met and became friends with Shirley Finn's youngest son, Shane. At the time, I was teaching a poetry class in Casuarina Prison, and Shane shared with me documents given to him by a sympathetic policeman. He encouraged me to write about his mother's murder.

The enquiries I made and the people I met informed the three crime novels I've now written—using crime fiction entertainment as a vehicle to explore the stories, characters and secrets of my hometown.

Initially, I had little idea what I was in for. However, the climate of fear and suspicion and the real threats of reprisal for writing about the murder were soon made clear. I mention this background only to express my great admiration for Juliet Wills and the evidence she has gathered, at great personal cost, here within the pages of *Dirty Girl*.

The overall picture of policing practices, and their connection to Shirley Finn's murder, is as damning as it is exhaustive and detailed. Her quiet determination and investigative skills, so apparent at my first and subsequent meetings with Juliet, are applied here in the best kind of journalism.

Juliet shines a light into the darkest corners, bringing clarity and vivid expression to the characters, the stories and the secrets that have hitherto remained unspoken, and so unknown. There is much that will surprise readers and much that gives flesh and voice to what was once only speculation, rumour and innuendo.

Dirty Girl is not only an exposé of this terrible and cruel unsolved murder, and its devastating effects on a family, and a community. It is a work of social history, covering a period and a stratum of society rarely examined in print. Much is new in this publication, including descriptions of close links between Sydney's organised crime and corrupt policing, and Perth's police service and criminal underworld.

We are presented with the statements of new witnesses and new evidence. The author's careful and structured application of these testimonies creates a damning timeline of events—involving those from the lowest level on the street to the highest office in the state.

This book is a highly readable, tough-minded and clear-sighted explanation of why it became necessary for vested interests to kill Shirley Finn, and then to cover up her murder, both at that time and well into the future. However, *Dirty Girl* is also a moving personal story—the story of the woman and mother behind the public persona, of her children, and of the damage done by loss and grief to each of their lives.

Dirty Girl is the result of over two decades of patient and often unnerving research. It is a great testament to the unwavering fight for justice by both Bridget, Shirley Finn's last surviving child, and the author, Juliet Wills. *Dirty Girl* deserves to be widely read and to endure as an important historical document that reveals the secrets and lies of powerful interests, criminal and political.

David Whish-Wilson, 21/02/17

PUBLISHERS NOTE
There are many characters and threads in this story. If you want a little help keeping track of *Who's Who*, please flip to the back of the book for a detailed description of the main players.

Introduction

The Kwinana Freeway runs alongside the Canning and Swan Rivers for almost ten kilometres before the city of Perth comes into view. The six-lane freeway is the main path for commuters heading to and from work. As the city comes into view, most eyes are drawn to either the broad expanse of the Swan River dotted with yachts, or to the city skyline ahead. But I always look to the right, towards the shrubs and trees on the side of the Royal Perth Golf Club.

Men and women tee off from the seventh fairway on manicured greens, mostly unaware of the cold calculated murder that took place just metres away, more than thirty years ago.

My mind pours through the statements of the many witnesses who drove past on the busy motorway on 22 June 1975. I try to work out the spot where it happened.

Four shots—point blank range. The small frame of a petite woman slumps behind the wheel of her luxury limited edition car. A trickle of blood runs down the side of her face from beside her ear, past her large hooped earring. Her styled, short blonde hair is stained red with blood.

She's just thirty-three years old, a mother of three. The shimmer of her glittering ball gown glistens through the window. Satin bell sleeves and cinnamon-coloured pleats fan out from just below her breasts over the leather seats to the floor below. Were it not for the revealing low cut, the design was the type you might find on a church choral singer; but Shirley Finn was no choral singer.

She was one of two police-protected brothel madams running an enormously successful criminal enterprise in Perth in the early 1970s. When police decided to organise crime by greenlighting certain criminal groups, it must have seemed like a good idea. They even coined a cute phrase to justify the illegal policy called 'containment' and sung its praises.

There were clear financial benefits to all parties in on the deal as long as it wasn't exposed. Gambling, prostitution, drugs, robberies, gold smuggling—if the police could shut down the opposition the protected businesses could thrive, and favours and benefits could be readily called in by those who offered the protection. Political friends were necessary for the scheme to succeed.

Did Shirley nearly unravel it all?

The day the news of the murder broke, the politicians that knew Shirley Finn must have breathed a collective sigh of relief, especially the man who would be Premier. Her diaries must have been a cause for concern. Conveniently they seemed to have disappeared.

Who sat next to her in the front seat and who held the gun to her head from behind? Who was in the three cars spotted near the crime scene; a white van, a large black sedan and a small green car? How wide was the net that closed in around her that night?

I know that I have more than likely sat face to face with her killer or killers, or at least those that conspired to have her shot. Dark secrets they prefer to remain buried. My mind sifts through the faces, and the words they spoke, and I try to sort out the lies from the truths and the available evidence.

I think of the families of police officers driven to drink and madness trying to evaluate who among them was capable of such a callous and brazen crime. From the commissioner at the time and all the way down, almost everyone I interviewed seemed to accept a police officer was, at the very least, involved. They just differed on which one.

Further up the Freeway, past the city that glistens by the Swan River, I pass the old Home of the Good Shepherd overlooking Lake Monger. What happened inside those walls? The heritage building now houses the Catholic Education Office. I picture the young girls working away in the laundries, sent there to bleach their souls. Dirty girls, clean sheets. Shirley's symbolic cleansing would cement her view of herself and help set her on a path that would ultimately lead to her execution.

Then I drive on. I wonder if I'm mad, but until the case is solved, I won't be able to pass by without asking: who killed Shirley Finn?

1

Goldfinger

The story is still dangerous. You will be stopped.
People will stop you.

— Goldfinger

When my youngest son confidently strode through the pre-primary doors on his first day of school, already laughing and joking with friends he had met through his siblings, we had both reached a milestone. After eight years of nursing babies, playgroups, casseroles, reading groups and Kinder-gym, his life, like mine was entering a new phase. I had enjoyed nurturing my three young children and only occasionally missed the excitement of the television news world that I had left behind with the birth of my eldest son. Interstate moves and my husband's long hours didn't allow for us both to pursue careers despite the hit to the family budget.

I was an experienced television journalist, having worked for all major commercial television networks before I had children. However, over the years my confidence had slipped away and, having moved twice, I had lost all contacts in the industry. Not to mention that I was fast approaching forty, and in an industry like television, age is not a virtue.

I felt like a kid straight out of university as I rang around the television stations, hoping to sell my credentials. The ABC told me to send in my resume, Channels Ten and Nine said not at the moment, but Channel Seven, the top rating news show in Perth at the time, invited me for an interview.

I had been living in jeans and tracksuits, and I couldn't wait for the chance to get dressed up again. I looked in the wardrobe at the faded, shoulder-padded suits that I hadn't been able to throw out, confident that they would one day come in handy again. I pondered the vagaries of fashion; that something that can look so 'in', so hip, so 'it' one year, can seem so drab and tedious another. Despite my misgivings, I succumbed to the latest fashion trend and purchased a smart new long-line grey jacket and pants (no shoulder pads) with a dusty pink blouse. The hairdresser told me that every client whose hair she had styled recently for a job interview had been successful.

As I walked into the throng of the Channel Seven television newsroom, I felt an adrenalin rush, remembering the thrill of a breaking story or a daily deadline. I had missed these more than I had been willing to admit. The haircut worked and I was offered a casual position.

In 2002, the Channel Seven newsroom was buzzing with rumour and the retelling of old cases in the lead up to the Kennedy Royal Commission in Western Australia to be held that year *into whether there has been corrupt or criminal conduct by any Western Australian Police Officer.* No-one knew what would make the grade. Organised crime, dirty deals and corruption. I wasn't from WA and knew few of the names, but the stories fascinated me.

Veteran crime reporter Alison Fan was working on the Mickelberg case. The three Mickelberg brothers – Brian, Ray and Peter – had been charged and convicted of the theft of more than half a million dollars' worth of gold bullion from the Perth Mint in 1982. It was a daring, brazen and sophisticated robbery, carried out with almost military precision. Three separate couriers bearing false cheques had arrived separately at the Perth Mint, in the centre of the city, where they were given forty-nine gold bars weighing sixty-eight kilograms, before delivering these to an office a short distance away. The couriers and the gold promptly disappeared. The case caused a sensation throughout Australia and had all the makings of a Hollywood heist. It was one of the most notorious corruption cases in WA criminal history. At immense personal cost, courageous journalist Avon Lovell had spent years investigating and writing about the crime and the conviction (on largely fabricated evidence) of the Mickelberg brothers.

Lovell's first book, *The Mickelberg Stitch*, was banned after the WA Police Union placed a levy on every officer to help fund their legal fight against the author. The brakes on his car failed, and his wife and son nearly died. He believes he was the target of corrupt police officers. His business was ruined, and then they worked on his reputation. Just one of many good men destroyed by the rat pack.

At the centre of his claims were the questionable tactics of Detective Don Hancock with the Criminal Investigation Branch (CIB) at Belmont police station on the day police arrested Peter Mickelberg, the youngest and considered the most vulnerable of the three brothers. Dubbed 'The Silver Fox', Don Hancock was later murdered in a car bomb attack in suburban Perth in 2001 after an altercation with bikies.

Tony Lewandowski was the junior police officer on duty the day Detective Don Hancock had secured his questionable confession from Peter Mickelberg. Lewandowski had, at the time, vehemently denied that Hancock had beaten Peter and fabricated the confession, as Peter had claimed.

After twenty years of pressure from Lovell, and after the death of Hancock, Lewandowski had finally rolled. He signed an affidavit admitting the confession he obtained with former Detective Don Hancock was fabricated.

Lewandowski and Lovell were now in hiding, and the media was in a frenzy trying to find them. Alison Fan was the newsroom's lead reporter, and the case had always been close to her heart. In 1987, a sack full of gold weighing fifty-five kilograms had been deposited at the front gate of Channel Seven with her name on it. A note was attached proclaiming the Mickelbergs' innocence and naming a WA businessman as the culprit.

Desperate to prove myself, and wanting to play a part in the story, I thought I might be able to help track down Lovell and Lewandowski. I'd met Avon Lovell, and I believed he trusted me. His son and my son were friends, and I suggested to the Chief of Staff that he might be willing to talk to me and reveal their whereabouts. He thanked me as I eagerly started making phone calls that went unanswered. Those in the know must have been smiling because Alison was, at that time, flying to Thailand where Lovell had Lewandowski in hiding. Channel Seven had already paid to get the interview from the pair exclusively, but I was a newcomer, and the deal was a closely guarded secret.

I had cut my journalistic teeth in the days of *The Moonlight State*, Chris Masters' cutting edge story that aired on the ABC's *Four Corners* program about police and political corruption in Queensland. The exposé resulted in the Fitzgerald Inquiry and the subsequent jailing of the Commissioner of Police. Chris Masters was the standard to which I aspired. Re-entering the newsroom in the lead-up to the WA Royal Commission into police corruption was reminiscent of those earlier days. Would WA politics and police be turned on their heads as they were in the heady days of the Fitzgerald Inquiry in Queensland? The prospect was enthralling.

I saw this as a time where journalism could do in Perth what it had achieved in Brisbane in the wake of *The Moonlight State*, creating a more transparent age and helping to redefine the line between criminals and those who investigated them. However, I later read this story gave Masters more grief than glory.

As the news of Alison's exclusive interview spread, the Chief of Staff smiled sympathetically at my naïve efforts to find Lovell. Strike one. I needed to make up ground and come up with a good story—and then it came to me. Whistleblowers! I needed to find those public servants who were willing to put their jobs on the line to expose corruption. I checked online and marvelled at the ease of research in the digital age. Bingo! There it was: *Whistleblowers Australia*. I rang and asked to be put in contact with any police officers on their books.

I was part-time, casual, which enabled me to conduct some research in my own time. I met former police officer Frank Scott who was suffering from the same problems that afflict all whistleblowers—feelings of isolation, persecution and stress—and was carrying numerous files to back up his claims. He didn't expect to be believed.

Few journalists have the time to analyse controversial claims and happily leave any investigating to the police and authorities. But I was fresh back in the game and eager to recut my teeth on a substantial investigation. Frank had been out of the Police Force for a while, and I was looking for something current to take to my boss.

Frank said there was another member of the Mickelberg investigating team that had allegations raised against him, and the Mickelberg investigation was the story of the day. The former police officer was now a Member of Parliament and back in the limelight due to the Lewandowski allegations of a fabricated confession. All I had to do was find an article Frank had seen in the *Western Mail*, a newspaper that would later merge with *The West Australian*. If I could find that information, Frank assured me, though he couldn't remember the exact details of its location and timing, it would be a great story. It was a long shot. A very long shot. But if I could do a bit of digging in my own time, I thought, I might find that nugget, and it could help redeem me. No-one needed to know if I failed; that's the beauty of a personal project.

The Battye Library is a treasure trove of little known but amazing stories. Back then there was no finger clicking to find an aged document; it took a lot of time and patience to find a single article with only an approximate year. It was the search for the proverbial needle in a haystack.

In a dark corner, small spotlights shone through microfiche film reflecting old newspapers onto a whiteboard screen. The only sound allowed in the library was the clunking of the microfiche as it spooled through the projectors. I found that I could get through three microfiches in an hour—if I didn't get distracted or stop to read the articles. But days of searching failed to find that story.

To this day, I have no idea if there was anything in the library about Frank Scott's politician. I became too distracted by another story on those pages, revisiting a murder that took place a decade earlier, the killing of a madam Shirley Finn in 1975. It kept cropping up over the years. It intrigued me. Her fabulous home in South Perth, with bay windows, leadlights, and a manicured garden. Her initials had been embossed on the bottom of the large oval pool, and the mosaics that made up the letters were said to be solid gold. Around the pool she had hosted fabulous parties attended by the who's who of Perth. Among her celebrity guests, on one especially notable occasion, was one of the world's greatest musicians, Elton John.

The newspaper said she knew too much and had high-level connections. In early 2017, the murder remains unsolved, dredged up every few years by a journalist hoping to make a breakthrough. Like the theft of the gold from Perth Mint and the setup of the Mickelbergs, the murder sounded more Hollywood than Perth.

In the newsroom, I spoke to my Chief of Staff, Mark Bennett, and mentioned I had been contacting whistleblowers. He recounted the tale of Spike Daniels, a police superintendent in the 1970s who tried to blow the whistle on corruption in the police force concerning prostitution, in the days of Shirley Finn. He said Spike had paid a terrible price for speaking out. "They destroyed him," he said. I wanted to find the superintendent and talk to him. Mark Bennett's father-in-law, Matt Stephens, a politician and friend of Spike Daniels, was another man who had fallen foul of the rat pack in the 1970s.

Another veteran reporter described the Finn case as the greatest festering sore on the side of the WA Police Force, suggesting it was the genesis of the corruption which followed and which was now being investigated by the Kennedy Royal Commission in 2002.

The Royal Commission was only looking at cases after 1985. I needed to focus on one of the cases they were investigating.

Frank Scott, the police whistleblower who'd inspired my microfiche search in the Battye Library, had more information for me. He thought he knew what happened to the Mickelberg gold, which had never been found and, of course, if the Mickelbergs didn't do it, there remained that other big question. Who did?

Frank believed a Northbridge Italian identity could have been behind the theft at the Perth Mint. He said he had personally witnessed the man bringing in large amounts of gold to a gold trader in Perth around the time of the swindle. He had advised senior officers and believed they intentionally bungled a raid on the gold dealer.

I was aware Alison knew more about the Mickelberg case than just about anyone, so I took her the name of the man Frank had identified and this potential new lead. I handed her the paperwork, briefly outlining the allegations, and hoped she'd give some indication as to whether they were worth following up. Alison was busy, and I was the new kid on the block. She showed no interest in the claims at all. Strike two.

I also mentioned the name of the gold dealer to a veteran cameraman, nicknamed Mouse, who knew the ropes.

"Mate, you need to read the book, *This Little Piggy Stayed Home*. It's about the Perth mafia!" He said the gold dealer was mentioned in the book.

"Perth mafia?" I couldn't reconcile myself with this concept. Mafia in Perth? I was originally from Sydney where Justice James Wood had exposed enormous corruption within the ranks of the NSW constabulary. Several Royal Commissions on the east coast had touched on organised crime, but I was fresh out of playgroup, and the idea of a mafia in a small place like Perth—I just couldn't get my head around that.

I checked all the libraries. All their copies of *This Little Piggy* were missing, but Mouse eventually found a copy for me. The book was about drug couriers Kevin Barlow and Brian Chambers who were convicted of trafficking heroin in Malaysia in 1986. Despite international pleas for clemency, they were hanged for their crime. *This Little Piggy* detailed the dealers and organised crime network, mainly operating out of North-bridge in Perth, that sent the pair to Malaysia.

The crime lord at the centre of the Barlow and Chambers case was Paul Mussari, a Mr Big of the drug world with links to crime groups interstate. Coincidentally, when I was part way through the book, an article appeared in *The West Australian* about Paul Mussari. He was on trial for conspiring to possess 524 grams of heroin. *JURY HEARS OF HEROIN DEAL TELEPHONE CALLS – Threats to shoot man in 'Caribbean shuffle' or break his legs*, the headline read. Almost twenty years on, and he was still allegedly plying his trade. And it was now more than fifteen years since Kevin Barlow and Brian Chambers had been hanged.

The next day I attended Paul Mussari's trial for possession of heroin. Mouse, a veteran Channel Seven cameraman, came along to help me identify some of the characters. It was like watching an episode of *The Sopranos*, the television drama about an Italian-American mobster who struggles to balance his home life with his criminal career.

One individual caught my eye: a tattooed Italian aged in his fifties who signalled to Paul Mussari in the stand. I wondered if he was John Asciak, a crook who, in 1988, was convicted of conspiring to import heroin with Barlow and Chambers. Said to be Mussari's offsider, he had provided a lot of information to *This Little Piggy's* author David Williams about the crime syndicates operating in Perth. Outside the court, I took the bold step of approaching him.

"Hi, I'm Juliet Wills from Channel Seven. Are you John Asciak?"

"No," he replied and gave me his name.

It was the gold dealer!

I must have looked startled, as I remembered him from my conversation with Frank Scott, because he asked, "How do you know my name?"

"I've been reading about you in *This Little Piggy.*"

He laughed, "It's all true that book."

"And still happening from the sounds of that court case… There's a sequel in that?"

"I could tell you a story or two," he replied.

I hadn't anticipated this—that the man allegedly linked to the Mickelberg gold theft by Frank, the former police whistleblower, would present himself to me. A combination of fear and the prospect of a scoop sent adrenalin coursing through my veins. "Can I buy you a coffee?" I asked.

We sat in the open-air café behind a columned heritage façade opposite the Magistrates Court. Another notorious crime figure sat a few tables away—in the centre of town surrounded by lawyers and crooks, alongside office workers sipping lattes oblivious to the theatre around them—I wasn't sure why I was there or where it was going, but the prospect of what Goldfinger might know held me transfixed.

We talked about the book, *This Little Piggy Stayed Home*, about the illegal gambling dens and drug deals. He told me there was still illegal gambling going on in Perth and that he was happy to show me.

He explained that among the Italians in Northbridge certain people were in charge of different areas of business. Gold trading and insurance were his specialties. He told me he was known to many as 'Goldfinger' and that he'd made a vast fortune from trading in illegal gold.

Goldfinger was an amiable storyteller. I went to bring out the tape recorder, but he said, "No," very firmly. I hoped he meant not yet, but I would soon learn that there would be no formal record of my conversations with Goldfinger, bar my notes when I returned home. Instead I just sat and listened.

While the Perth Mint robbery is well known, largely because of the work of Avon Lovell and his crusade to clear the Mickelberg brothers, what is less well known is that hundreds of millions of dollars of gold was systematically looted from WA mines in the seventies and eighties. Gold bullion disappeared from flights, was looted from mines, and police reports emerged of armed ships with concealed cargos of gold off the Western Australian coast. Illicit gold from WA was reportedly used in the purchase of heroin from the golden triangle. Gold was the preferred currency of organised crime, and many a nugget was discovered on a patch of dirt in WA, illegally melted and delivered to the mint as a 'discovery', dirty money washed squeaky clean. Gold and organised crime in WA were intrinsically linked to international crime syndicates.

Goldfinger was in the big league and just being around him made me nervous.

He said he did take gold to the Gold Exchange where whistleblower Frank Scott had seen him bringing in large quantities of gold. I asked him if it was from the Perth Mint heist. He said it was not. He was adamant about who did steal the gold and said it wasn't him.

As he listed off stories about people notorious in Perth for drug trade and corruption on a grand scale, I began to wilt in my enthusiasm. A part-time working mum taking on organised crime did not seem like a sensible option. I had read of journalists in other countries who had died for similar stories. Nonetheless, without venturing too far into this treacherous terrain, I thought the story of Paul Mussari still plying his deadly trade almost twenty years after the death of Barlow and Chambers could be worthy of a yarn, especially since it had gone through the court process. In retrospect, perhaps I should have just sat back, for my enthusiasm was not well received.

I bowled into the office of Mario D'Orazio, the Executive Producer of *Today Tonight*, to run my idea by him. He didn't seem overly impressed.

He'd done plenty of heroin stories before, he said, even had reporters going in with button hole cameras in Northbridge to catch the crooks out. He didn't think they rated that well. He said he'd think about it. By coincidence, or design, the next day my casual shifts were cut, and I wasn't asked back to the Channel Seven newsroom. I was never given a reason.

That same year, in 2002, author and journalist Avon Lovell was charged with contempt of court for refusing to answer questions at the Kennedy Royal Commission into police corruption. His years of investigating and trying to expose corruption surrounding the Mickelberg case continued to cause him grief. No credit was ever given for his bravery and tenacity in exposing corruption, despite the enormous emotional and financial price he paid.

Heroin dealer Paul Mussari, whose trial I had attended months before, was now serving time behind bars. He was also called to answer questions about police corruption at the Royal Commission. He too refused, banging his head against the wall saying he couldn't remember. He was not charged with contempt.

Brian Mickelberg had died in a helicopter crash in 1986, having served nine months in jail. Ray and Peter served eight and six years, respectively. Their convictions were overturned in 2004, and they were awarded one million dollars in ex gratia payments for their wrongful incarceration. Whoever stole the gold from the mint remains unknown.

Perhaps people had heard too much of Royal Commissions and corruption, or perhaps because few names were revealed, and the crooked cops and crims were not identified, the public couldn't relate. The Royal Commission soon faded into obscurity with seemingly few repercussions.

I met with Goldfinger at another café in James Street, Northbridge. He pointed to a door that he claimed still led to an illegal gambling club and offered to take me one night. I made excuses. I was without the support of a television network. Goldfinger was in tight with the Northbridge crime set, and I wondered if he knew Shirley Finn. It was a name that everyone in Perth seemed to know.

"I can tell you who killed her." He paused and—thinking he might change his mind—I allowed the silence to hang between us. He seemed to be reassessing. "I won't tell you who did it, but I'll tell you who ordered it." Another pause. Then he spoke. The name he gave me swam in my head. It went to the very top at that time. I didn't know whether to believe him. It seemed too big to be true, and besides, he couldn't back it up.

I ran Goldfinger's allegation by a few well-known journalists from the era. They had heard the rumour too. In fact, they tended to respond with a degree of surprise that I hadn't. The common belief was that the police investigation had been so flawed and corruption so rife, at the time of her murder, that there was no prospect of ever finding out exactly what happened to Shirley Finn.

Foolishly, I decided to try, in spite of being told by Goldfinger, "The story is still dangerous. You will be stopped. People will stop you."

So began a journey that would take me more than ten years, as I trawled through the life and times of this Perth madam. I was to dig through mountains of historical documents; meet her friends, her family, and her business associates; interview police, politicians, lawyers and some of those who were said to have had a hand in her death.

Along the way, I received many threats and warnings including this anonymous one:

```
You have no security and no confidentiality or
privacy due to the subject matter you are working
on. You are being tracked and monitored every
second of every day and your wellbeing is not
safe.
    Watch your back at all times. Continually check
your car for interference and fuel contamination,
check all your mail for interference, any anomaly
at all with anything, record it and include the
date, even unusual phone calls. Say nothing of
value on your mobile.
    Keep the video eye in your computer/
laptop covered at all times. If you don't they
will video you through your own computer and use
```

it against you at a later date. They can see and hear everything you do WITHOUT YOUR KNOWLEDGE.

If you have NO suicidal tendencies and never have had them, write a letter and explain that "under no circumstances would you ever commit suicide" and give copies to your family and friends to keep in safekeeping (in case of involuntary suicide).

2

Bridget

It is such a secret place, the land of tears.
— Antoine de Saint-Exupéry

Flying into the city built on sand, Bridget gazed below, with a mix of hope and relief, at the patchwork of parched yellow land cut by the Swan River as it seeped into a turquoise ocean. She was coming home. It was 1972 and two years since the 10-year-old had seen her mother. Too long for one so young.

Her brothers, Shane and Steven, were squabbling in the seats beside her and her father clipped Shane over the ear. He yelled out. Bridget looked the other way, hoping people wouldn't think she was part of the same family. Boys!

Her mum, Shirley, had written every week and had also sent the money they relied upon to live in the UK. The highlight of the whole trip had been when her mum turned up to take them to Spain. She hoped her mum would be pleased to see her.

Des Finn had taken the three children back to England to get to know his family and somewhere along the way Bridget learned her parents' marriage was over. It had been a very long trip away. She remembers there were fights, and plenty of them, in the lead-up to the trip to Europe, mostly over money. She recalls little affection from either parent.

Des Finn had a good job in the RAAF when he married Shirley, but a few years after Bridget was born, the third and youngest child, an accident left him badly injured and suffering from depression. He broke down completely and was hospitalised at Heathcote Mental Hospital for long periods. Shirley was left with three young children and a sick husband. The bailiff was knocking at her door, and the children were hungry.

She had to try and support the family financially. She desperately wanted to get ahead and to end the hardship the family had endured since Des' accident. So, in the years her family lived in the UK, getting ahead was exactly what Shirley had done.

The boys had been a real handful, and Des had had enough. It was Shirley's turn to care for the kids, but she wasn't expecting them.

When Bridget saw her new home in South Perth, she couldn't believe it. Landscaped gardens with a pond and statues led up to the entrance of the Federation-style home. An archway framed the verandah, and inside, the entrance hall was like walking into a church. Ornate leadlights framed by carved dark wood architraves, a high ceiling with an ornate brass chandelier; the walls looked like marble and held candelabras in recesses. Shining glass doors led through to a lounge, where woodwork and leadlights framed an arched fireplace, with window seats either side. The finest quality antiques were featured throughout, with curios from around the world. More glass doors led to a large dining room. Out the back, a bar room opened onto the backyard.

Her mum's dressing room was the biggest Bridget had seen, filled with designer clothes and rows and rows of shoes. In the bathroom was a floor to ceiling mirror and gold taps in the shape of swans.

Shirley extended the house upstairs to accommodate the children and she bought Bridget a wardrobe full of the prettiest dresses she'd seen. Not that Bridget was a dresses kind of girl, but she appreciated the sentiment.

Des was in need of a job, and Shirley hired him to work on renovations at her Northbridge nightclub and extensions to her new home.

By next summer their new pool would be finished. The tiler was placing the solid gold tiles on the bottom that would form her mother's initials, 'SS', for Shirley Shewring, her mother's maiden name.

Her brothers, Shane and Steve, were more impressed with their mum's new limited edition Dodge Phoenix with a black vinyl roof, a white body and all the latest luxury trims. Only 400 were made each year, and the Dodge Phoenix was the most expensive Australian-made car of that time.

Bridget wasn't sure what her mum did for a living, but about a year after they'd arrived back in Perth when Bridget was in Grade 7, there was an article in the newspaper with her mum's name in it. She can't remember who pointed it out, but she does remember feeling embarrassed.

At school, it seemed her teacher had read it too. Looking straight at Bridget she asked the class to write an essay about what their mother and father did for a living. Bridget wrote that her parents owned a lolly shop.

Bridget was still in primary school when Shirley's friend, Rose, began sleeping on the sofa, in the summer of 1973. Bridget didn't like Rose; she thought she was a man. She was shocked when she later saw Rose swimming topless in the pool. Bridget had cried with her mum at the movie *Sunshine* and danced and sang with her mum at a Status Quo concert. Bridget had wanted to be the special girl her mum spent time with.

Soon after Rose started sleeping over, Bridget was shipped off to Kobeelya, an exclusive girl's boarding school in country Western Australia. It was the beginning of 1974 and Bridget's first year of high school. Bridget didn't like living away from home and blamed Rose.

Shirley was furious when she received a call from Kobeelya in April 1975. They were expelling Bridget. She had been sneaking out to catch up with friends, and the school couldn't risk having students roaming the streets. Shirley was in Hong Kong at the time and had to fly back to fetch her daughter.

Bridget was sent instead to Kent Street High within walking distance of their South Perth home.

Her brothers had been kicked out a fortnight before for stealing money. Shirley had bags of it, stacks of $50 and $20 bills lying around, but when the boys started helping themselves, she had a new safe installed; not that this could stop Shane. He was wily and resourceful and answered to no-one. Both his parents and the adults that came in contact with him struggled with his temperament. The house was quiet and relaxed without the two boys.

The Sunday night that Bridget's world was turned upside down had started out peacefully enough. There was no indication of what was to come, or not one that Bridget recalls. A relaxing family get-together—Shirley, her partner Rosalie Black (a.k.a. Rose Dean) and Bridget had sat on the terrace beside the beautiful oval pool and enjoyed a barbeque.

The night before, her mum had allowed Bridget's boyfriend, Kim, to come over for a roast dinner. Shirley didn't approve of Kim who was five years Bridget's senior. Bridget had been sneaking out to see him, and Shirley had agreed to the dinner invitation in a bid to stop the secrecy. Bridget was happy her mother had finally allowed Kim into the house. The fights over her sneaking out would be over.

Bridget can't remember if they talked about Kim at the barbeque the next day, or if her mum had approved of him. Much of that night remains a blank to her. In the coming years, Kim would stay by Bridget's side and father her three children, but on the evening of her mother's murder, he was not there.

On the night of the barbeque, Bridget was back home with her mum, she was going to the local high school, and she was in love. Even if Rose was there with her mum, life at that point seemed OK.

Bridget had school the next day, so was sent to bed early. Her mother was in jeans watching the TV with Rose when the teenager headed upstairs.

Bridget didn't see Rose leave. She never saw her mum get dressed up in her finest designer ball gown. She didn't hear the car start. She didn't know her mum had left the house. Why would she? Her mum had never left her alone before.

Police records say Shirley sent Rose away saying she had an important meeting. Worried about leaving her daughter alone, Finn called a babysitting service. They had no-one available that evening, so Bridget was left home alone.

Rose called in the middle of the night concerned about Shirley's whereabouts, and Bridget answered the phone. Rose asked her to check on her mum whose bed was empty. Bridget was worried but wasn't quite sure what to do, so went back to bed. In the morning, Rose was in the kitchen, but she didn't say much. The 13-year-old took herself off to school.

Later that morning, the headmistress at Kent Street High knocked on the door of the Year 9 Social Studies class and asked for Bridget to join her. Bridget had no idea what it was about or why the headmistress was looking at her so strangely, but the level of sympathy in her eyes led her to believe something was wrong. As the shy teenager stood up, she felt all eyes upon her.

She stepped out into the hall. The headmistress wrapped her arms around Bridget's shoulders, which made her feel a little uncomfortable. Her eyes watering, she said in a motherly way: "I don't know how you're going to live through this."

Guided into the principal's office, Bridget was greeted by what seemed like a large wall of detectives all looking down at her. "Your mum's no longer with us," said one amongst the crowd. Bridget went numb.

"Bridget, we're going to need you to answer a few questions," one of the detectives said. Everything seemed a blur after that. It was one in a series of tragedies that would beset Bridget Finn's life. She would not step back inside her beautiful home again for forty years.

"What happened?" she asked the detectives. In 2017, she's still asking.

3

Cleansing Shirley's Soul

Some rise by sin and some by virtue fall.
— William Shakespeare

The man sitting opposite me was well groomed and polite. He had blue eyes. I imagined Shirley's had looked the same.

"Please don't mention our family name." Shirley's father, Jo Shewring, pleaded with me and I agreed so long as they were alive. Our interview was conditional upon protecting his family's privacy.

Shirley had grown up in a leafy middle-class neighbourhood not far from the banks of the Swan River in Mount Pleasant. The eldest child, she had been a good girl, helpful, vivacious and bright. Shirley's mother had erased her eldest daughter from their lives, refusing to talk about her or speak her name. "Her mother is still devastated!"

I thought it was their daughter's murder that upset her, but the rift went back much further. "She must never know I spoke to you!" Shirley's father told me, and I kept his wish, only writing up this part of the interview after they had both passed away.

I wanted to understand where it all went wrong for Shirley.

He said they had been worried about the impact Shirley's behaviour might have on her two siblings, particularly her brother who was much younger. "He doesn't even know about Shirley!" he explained. "We tried to protect him." Shirley's name had been banned in the house when she was still a teenager, well before her mysterious death. For as long as her mother and father were alive, Shirley was wiped from their family's history. To Mrs Shewring, her daughter didn't exist. It was how she coped, a 1950s housewife, unable to bear the shame Shirley had brought on the family.

The other two children grew up without a hitch, both well-adjusted adults Mr Shewring assured me. Neither parent drank nor smoked.

Born in 1941, Shirley was a wartime baby. "I was away a lot. It was the war!" I noted the flying badge pinned to his jacket. "I was a bomber pilot," Mr Shewring explained. He rarely got to see his little girl and, though he didn't admit it, like many wartime veterans, probably suffered a degree of trauma for his experiences. "Perhaps if I hadn't been away so much things would have been different."

She helped around the house, got good grades and was a likeable but spirited child, he explained. "With me being away she got used to not having a father telling her what to do. Her mother wasn't very strict! She didn't really like it when I came back and started trying to put in some firm rules."

Shirley hit her teens in the era when the term teenager was coined. The 1950s represented a new rebellious phase; peace, plentiful jobs, cars and rock and roll. Her parents were part of the wartime generation who looked on with disdain. Like many who endured the war years, they were suffering from a collective postwar trauma, trying to rebuild, but haunted by the loss of friends and family, the lonely brides, deprivation, horror and hunger of the war years.

With a new baby brother and a house under construction, her parents were distracted.

Shirley topped nearly all her classes, and in another time she may have been put in a gifted program, but this was 1955, and the parents of this generation thought the best a young girl could hope for was to find a good husband. Shirley just started a bit younger than many of her peers. She was fourteen; boys noticed Shirley and Shirley noticed boys.

Her father said he wasn't aware of Shirley's early interest. She started sneaking out. "One time I couldn't find her. I reported her as a missing person." Mr Shewring explained that as a result of running away she was put in the Home of the Good Shepherd at Leederville. "She learnt to smoke and put on make-up. She changed," he said.

What happened to Shirley before and during her stay in the Home of the Good Shepherd is partly recorded in her welfare papers. Perhaps relating to the night her father reported her missing, these documents say Shirley was caught in the company of a 20-year-old man, Tim; that she was interviewed by police and admitted having sexual relations.

She was fourteen years old. The 20-year-old, to my knowledge, faced no consequence despite the fact that it was he who committed the offence by having sex with a minor. Shirley and her parents were hauled before a magistrate. Shirley was said to be a neglected child. Her parents were asked to explain how they had let their daughter get so out of control.

Shirley's father described how they had banned her from going out. *"She is very strong-willed,"* he told the magistrate. All recorded for posterity.

"You're her father, sir. It is up to you to keep control, and clearly you have failed in your duty," he admonished.

It's an age-old story—the battle between a teen seeking freedom and her parents wanting to protect her innocence. The pill did not exist in 1955, and a teen pregnancy was considered a family shame that could result in being ostracised from the community, but Shirley didn't understand the risks of her actions. Her parents wanted to stop her travelling the path that she was choosing to follow. She argued heatedly with her father.

There is nothing in her welfare records to suggest abuse. But they did record and judge her parents' attempts to discipline their daughter.

When Shirley first started staying out late, her parents had tried to stop her. *Once, her father forced her to remain at home on a Saturday afternoon, after which she admitted she deliberately used her wits to defy him. Keeping company with undesirable lads was a further means of expressing her defiance*, her welfare records explained.

According to the records, 'Tim' would be her first dalliance. He kept inviting her to the park, and eventually he succeeded in getting her there. Shirley lost her virginity at the park. She was puzzled by this experience, did not understand it, and she got nothing from it. It never occurred to her that it might be wrong, because her mother had never told her so, but following this, she refused to go out with the boy again. She later told her mother, "It was awful."

Like many mothers of her era, talking about sex was uncomfortable, and there was no sex education to explain the feelings. Pregnancies happened, but they were hidden; young unmarried women were sent to 'the country', their babies put up for adoption. Child welfare authorities could see the dangers that might befall a sexually active 14-year-old, even if Shirley couldn't.

Her parents' efforts were successful in the first instance. The young man stayed away, but this only made Shirley more determined.

She seemed to quieten down for a while, and she asked that they trust her. They gave her the benefit of the doubt and, with an agreement to ensure she was home on time, allowed her to go to the pictures with her girlfriends. Here she met Pete, though her parents didn't find out. She was back on time, agreeable and helpful, and therefore she was allowed out again.

Shirley wanted to act like her peers and to impress them; they were older than her and told her that having sex was normal. Two months later she had sex with Pete. The magistrate showed no interest in the fact that the older boys had committed crimes. Shirley was the victim of carnal knowledge, but this was the 1950s. It was up to the girls to maintain the standards of propriety so Shirley and her family were treated like criminals.

Her parents pleaded with the magistrate. They had been distracted, but they had always believed they had given her a good home. They agreed to educate her on the dangers of sex, promised more supervision and urged that she stay in school and not be taken out by the authorities. Shirley wanted to join the marching girls, go back to church club and, perhaps, play tennis in the summertime. They would ensure this would happen they told the Catholic magistrate. It wasn't enough. He recommended she should listen to her parents and go to church more often and then ordered that the 14-year-old be committed to an institution. A dose of the nuns at the Home of the Good Shepherd was his answer. Her parents were horrified and ashamed; the move later being described as *"shock therapy"* for the family.

Shirley was led away from her middle-class family in leafy Mount Pleasant, her home, her school and her friends, and delivered into the hands of the nuns at the Home of the Good Shepherd in Leederville. Shirley was a dirty girl in need of a little religious cleansing.

The stated aim of the convent was to *provide shelter for girls of dissolute habits, who wish to do penance for their iniquities and to lead a truly Christian life.* Shirley was to join other girls working in the laundry, the idea being to combine rehabilitation of supposed delinquents with the chance to earn a modest profit. There was an element of symbolic cleansing in such employment—the washing of sheets suggesting a search for purity.

In 1955, when Shirley cleaned sheets for WA hotels and hospitals without receiving a wage, the Good Shepherd laundry had its most profitable year. The institution was slated in the newspapers at that time for profiteering from the girls' cheap labour.

The home had been set up in 1904, following a plea from the WA Catholic Bishop in 1898 to rescue females from the predominately male population who had come to Western Australia, in search of gold. *We have an overwhelming majority of a male population, in consequence a great deal of depravity. Come to the rescue of weak females, or utterly perish,* Bishop Gibney wrote. More men than women would be an ongoing problem in the mining state.

Shirley was assigned to the mangling room where, instead of an education, she would spend her days putting sheets through compressed rollers, ringing out the water and soap. It was hard, unpaid work in hot, steamy conditions. Accidents were not uncommon with at least two girls losing their arms in the mangle.

Women punished for running away by placement at the convent laundry in Leederville recalled their stories to Pam Casellas of *The West Australian*, in 2004. Many felt they had done nothing wrong, but were still locked up. There was a sense of rejection and abandonment. A woman named Paris (because she never made it there) was incarcerated for running away from her strict European home where she was banned from mixing with Australians. *"I was watched over by a nun like Hitler and ironed millions and millions of shirts. To this day I cannot iron a man's shirt."*

Another girl worked a steam press; any tiny crease meant she'd have to complete the task again. *"It was like a scene from [the television series]* Prisoner."* The girls were not allowed to speak, a former Good Shepherd girl explained. *"It was a bugger of a life,"* Mary de Sales recalled to *The West Australian. "The nuns were cruel, they belted us, hit us with bunches of keys and put us in straitjackets like Chinese dolls. I'm still deaf in one ear after a belting. I cut my plaits off so they couldn't pull me up by them."*

It must have felt like a prison to Shirley, and she was not one to be confined. A week after she arrived, she joined three girls who'd planned an escape. While the other girls in the dormitory were sleeping, they broke a pane of glass from a window using towels and bedspreads to absorb the sound. Nobody heard them leave, but a few hours later the night staff were alerted by a *mysterious phone call from a Jean Dean.*

The police were notified, but Shirley and her friend Margaret turned up at the front door around 2:45am, explaining to the nuns the other two girls were going back to Fremantle to build a fire on a vacant lot and sleep there. Margaret and Shirley apologised profusely and were sent to bed. Like her parents, the nuns had failed to keep Shirley in. Police found the other two girls later that morning, returning them to the convent where they were placed in detention.

A friend of Shirley's, from the Home of The Good Shepherd, contacted Bridget many years later. According to Carol, on weekends the girls were sometimes taken to the Swan Valley and handed to paedophiles for sexual favours. They were given lollies in return.

In a recorded interview with Bridget and me, Carol said she was one of the girls who ran away with Shirley. When they were picked up, the police officers told the teenagers they wouldn't take them back to the Home if they had sex with them. The girls agreed but were returned anyway.

Six months of laundry work and life at the Home took its toll on Shirley. A psychologist provided a report to Child Welfare on her progress while in the home—far from cleansing her soul, it blackened it. *Normally, Shirley is an outgoing, lively kind of girl, but her recent experiences have depressed her natural vivacity. Previously, she could have been impulsive at times, but recent experiences have deadened her liveliness and she has become somewhat apprehensive and anxious. As may be expected since her committal to the institution, she has felt bad, dirty and contami-*

nated. During her stay at the Home of the Good Shepherd she felt alone and deserted and has become increasingly unhappy.

Tests revealed disturbing signs of depression, which showed that continuing to stay in the institution could be harmful. *She is naturally a fairly well balanced child, but these morbid signs of depression are disturbing in a child of her age,* the report stated.

Shirley recognised her downfall was due to her disobedience. *Shirley now wants to put the past behind her and is prepared to agree to almost anything to get home again,* the psychologist wrote.

Bad girl! Dirty girl! Wash away your sins.

In the era where reputation was everything, Shirley's confinement took a heavy toll on the Shewring family. Welfare papers reveal: *The court action and consequent committal to the Institution have been shock therapy of a kind for the whole family.*

Shirley was aware of the shame she had brought on her family. She tried to make amends. On Mother's Day that year, she sent her mother an acronym poem, which read:

> *Dear Mum,*
>
> *M is for the million things you gave me,*
> *O is for I am sorry you are getting old,*
> *T is for the tears you shed to save me,*
> *H is for that heart as pure as gold,*
> *E is for those eyes with love light shining,*
> *R is for right and right you will always be.*
>
> *Put them all together, they spell*
> *MOTHER a word that means so much to me.*
> *With lots of love from your daughter,*
> *Shirley.*

The family was shattered. For parents doing what they believed was best, there can be no greater shame than having the child you loved being declared unloved and neglected. Her parents couldn't speak about it, not even to her brother and sister. Having been deemed a failure as a parent to Shirley, her mother threw her energies into the younger children, aged six and two at the time of her release, hoping things would turn out better for them.

On her release, the psychologist warned it would be unpleasant for Shirley to have to explain her eight-month absence at her old school and suggested she try a new one. The laundries effectively ended her education. She was enrolled at Kent Street High School, the same school her daughter, Bridget, would later attend. The bright young 15-year-old, who had once been in the top group at school, achieving the highest possible scores in reading, writing and maths, was so far behind that she saw the year out and then, against her parents' wishes, left, finding work at a frock shop.

Things were okay for a while at home. Her parents felt intense pressure to keep her in check and Shirley began again to feel claustrophobic, as a result of her father's strictness and "moralising". She tried hard to be a "good" girl, staying away from boys and doing as her father said, but she felt her parents judged her for even the smallest things, and she soon got bored.

Working at the dress shop one day, she met Des Finn, a handsome 22-year-old Air Force mechanic, who swept her off her feet.

4

Behind the Lace Curtain

She is free in her wildness, she is a wanderess, a drop of free water.
She knows nothing of orders and cares nothing for rules or customs.
'Time' for her isn't something to fight against. Her life flows clean,
with passion like fresh water.

— Roman Payne

In 2003, I found Des Finn living in an isolated wooden cottage near a railway track just outside Bridgetown, a semi-rural town with rolling hills on the Blackwood River, south of Perth. He preferred to live away from people.

The kitchen was a picture out of yesteryear. An old fashioned wood stove stood in the fireplace. Above the sink, there were wooden sash windows with peeling paint and in the centre of the small room was a home-made wood table, well-worn. Wooden toys he made for local charities and home-made silver jewellery, mostly Celtic symbols, lay on narrow bench tops.

He offered me a cup of tea and agreed I could record the interview.

"Maybe I'm naïve," I confessed to him. "I've been a little bit surprised at what went on."

He raised one eyebrow. "I've always likened life to walking down the street in St Kilda, all lace and curtains, with the light shining on them on a Sunday afternoon. What's behind those curtains will terrify you."

He was intelligent and introspective but seemed to carry the weight of the world on his shoulders. Like many people scarred by nasty breakups, he denied he ever loved his former wife, but I held letters from his past, a window into his 22-year-old soul, which showed otherwise.

"She had a beautiful figure," Des Finn recalled, "not overly tall, well curved, well developed, she may have been fifteen, but she was a woman. She had a good job in the city in a nice dress shop in the Piccadilly Arcade."

Shirley's father, Jo Shewring, hadn't approved of their relationship. "He definitely did not like me," Des recalled.

When I'd met with Shirley's father, Jo had told me he thought Des was no good, and he hadn't liked the way he spoke.

Despite her father's attempts to stop her from seeing Des, Shirley would always find a way for them to be together, climbing out the window in the dead of night if necessary. She had become quite the escape artist. No-one was going to keep this determined teen in.

Des had few fond memories of Shirley. When I asked him if he loved her once, he scoffed. "She wanted the finer things in life. She was willing to strive for it and sacrifice other people for it. She used me."

Shirley craved legitimacy, and she thought that money could buy it. In a place like Perth, she was probably right. Money could buy you a home in a respectable suburb, a thriving business and respect.

He showed me some photos of when they were younger. On the back were handwritten messages that spoke of a time before the bitterness. *Caught me*, said one with Shirley's written reply, *Did I ever*. On the back of another photo of Des in uniform, *Serious ain't I*, to which Shirley had added, *Thinking about me I hope*.

Des Finn had left behind an abusive childhood in Brixton, England, migrating to Australia in 1951 after his father had died. Soon after, he joined the Australian Navy, before joining the Air Force. When Des was posted to Melbourne, he missed Shirley terribly. He would try and sneak calls through hoping that Shirley, and not her father, would answer. So desperate was he to be with Shirley, he went AWOL, hitchhiking back to WA. Scarred by the magistrate's accusations of neglect, Shirley's father fought tooth and nail with his daughter to stop her seeing Des.

Shirley sneaked out. They headed up to the Snake Pit in Scarborough, dancing with the bodgies and widgies on the Scarborough beachfront. She was young and free.

When she finally came home, she fought with her father. Shirley was furious she could not be with the man she loved, and her dad said she was not allowed to see him again. The fight escalated, and Shirley's father told her she was not to leave the house. Hot with rage, Shirley went out anyway, running to her welfare officer and refusing to go home to her parents. She showed a bruise on her arm, which she said was from her father's smack. Welfare interviewed Jo Shewring who expressed his frustration that Shirley could run to Welfare whenever they had a row. Her mother, interviewed separately, agreed Shirley was using the authorities to get her way, and she did not accept her husband's smack had been excessive.

Shirley won, or lost, depending on how you look at it. She was no longer under the care of her parents. Placed back under the care of Welfare until she was eighteen, her father was again reprimanded for failing to control his daughter. Her parents retreated bruised, weary and ashamed.

The magistrate told Shirley that she was to go back into the care of the Child Welfare Department but was to have nothing to do with Finn. *"But that's past, we haven't done anything—we've reformed,"* Shirley pleaded with the magistrate, but the magistrate threatened that if Des Finn had anything to do with her, he'd be sent to jail. *"It's not better for me! Please!"* she begged, but her words fell on deaf ears.

In the next year, she would be farmed out to several foster families, all the time refusing to speak to her parents who told her she was always welcome back home as long as she was prepared to abide by some rules. Banned from caring for their daughter, they also stopped speaking to her or about her. It was Shirley's choice, the welfare papers record. Her foster parents were no more successful at keeping the young lovers apart. She was free to roam the streets as she pleased with whom she chose.

Shirley just wanted to be with Des and wasn't able to get over her sense of abandonment to the nuns when she was fourteen.

Des wrote a letter to Welfare in June 1958 declaring his love for Shirley and apologising for any trouble he caused. *This is the only trouble I have ever got mixed up with. Frankly I don't like it. But what was asked of me was not exactly impossible, just improbable for my part. I love Shirley and I couldn't find it in my heart or brain not to be able to write or communi-*

cate with her for two years. He said he had the means to support her and wanted to take her back to Melbourne. *I am very much in love with Shirley and I know she is with me. We would get married when the first opportunity arose, that might take a long time and we both feel that it would be a waste of time and happiness to wait.*

The young lovers had to wait until Shirley was seventeen to wed as she was still under the care of Welfare. Des was twenty-three. They married in a registry office in November 1958. Shirley's parents had lost any authority over their daughter long ago. They attended the occasion. Des took his bride back to Melbourne where he continued to work with RAAF and Shirley went to work at Buckley and Nuns Department Store selling clothes. She was soon pregnant with their first child, then hospitalised with toxaemia (blood poisoning), which threatened both her life and the baby's. Steven came into the world seven weeks premature and struggled with his developmental milestones. Shane was born a year later in 1960.

Shirley and Des were transferred back to Perth where Des continued to work for the RAAF at Pearce airbase, and in 1961 Bridget was born. The three children were demanding and exhausting. The couple began to fight and then things got worse.

Groin injuries sustained in an accident on an aircraft in 1962 left Des partially castrated and with depression. He was unable to work and emotionally unable to help with the care of the children. He lost his temper often. He spent most of the following year in the Heathcote Mental hospital.

At twenty-two years old, Shirley had three babies, a husband in hospital, and no income to support her family. She wasn't coping with the children, particularly Shane who she found to be persistently demanding. The house-proud mum had to work to survive. She later admitted that she broke down and howled on occasions. Shirley had bills to pay and wanted more than laundry work. She found a job at the Oasis nightclub in Mount Hawthorn run by Don Mack, an SP bookmaker, who she would turn to in the days before she died.

Shirley was a ticket dancer. She played the crowd, and her dance ticket was always full. Go-go dancing was sweeping the world, and it was just the escape the young mother craved. Wearing mini-skirts and boots, Shirley left the problems at home behind her. Her aggressive, depressed husband could be left to manage the unruly kids when he was well enough. Not only did the nightclub get her out of the home, but it was also a chance to make some much-needed money. Shirley needed to feed her family. Ticket dancing enabled her to do both.

Shirley took on the tutelage of a young, tall, leggy waitress called 'Scherry', who started out as a ticket dancer and later became the floor-show; wearing exotic costumes and stripping down to a G-string to a cheering crowd on a tiny corner stage.

When I met with Scherry, she told me she had happy memories of the 1960s working at the Oasis with Shirley Finn. "When I was offered the job, I was a teetotaller. I'd never got into a bikini. I was a cowgirl from the bush, but the owner was desperate, as two girls hadn't turned up for work," she told me. A barman dared Scherry to go topless, offering a hundred dollars. "The gay guys put me out the back and pulled half a curtain down and draped it over me. They made a frilly little bikini and wires under here, because I was still breastfeeding, and gave me a couple of brandies and, well, I'd have done anything. Don [Mack, the owner], was saying, 'You're the best go-go dancer we've ever had.' Shirley was saying, 'Natural talent, Don! Natural talent!' We laughed, and I stayed on in the job. When my husband found out how much money I made, he was all for it." Scherry and Shirley became close friends, and Shirley watched out for Scherry.

The Oasis was an escape from the demands of home life, and work was where Shirley preferred to be, but she had to pay for babysitters, a family and medical bills. Friends of Shirley said Des encouraged her promiscuity; he knew how much they needed the money. The club's owner, Don Mack, would remain friends with Shirley. She would turn to him for help in the days leading up to her death.

A *Daily News* photographer asked Scherry and Shirley to pose nude for overseas magazines. Shirley handled the negotiations and made sure Scherry was well paid. "I was on Quinns Rocks beach. I was nude, and it was very hot. It was very private. I thought he'd deserted me. I turned around and said, 'Where in the fuck are you,' and 'click', that was the photo. The photographer won an overseas photo competition with my photo. That started my photographic modelling career and his photographic career," Scherry said.

Scherry soon had a modelling and photographic studio in Wellington Street, in the city. "We were skylarking in my studio, and one of the photographers was there, and I said, 'Let's do something different.' I got hold of some of these paints, and I painted these designs on myself and that is where Shirley got the idea of body painting."

When Des left the hospital, he wanted to study. "I love anthropology. I was going to be an archaeologist. I even started studying at university. I got in contact with the curator of the museum, and I was going to get a job, but then they [the museum] needed the money to build a pontoon to dive for the Gilt Dragon [the 1656 Dutch shipwreck discovered in 1963]," he said.

Des says it was his interest in old English history and paganism that led the pair to dabble in witchcraft. It seemed decadent, wild and free—a world away from their struggling life in suburbia. "Life was simple. Just things like walking round naked and being a witch was so exciting," he said.

The coven mainly met in Kings Park in the centre of Perth. Amidst the bushes in the dead of night, they would join others, some respected businesspeople, dancing naked in the moonlight. Witchcraft was prevalent in the Perth at the time; covens even advertised in the newspaper urging witches to meet: *Ever seen a virgin witch—go to the Grand*, one ad read, and another: *Black magic and sex! It's all in virgin witch*. Shirley continued to practice witchcraft until she died, despite her teenage years in the hands of nuns who had tried to cleanse her blackened soul.

Scherry said the coven was not always as innocent as Des claimed. She remembers Shirley's distress when a doctor apparently brought an aborted foetus to a coven meeting for symbolic ritual sacrifice.

Shirley longed for a better life. She cultivated contacts, using her curves.

Des applied for the Army but was rejected. He took odd jobs, but Shirley argued that, because she earned more, he should stay home and look after the kids. The cost of babysitters ate into their income.

Life at home didn't improve. They argued more and more, and both sides claimed abuse. In 1966, Des was again hospitalised—this time at Heathcote, with severe depression. Shirley found Shane's behaviour difficult and the more she rejected him, the worse he became. Trying to manage on her own—with only one income—her husband sick in hospital and unable to cope with the children, Shirley had had enough. There wasn't childcare in 1966, and she needed to earn a living. She handed the kids to Welfare and joined the show circuit.

George 'Slim' Stewart was a fixture at Perth's annual Royal Agricultural Show, running boxing tents and building rides including the iconic Ferris wheel, which still stands. Dyslexic and illiterate, he'd joined the Merchant Navy and travelled to the world's port cities where he learned to survive by the use of his fists, earning a living from boxing. What he lacked in brawn he made up for in height and determination. George Stewart got to know Shirley through the racing crowd at the Oasis. He liked the way Shirley danced and, when she danced topless for some of the crowd in his boxing tent at the Royal Agricultural Show one night, she was a huge hit. The next time she got in a girl and allowed men to paint her semi-naked body. The body painting drew an even bigger crowd. She opened a tent of her own next door.

The men that filled George's boxing tent would flow straight out and into Shirley's. Business thrived, and George's boxers provided security for Shirley's girls. The money poured in. Des was glad for the money as he still wasn't working.

My search for George began early on. Retired Country Party politician, Matt Stephens, spoke to Stewart about the Finn murder back in 1988, while still a Member of Parliament. What he heard alarmed him. George told Stephens he thought a senior detective and a senior politician were behind Shirley's death. "He [Stewart] said I don't believe either of them pulled the trigger, but they would have been involved in the decision to get rid of her," Matt Stephens told me.

Stephens urged Stewart to give evidence. "That's when Stewart told me, 'I'm seventy years of age, and I want to die a natural death, and I've already on two different occasions found a live hand grenade on my front lawn. I work in the bush on my own. I'd be the easiest one in the world to knock off,'" Mr Stephens recalled.

His story was hearsay. It proved nothing. I needed to track down Stewart.

George Stewart was no longer the tough man that had dominated the boxing ring in his younger years when I interviewed him in an aged care facility in Bentley in 2004. Tall and frail, the years in the boxing ring had taken their toll. He tended to repeat himself, but what he could remember he remembered well.

George and Shirley travelled around the state as part of the show circuit in 1966. The show days where George had run his boxing tent alongside Shirley's body painting tent were happy days. "She was a great ol' bird. She was very attractive; she had a lot of character. We got on very well," George said of Shirley. "I told her she needed to be careful of the way she handled herself because she was a very well-developed woman." He smiled as he remembered a young, vivacious Shirley.

Shirley knew how to get attention, and the laughs were matched by community outrage. Complaints grew about Shirley's show, and eventually, the body painting tent was shut down. The pair remained good friends right up until her death. George said he was shocked and angered by her murder, but most of the story he either wasn't able to remember or chose not to revisit.

I asked him about Shirley's friends and associates in those days, but the 85-year-old said he couldn't recall. However, he did remember Detective Bernie Johnson. Shirley spoke of him often. "He was a red-hot copper. He was into anything." George did not or could not elaborate.

"Do you know who killed her?" I asked.

"No!"

"I've been told you do." I paused and waited for him to respond.

"I don't know who killed her. Lots of people reckon they do, but they don't."

"Is it true you had hand grenades put on your lawn?"

"Hand grenades…yeah…had to move them out of bounds…I got the right sort of people in to look at them. They wouldn't have gone off, but I didn't know that."

I asked him who he called in. He said, "Not the police, they cause too much trouble."

George was tired and didn't want to be drawn any further. "Memories left behind shouldn't be brought back and exploited," he said.

He died a natural death, as he had wished, in 2009.

When Des left the hospital, he was furious with Shirley for leaving their children in Welfare while she travelled the state with George Stewart. He's not sure of the year or how long the children were in care, but he remembered immediately marching down to the Swanleigh Home where she had left them.

"It was one step up from a Dickens," Des recalled in 2003, still distressed at the thought of his abandoned children. "I saw the medical officer and I said, 'I gotta go down and see 'em', and I went down and it was winter, July, and it was raining and they had mumps, no, it was chicken pox, sores all over them, ill-fitting clothes.

"I said, 'Get these kids dressed, I'm taking them home.'

"They said, 'You can't do that.'

"I said, 'I can. Do you want me to go and get the police?' I can be a very imposing thing when I lose my temper. I said, 'Get them dressed now.'

"It was about half past five. It was raining and I sort of picked up Bridget, I suppose she was five, I walked down to the railway station, all the way through Perth and these people looking at these kids. All the way from station to home, they were sitting there quite happy, and I almost kicked the front door in. She [Shirley] looked at these kids, and she burst out crying. I said, 'You ever do this again, I'll bloody kill you.'"

Domestic violence would continue between the pair, with a social worker commenting that Des might, *one day kill his wife if the present pressure on him is not alleviated.*

Without the show tent, money soon ran out. Across the world body painting was being popularised by the 1960s hippy movement and models like Verushka. Shirley considered it an art and sought to emulate this new, liberated trend.

Spurred on by the success of the body painting at the Show, needing an income and trying to hold their marriage together, Shirley and Des started a body painting and escort business on Albany Highway, Victoria Park, opposite the Victoria Park police station. Regency Escorts, opened in 1969, was painted red and black, Shirley's favourite colours.

"It was so open and above board, although it was frowned on. They had me into the ABC, me painting this girl," Des said.

Detective Ron Whitmore and Detective Bernie Johnson turned up soon after Regency Escorts opened. Shirley was charged with *keeping premises for the purpose of prostitution* in March 1969. Des was there when the raid took place. He had the paintbrush in his hand and insisted the business was body painting. Detective Whitmore later described the raid as a pioneering move. Shirley's conviction would lead her into the big league as one of three police-protected madams in the state.

Shirley was outraged by the charge and wanted out. Des Finn said lawyer Ron Cannon had told her that there was no point fighting it, she was going down. From the moment the conviction was recorded, Des felt they became pariahs. The newspaper published Shirley's conviction. Friendships they had built from Des' days in the RAAF when the family had held some degree of respect all disappeared. No-one wanted to associate with them.

The Finns were asked to remove their children from the Catholic primary school, and the couple's arguments escalated again. The boys were put back into the hands of Welfare, this time at Castledare. Des was ousted from the local scout group, and he said Shirley was in the hands of police. With a crime sheet she had no choice but to do their bidding.

"It's like all of a sudden you have strings attached to your finger from the puppets down there. Until then the puppet's on its own. It's doing its own thing, once you've got the strings there, you control it," Des said.

Within six or seven weeks of getting busted over her body painting business, Shirley asked Des to take some clothes up to Kalamunda, in the hills some distance from their house. Des said the trip was a diversion to get him out of the house while she sealed a deal with the vice squad.

"I was just coming along the road there, and I saw this car in the drive and smelt the police. So, I just drove past and parked up the end of the road, and after about ten minutes this car pulled out, and I drove back again and saw the drive was empty, so I came down."

Des was furious the police had been at their house, and he demanded to know who they were. "What kind of a game are you trying to pull," he recalled shouting. She eventually confessed they were the vice squad and that "everything was sorted".

Shirley was secretive which made Des angry. She was pulling away from him, and he wasn't coping. An unexplained overseas business trip made by Shirley became the catalyst for an event that finally ended their turbulent marriage.

It was a public holiday in the spring of 1970. Dutch Consul Thomas Dercksen and his wife, Shirley, said they would never forget the day they got lost on a country drive north of Perth and came across a distraught naked woman.

They were taking their daughter and a friend to see the Pinnacles, a vast field of ancient limestone needles about three and a half hours north of Perth when they took a wrong turn. They found themselves on a rough dirt track with the Pinnacles nowhere in sight. They were about to turn around when an angry-looking bedraggled woman, clad only in a blanket, appeared from the bushes waving at them to stop. Mr Dercksen slowed down. "She looked like she'd been around. She had no make-up on, and her hair was all disheveled, and she looked very, very angry," Mr Dercksen recalled.

"I was reluctant to stop because of the children. She begged for help. She said she'd been tied to a tree by a man who had threatened her with a rifle. She showed me her wrist; you could see the tie marks. We were worried about the chap with the gun, especially because we had children in the car."

Apprehensively, they let her in the car and agreed to take her to the Lancelin police station.

Shirley Finn had spent a terrifying night trapped, exposed and fearing for her life. Mr Dercksen recalled her fear. "She said she kept imagining snakes all around her."

Despite her ordeal, Mr Dercksen remembered that an upcoming business trip was playing on Finn's mind. "Shirley was very worried about missing her flight to Singapore. That's what had started the fight. She didn't want him to go [with her] because it was business. Given what she'd been through, we were a little surprised she was so worried about her trip."

I was intrigued by the Derksen's account of Shirley's desperation to get to Singapore. Shirley made a number of trips to this destination. I wasn't able to confirm why, but there is evidence to suggest it was to launder dirty money.

The Dercksens didn't know who 'he' was. They drove Shirley to the Lancelin police station, and Mr Dercksen took her inside. It was empty, but he heard a lawn mower around the back. He went around and explained to the police officer that he had picked up a naked woman who had clearly been restrained against her will.

"Look, I'd rather my family not get involved, but I don't want this story taken the wrong way. So I'd appreciate if I could make my statement and we'll be on our way," he said to the police officer.

Mr Dercksen and the police officer entered the station and Shirley joined them, immediately shouting instructions, ordering the young man to call Bernie Johnson and sort it out.

The young constable handed the woman a form and asked her name and address. She again ordered the officer to call Bernie Johnson. "I thought this woman had connections and she's not prepared to deal with any country cop," Mr Dercksen recalled.

He was not happy involving his family in this situation. "I was concerned I could be wrongly implicated and asked that, before he called up the senior detective, he allow me to make a statement. I wanted to return to the family."

Mr Dercksen was staggered the policeman would not take a statement and insisted on leaving his name and phone number. "This woman was kidnapped at gun point, and the police didn't even want a statement." Mr Dercksen returned to the car and said to his wife: "I don't know who the hell she was, but she certainly has connections."

They never heard anything again about what happened to the woman. There was nothing in the paper and, to their knowledge, no charges were laid.

The trip to Singapore was important to Shirley and may have been connected to her tax problems. It was around this time (1970) that the Hong Kong syndicate money said to be the central motive in her murder began arriving into her account. Financially, Shirley had started to make big money.

It was ten years after speaking with the Dercksens before I found out who kidnapped Shirley. Des Finn had told me how angry he was, after she got busted, about her meeting with police and not telling him what was going on or where she was going. But Shirley confided to a close friend who had tied her up that night.

While omitting the catalyst of their marriage breakup, it was Des Finn who filled me in on what happened next. Shirley had called on her new connections after recovering from her overnight ordeal, then invited Des out to the Zanzibar Nightclub. It was a trap.

5

The Duchess Arrives

The major civilizing force in the world is not religion, it is sex.
— Hugh Hefner

Dorothea or 'Dorrie' Murray and her coterie of good time girls arrived from Sydney's notorious Kings Cross in 1968. 'The Duchess' as she became known showed Shirley where the party was, and Shirley wanted in on the action.

Perth was raining money and men on the back of the mining boom in the North in the late 1960s. Dorrie was sent west by police in the wake of Sydney's notorious brothel wars. She visited Detective Bernie Johnson in WA's Consorting Squad. The Duchess was soon reigning over Perth's sex industry.

Her outfits were legendary: a red leather 'wet look' super short mini dress just covered her crotch with high white patent leather boots that reached to the top of her thighs. Her wigs would always match her outfit. A white dress, a white wig in the latest sixties bouffant style, suede boots and a suede mini, or a sequin number, worth thousands of dollars, with high platform shoes. Dorrie knew how to stand out in a crowd. Where Dorrie went, the party followed, and her home hosted the most talked about parties in town.

At a Roman orgy party for Easter, as long as you dressed up you were welcome. A toga, or a Roman Catholic nun, or priest costume guaranteed you would be anointed with copious quantities of alcohol. The party would last for days: the bathtub, the pool, the shag pile carpeted lounge room with leopard skin prints, the marquee brimming with exuberance.

Dorrie transformed the brothel business in Perth, creating themed rooms such as, 'An Arabic tent', 'The Marie Antoinette Room', 'The Spa Room', 'The Jungle Room' and 'The Dungeon'. She situated herself in Newcastle Street and Lake Street, in what was then still known as North Perth, now Northbridge.

Her gay friends nicknamed her 'The Duchess of Newcastle and Lake on Swan.'

The men lined up, and girls would service up to thirty-eight men a night. Business was booming.

Kim Flatman was straight out of Bible College heading for life as a missionary when Dorrie turned his life upside down and showed him a world he didn't know existed. He was twenty-one, she was forty-two.

Dorrie's husband lived in Sydney and heard about Dorrie's involvement with Kim. Her husband "went to Billy Green to get her dealt with." Dorrie had connections so he would never get the chance to deal with his wife. They travelled back to Sydney where the mother of four dumped her husband then drove with Kim back to Perth. When the divorce papers came through, she married Kim in 1971, setting up house in the beachside suburb of Scarborough.

"It was life in 3D. She was the life of the party, all night every day of the week she would party," he recalled. "She would have a wig to match her clothes. Green dress, a green wig, red dress, red wig, purple wig, purple dress, gold dress, gold hair but mainly blonde. The coloured ones were for special occasions. The nightclubs finished at 3am Then we'd have parties at home."

The Village Theatrical Group, a group of Dorrie's theatrical friends, would emerge wearing Dorrie's outrageous outfits and perform drunken antics to the delight of the party crowds. Wives would find their husbands with other men, and almost anything went. Homosexuality was still illegal in Perth. The clandestine nature of these meetings somehow added to the excitement.

"Dress up in sequins and wigs. The party would start on Friday and finish on Monday. The parties were full on; they were just insane. We didn't know half the people. We had a twelve-foot bar. Non-stop alcohol. She loved Chubby Checker. She taught me how to jive. On summer nights everyone would end up in the pool. Naked of course, and then back in the house to drink and eat and party on. It was outrageous," Kim recalled.

"We loved to travel. I used to go round in a big kangaroo fur coat, and drive a Buick Riviera like out of Butch Cassidy and the Sundance Kid. I had big flare trousers and platforms with six-inch heels. She'd have a big white coat with higher platforms and a white wig, walking down the Champs Elysees. We would have been quite a sight," Kim recalled. "Quite a lot of senior political people were her clients. Extremely famous people would come into the business. Then some girl would say, 'aren't you such and such', the minute someone said something it was all over. You couldn't talk. Discretion was important."

The Member for North Perth, Police Minister Ray O'Connor, was a client.

The Zanzibar nightclub was *the* place to go in Perth in the late sixties. Long queues meandered down William Street on a Friday and Saturday night, though politicians, senior police, journalists, and VIPs did not need to line up.

Dorrie Murray was the club's biggest spender, considered one of its most important patrons. She spent up to a thousand dollars a night. She sat at the 'Captain's table' which was always reserved for her. She was the club's drawcard because where The Duchess went the party followed.

"If she wasn't there the place was dead. With her, it was jumping. They needed her," Kim Flatman explained. The money she had to spend on alcohol never seemed to run out. Every night a new outrageous outfit and wig and a bevvy of beautiful girls would accompany her. Police, politicians, journalists and businessmen would join the table, and the party would go on well after closing time. Girls, boys, whatever they wanted, Dorrie could organise it. "Everyone was scratching each other's back. You let me do this to you, and I'll do this for you."

She'd get front row for the floorshows. A long-legged girl in a tiny sequinned outfit would ride onto the floor atop a Harley Davidson that spilt smoke and fumes. She would strip naked to the cheers of drunken onlookers.

The club's owners, Bert and Laurie Tudori provided security at Dorrie's brothels. Their businesses complemented each other, and they worked together. No-one would cross the Tudoris and their henchmen without serious consequences. "They'd pulverise them, break their arm." They were handy security for the brothels. Detective Bernie Johnson would sometimes work on the door at the Zanzibar, and he'd also help out Dorrie Flatman if she had trouble.

The Tudori's were generous people, and people were generous back. As long as you were loyal and discreet, you could enjoy their generosity.

Shirley knew the Tudori brothers. Like much of the young social set in Perth, Des and Shirley Finn frequented the Zanzibar. Des recalled, "she was very attractive all done up and always sort of pushing it up to blokes. Everyone wanted to get into her knickers… One night we went out, we got some babysitters, and we went to the Zanzibar. It was a trap.

She worked it out with these blokes. They were going to do me over and give me a bloody good hiding. Luckily, I knew a couple of the blokes. One of them said, 'I wouldn't hang around here if I was you,' out the corner of his mouth. I said, 'Why?' He said, 'They're going to get you in a minute.' I went out, and about four or five of them came thundering after me. Luckily, the car was parked outside. She came out and said, 'What are you going to do? What about me?' I said, 'I don't give a shit about you.'"

When Des told me about the beating he believes Shirley had arranged for him at the Zanzibar during our interview in 2003, he omitted the likely reason. A close friend of Shirley's, Glenn Properjohn, later told me that it was Des Finn who had tied his naked wife to a tree in Cervantes and left her there.

The marriage was over. Des wanted to take the kids to England to meet his family and Shirley agreed. Shirley moved into a small flat in Yokine in 1969, and the rest of the family left for England. She became the sole breadwinner and sent him money.

Shirley joined Dorrie's party and started throwing a few of her own.

The quietly spoken, and immaculately dressed English woman who sat opposite me in 2004 seemed more like someone's wealthy grandmother than a flamboyant brothel madam. Dorrie Flatman drank tea from a fine bone china teacup decorated with English roses.

"I introduced Shirley to the business," she said.

Aphrodites, the ten-bedroom brothel located in William Street, Northbridge, was still running at that time, after thirty years. Shirley Finn had converted the premises into a brothel shortly before her death. Dorrie took over the brothel two years after the murder, and her daughter was running it when I interviewed her.

"I think she went up to the Vice Squad and said: 'Well I'm here, I'll abide by the rules and I want to open up a small place.' So she got the go-ahead, but there was no training, as such," Dorrie recalled.

'Madam Sin', as Dorrie was known in Sydney, had run brothels in Kings Cross before she headed west. Two security guards had kept her safe from the crooks.

Dorrie Murray arrived in Sydney with her husband and four daughters from England in 1963. Her husband was out of work and an alcoholic. Dorrie needed to pay the bills. After a brief stint at door-to-door fashion sales, she applied for a job as a masseur. A hairdresser by trade, she said she thought it was straight massage. "A young girl answered the door. I was about forty. She took one look at me and said the position's been filled."

As she was about to leave, the owner of the business approached her. "Have you ever managed staff?" he asked, and she nodded. Dorrie took over the management of the massage parlour, The Continental in Chinatown, while the owner went on an extended holiday in Europe. By her account he never came back, offering her the place. She bought it, soon expanding her Sydney empire to at least seven brothels.

Dorrie Murray was growing her brothel business in Sydney at a time when underworld figures were jostling to take control of the vast illegal empire of drugs, prostitution, smuggling, gambling and race fixing. They were spurred on by the burgeoning demand of US troops on leave from Vietnam. Names like Abe Saffron, Perce Galea, and standover men Lennie McPherson and George Freeman ruled the Cross, some of their stories immortalised in the Australian hit series *Underbelly*.

Kingpin of the brothel underworld in Sydney, Joe Borg was blown up in his van in 1968. Joe 'The Writer' Borg was a gunman, thief, shop-breaker and pimp. He arrived in Australia in 1952 and, in the 1960s, began buying up terrace houses in East Sydney and converting them into brothels. By 1967 his business was turning over millions of dollars.

Borg was in the middle of organising an appeal against his conviction (for having bribed a Consorting Squad detective in 1968) when he was murdered. The New South Wales consorting officer who arrested Borg was alleged to have sent Dorrie to Western Australia with a letter of recommendation to be handed to a detective in the Vice Squad on arrival. This allegation was dismissed by the 1975 Royal Commission into prostitution in WA.

Borg's death was described by police as the climax of a 'reign of terror' as a rival gang angled for control of prostitution, and a number of gangland executions ensued. After Borg's murder, his brothels closed and rivals immediately began charging his girls $48 an eight-hour shift—more than double Borg's rate. Seven other terrace houses in the 'Doors' district were firebombed; killing followed killing and many of Borg's gang fled, to the West.

Sydney prostitutes remember this period as one in which police corruption and abuse was particularly heavy. In 1968, the East Sydney brothels were closed down and, to prevent an increase in street prostitution, a new law was introduced making it an offence to loiter for the purpose of prostitution. The impetus for these legislative changes was to 'protect' American soldiers on R&R leave from Vietnam and to curb the increasing drug dependency of streetwalkers.

The 1970s witnessed the highest numbers of arrests specifically for street prostitution in New South Wales. In addition to having to endure repeated arrests, street prostitutes at this time complained that police extorted $150 a week from each woman to keep arrests to a minimum.

Sydney madam Shirley Brifman died in Queensland in 1971 after naming the head of the New South Wales Special Breaking Squad, Fred Krahe, as the man to whom she paid $1000 a week protection money for several years. Brifman alleged Krahe and 33 other police, also named, had variously received stolen goods, organised bank robberies, distributed counterfeit money and fixed court cases. Police treated Brifman's death as suicide. At the request of Queensland police, no inquest was held at the time. The death left other madams nervous about speaking out.

Dorrie Flatman said she did not know of the violence amongst underworld figures at this time. She never met Joe Borg, but she did know some of the NSW detectives. Her brothels seemed remarkably immune to the turmoil at the time. By her account, she said she was "too small" to attract the attention of the standover men. Perhaps had she paid enough money to avoid trouble from them, or perhaps, with police on her side, the criminals left her in peace.

Organised crime king, Abe Saffron was sealing his grip over the brothel trade in Sydney's Kings Cross when Dorrie was there, and he continued to expand into Perth and Queensland in the 1960s. He was already established in the hotel trade, owning four pubs in the West, most notably the Raffles Hotel on the Swan River at Applecross since 1953, a favourite drinking spot of WA detectives. Abe Saffron had extensive criminal links, but for many local politicians and police, he was a pub and club owner, and they were mostly pleased to enjoy his largesse.

Both police and Saffron may have helped orchestrate Dorrie's move west, along with another police protected madam from Kings Cross, Stella Strong, allowing them to set up their trade monopoly in Perth. Dorrie denies this, saying she operated alone and paid no franchise fees. Stella admitted she stayed with Abe the week before she travelled to Perth, but was clearly still terrified of the man when I interviewed her in 2004.

After Abe died in 2008, his son Alan wrote an exposé on his father titled *Gentle Satan* revealing how Abe took control of vice in NSW. Premier of New South Wales Sir Robert Askin and Police Commissioner Norm Allan made a deal with Abe, to keep control of vice without risking their reputations. *They knew they'd reliably get their cut and would never be exposed. In return, my father [Abe Saffron] was now completely protected. Unlike the Mafia gangsters portrayed by Hollywood, my father didn't preside over a criminal gang that guarded him against rivals and the law—he didn't need a personal army or bodyguards because he was protected by the police themselves.*

I contacted Alan in Los Angeles. He recalled collecting money from Dorrie and Stella in Kings Cross. "If my memory is correct, they both worked for my father and ran a brothel in Kings Cross for him. Wayne and I collected money from them for my father. I believe my father set up Dorrie in Perth in another brothel."

I said to Dorrie that it was hard to believe she could run a large number of brothels in Sydney where extortion was the rule, not the exception, and be one of the few operators not having to pay for the privilege. She continued to insist she never paid a penny. Dorrie said they did *try* and collect money from her and that's why she left Sydney for Perth.

The evidence suggests Abe Saffron struck a deal in Western Australia similar to his NSW deal with the Premier and Police Commissioner, as outlined by Alan Saffron. That is, police would protect his business and, in return, fees would be paid up the line while political reputations were protected at all costs.

Brothels went upmarket across Australia. Girls were a commodity moved across the country to meet supply and demand, and the charges paid for police protection from Sydney to Brisbane and Perth were the same. They needed business savvy individuals to run them—ones who knew how to keep a secret.

Dorrie's arrival in Perth was a game changer. The Duchess was at the helm joined by Stella Strong and local recruit Shirley Finn. The Duchess brought with her Sydney working girls, including Joe Borg's wife Irene and Jan who would later run January's brothel next to the Tudori's Il Trovatore illegal casino in Northbridge.

The madams who had been operating in Perth for decades were raided and shut down, and there was nothing they could do to stop the takeover. Australia-wide, crime was becoming highly organised, and police were organising it. The inner sanctum of the WA Police, mainly Consorting Squad officers, was in control of crime in Perth and no-one dared to cross them.

Dorrie first set up in Lake Street, North Perth. Detectives John Skeffington, Bernie Johnson and Ron Whitmore visited the brothel to check out the girls. "I don't know whether they rang up Sydney or how they checked them out, but they just took the girls' names and addresses, where they were living here, if they were married, if they were living with anybody," she recalled.

Kim Flatman provided the Consorting Squad with a list of girls that worked for Dorrie each week. They needed to keep a close eye on things. The girls couldn't start until they had an interview with police, who would let them know the rules.

Dorrie said she stuck to the rules, one of the reasons she was given preference. She admired the strong hand of the Vice Squad in those days, particularly Bernie Johnson who, as head of the Vice Squad, enforced strict rules on the contained brothels. "He really ruled with a thumb; keep things quiet; you have two girls on each shift; you don't open on a Sunday; don't open at Easter; don't open on Christmas Day. If anyone threatened the girls, you could ring up and he was fair." She is adamant she has never paid him a cent.

The Western Australian police shut down all her opposition, and she said it was less violent here than Sydney, because men were kept out of the business. "Because madams will behave like women. They will bitch at each other, but they will never get guns out and try to take over each other's places, where men do. This [violence] is what happens in Sydney."

Dorrie also helped police out with intelligence on other crooks. An example used in the Norris Royal Commission into prostitution was that Dorrie had dobbed in a brothel operator running two doors up from her in Lord Street, Perth. Police acted immediately and forced the operator to return to New South Wales. On his return to the East, he was shot and killed.

She said some police did take money, but they were caught. She insists Bernie Johnson was not one of them, "Bernie Johnson never received payment from me, directly or indirectly." When asked about Shirley Finn, she explained, "Me and Shirley were good friends at the beginning. She was very fun-loving. She loved a good time, and the girls liked working for her."

But their relationship soon turned very sour.

6

The Puppet on a String

I've always likened life to walking down the street in St Kilda, all lace and curtains, with the light shining on them on a Sunday afternoon. What's behind those curtains will terrify you.

— Des Finn, 2002

Dorrie showed Shirley the ropes. After gaining police approval and agreeing to abide by their rules, Shirley got the green light to run her highly lucrative business. She ran a brothel in Aberdeen Street and then moved it to 454 William Street in 1971.

After leaving Des, Shirley moved into a small flat in Yokine with George Webber. George said Shirley would regularly meet with Detective Bernie Johnson behind their flat. "I saw Shirley placing hundreds of dollars into an envelope that she would take in our car to the edge of the park where we lived. There was a real big park right behind us. Bernie used to go there and crawl into the back of her car like a mongrel dog to get his pay packet," Webber told Bridget in a recorded interview in 2016.

Shirley paid Dorrie and police so she could operate her business. Gladys Harding, a former Roe Street girl who worked for Shirley as a cleaner, was babysitting one of the prostitute's children at Shirley's brothel. She saw three envelopes and asked Shirley what they were for. She would later testify at the Norris Royal Commission that Shirley told her, "One is for rent, one is for Dorrie, and one is for the fucking cops." The envelopes had written on the front, Dorrie, B.J. and Rent. Presumably, B.J. was Detective Bernie Johnson.

Shirley's driver was a young man from Kalgoorlie, called Harry Varis. "It [William Street] was just a room and clients would come in and pick a girl. I used to make coffees and teas and wear a little apron. When the girls got a booking, they'd give me two dollars, and I'd take them in my car and drive them to the motel, and afterwards I'd bring them back again. You'd book two or three motel rooms for the night."

Harry has made the transition from man to woman, from Harry to Leigh, from prostitute to madam and then from the brothel to the council chambers. She won her spot on council in 1999 with the catch cry "dare to be different". Kalgoorlie's most colourful councillor said she could relate to more people because she had looked at life from both sides. In 2004, Leigh was working for Langtrees brothel in Perth. We met in the State Library café.

"Shirley was one of the nicest people you could ever find. She could be a bitch if you did the wrong thing by her, but if you did the right thing by her, she always looked after you. There weren't enough girls in Western Australia at that time, so the girls in Sydney would come across. Tell their parents they were coming over to be jillaroos or barmaids and they'd work as hookers." The links would be through the Kings Cross crime networks, crooked police and major crime figures in the mix.

"Back then, girls used to line up to be arrested. The cops would say, have two girls ready, and girls had turns, but Shirley always looked after the girls," Leigh said.

The girls never gave their real names when arrested. Mandy Rice Davies and Christine Keeler were two famous names adopted by prostitutes in the West and noted on police records. They were pseudonyms borrowed from two women caught up in a spy scandal in the United Kingdom, known as the Profumo Affair.

"The cops were fine, as long as they got paid their money. There were only a handful of cops that you couldn't bribe. We don't pay cops these days. It stopped around the Royal Commission [1976 Norris Royal Commission into Prostitution]. In 1972 –73 I went over to the Cross with a girlfriend. We were working the streets. Every Thursday, in the Cross, this copper got out of his car. He had tartan shorts, socks and white shirt. He went from girl to girl, and each girl handed him forty dollars. Within ten minutes after he got to the end of the street a police van would rock up and the girls who hadn't paid all got arrested. We'd be doing well then two guys called us over one night and said, 'As from tonight you work for us.' Then I decided I'm not working for no bastard, so I decided to leave and go back to WA. I left that night. My girlfriend stayed. She lasted eighteen months. She was dead. They got her hooked on drugs." Leigh sighed, "She was stunning. There were no streetwalkers here. It was all brothels. Coming back probably saved my life."

Leigh was part of a female impersonator comedy act, known as 'Les Coquettes' that performed at Shirley's Striparama nightclub in Northbridge. Kings Cross crime boss Abe Saffron had introduced transexual dance troops and strip clubs to Australia.

Leigh was Shirley's driver. She says she regularly drove Shirley and Ray O'Connor, the member for Mt Lawley and the Police Minister. He would later rise to become Premier of Western Australia. She said it was clear the pair were having a relationship. "I would be prepared to stand up in court and say, 'Ray O'Connor, you were on with Shirley Finn. I drove you around Perth.'"

In the Brand government, Ray O'Connor was Minister supporting Sir Charles Court. Colleagues remember him as a chronic womaniser.

Leigh Varis said she was too frightened to say anything about it at the time of Shirley's death. "Back in those days, he was on top of his game. He was the politician that was going to the top. He was Police Minister. What could you do? You didn't talk about people like that. I took them to pubs, clubs, wherever they wanted to go. She was going out for quite a while. I wasn't in town when Shirley was shot. I'd gone up north. Mum had suggested I go up there to find myself." She recalled an argument between O'Connor and Finn. It was over the tax debt. "If I go down, you go down," she overheard Finn say.

Scherry also said she saw Ray O'Connor with Shirley at the brothel on at least one occasion. Ray O'Connor adamantly denied any connection with her. "It's a joke. I have never even met Shirley Finn," he told me.

Politicians and businessmen were said to be present at a party in Wanneroo where Shirley and her girls provided the entertainment.

Shirley apparently kept a diary with the names of her clients.

When Shirley needed extra girls or exotic dancers for parties and entertainment venues, she would call on Scherry who had a photographic modelling studio in Perth. Football clubs were there biggest patrons.

A friend put me in contact with Scherry. The former showgirl had a black and white portrait of herself in the show days on the wall of her flat, a skimpy outfit, glitter, feathers and impossibly long legs.

"They'd have gaming wheels. Shirley would do the topless waitressing, and I'd do the show. Then the brothel girls would come in after and finish off the night," Scherry said. The police provided security. "Up to six blocks, before you got there, there were guys with walkie talkies checking out who was coming in. They were cops. Plain clothes cops.

"We'd go along to the university parties; we went as Egyptian and harem girls. We didn't have enough girls and sometimes had to fly them in."

At a university law ball, Shirley painted one of her girls with psychedelic fluorescent paint; she stole the show. The girls were the toast of the town. The up and coming lawyers, the footballers, the businessmen and the politicians, who so enjoyed Shirley's services, would deny knowing her in the years to come.

Police arrested Scherry over a football club strip show. She claims charges of prostitution were trumped up and her statement altered so police could get money from her. Scherry alleges the officer who charged her offered to drop the charges if she agreed to pay graft.

"I agreed to give the judge the name of the cops running the corrupt shows. I gave him the names. They were trying to get me to run the brothels like Shirley, but I refused," Scherry claims. She was fined and said the police threatened the charges would continue until she came on board. Fed up, and fearing ongoing harassment, she left the country the day after appearing in court and began working in Singapore and later the Middle East as an exotic dancer.

When Sir Elton John arrived in town in 1974, Shirley was called upon to organise the party.

Crowds spilt onto the back terrace. A live rock band and dancing girls provided entertainment. Alcohol flowed as did the food. As well as the famous entertainer, actresses, lawyers, doctors, politicians and businessmen danced around Shirley's beautiful pool and gardens. That night they were her friends.

The Hollywood-style party was regarded by many as *the* social event on the Western Australian calendar that year. Leigh Varis was there. "It was outrageous! I was quite young and new to the gay scene. The day of the party I helped put lights behind the plants. There were a lot of dignitaries there, a who's who of the gay scene. There was a priest, all sorts of different people. I was so in awe of Elton. It was so much fun, but he wasn't interested in us local boys. They were the good ol' days."

I contacted Sir Elton John's manager via email. He advised Elton could not remember the occasion.

Family, friends, employees, colleagues and enemies all recalled Shirley's extraordinary sense of business. Des told me, "Shirley was all about business."

The brothel business was making good money, and her business trips to Singapore supported claims later made by lawyer Jim Kenneison that she was laundering money for the big end of town.

Getting police onside proved lucrative for business in Perth. Shirley purchased the Pepe Lopez nightclub in the heart of Northbridge in 1971 and decked it out with the latest trims and fittings. She renamed it Striparama, a name synonymous with Kings Cross in Sydney and possibly alluding to her new criminal connections through Dorrie Flatman.

The lively Northbridge club was packed every night with cabaret acts, striptease and drag shows. Liquor was sold, although the club didn't have a licence. Built in a church, today the nightclub is called The Library.

Des Finn, who'd returned from London in 1972 with the kids and needed work, helped with renovations to the loft of the former church. The religious association was not lost on the practising pagans. Shirley wanted this sealed-off area, intended for the escort business, to be accessible only from outside.

"They had a bar at the back of the church. There were steps going up the back to the choir loft. She said the door at the top had to be locked.

She wanted me to drive screws into it, so patrons would have to go up the outside steps, because she didn't want the escort business to impinge on her application for a liquor licence," Des explained.

Consorting Squad Detective Arthur Simms checked in on Shirley regularly. "She was my informant," he said. "I don't think before the business she was ever a prostitute. She just did the body painting. It's because of her we were able to arrest some of the Croatians involved in terrorist activities in Australia. The women that worked for her, some of them worked as cleaners and one saw a coffin and foreign uniforms. We began to watch them and we found eighty-six sticks of gelignite, detonators and photographs in the car of a man called Maric."

Two bombs exploded in George Street, in the centre of Sydney on 16 September 1972, both allegedly linked to a group known as the Croatian National Resistance in Australia. Two migrants associated with the Yugoslav government were the targets of these attacks.

Angelo Maric was arrested in Perth in November 1972 and extradited to Sydney where he was convicted and jailed for exploding the devices and injuring people and property. Maric appealed in 1979 claiming he was verballed and that the judge had mishandled testimony. His appeal was upheld.

Shirley ended her defacto relationship with George Webber after a couple of years. The pair separated amicably.

When Shirley bought her home in Riverview Street, South Perth in 1972, she finally felt she had made it. She filled it with all the finest fittings and grandest luxuries she could find and hosted parties that kept Perth talking for days. Dorrie had shown her the way, and now she was forging a path of her own.

Shirley's home was a sanctuary, and she took great pride in it. She commissioned ornate leadlights—featuring symbols to ward off evil—for all the windows and doors, inside and out. The entrance hall was like walking into a church, with stained glass windows framed by timber panelling, recesses for candles in marble textured walls, a huge brass candelabra hung in a vaulted ceiling, solid wooden trims, and antique furniture.

Each room was decorated with the finest fittings and antiques from overseas, using the best craftsmen available at that time. The landscaped gardens featured roses, palms and ponds. Palm trees and nude statues set into brick arches were lit up around the huge oval signature pool. The large glass doors, which opened onto the back, were slid into the walls to open up the bar area onto the pool.

In just a few years, Shirley's fortunes had dramatically changed. Newspapers reported that Shirley had greater ambitions for her luxurious home: an outdoor sauna and a wine store, plus a huge statue of two nudes embracing in the swimming pool. Roman-style wall paintings and covered walkways were also in the plans. Nude paintings were to hang on the walls inside; and each room, including the bathroom, would have a telephone.

Shirley also purchased a block of ten flats in Mill Point Road, just around the corner from her Riverview Street home, as well as a block of land in Bunbury. A man who made dresses for her and counted her as a close friend said her favourite saying was, "I love life". He felt this saying summed her up.

The 24-year-old Rosie Black (a.k.a. Dean) returned with Shirley after a trip to Melbourne in the summer of 1973 and worked in one of Shirley's brothels. This attractive young woman had grown up on the hard streets of Melbourne, arrested for theft and housebreaking at the age of fourteen, her criminal convictions mounting year by year. In 1966, aged just seventeen, she was working as a prostitute in St Kilda, where she was arrested almost every month for the next three years. She arrived in Perth in 1973 with a drug habit and nowhere to live. She worked for Shirley for a while and slept on Shirley's sofa occasionally. Rose appreciated Finn's support and the pair became close.

Rose moved into Shirley's South Perth home in 1974, forming a lesbian relationship with Shirley, but her drug use was a constant source of tension. Shirley battled to free her lover from the grips of heroin and was successful for a while. Bridget heard some of the fights when Rose transgressed and said they were very heated.

I have spent many years trying to find Rose, trying to get a sense of her and her relationship with Shirley. Did she love Shirley? Does she know what happened? If she does, has her silence been bought with heroin?

I managed to get her on the phone a couple of times. The last time, one of my messages, letters or notes must have hit the mark. It was a silent number. I was driving and had to pull over. "This is Rose," the voice said. A million questions ran through my head, I asked a few, but she was understandably guarded, so I attempted to set up a meeting. She refused but promised to call back. She never did.

7

The Whistleblower

There are two great teachers in life, son.
One is university and one is adversity.
One breeds scholars, the other breeds men.

— Spike Daniels, 1972

Shirley and Dorrie's business activities attracted some unwanted attention. They had the Vice Squad onside, but uniform officers often had to deal with the questions that came with a handful of madams running a relative monopoly. Superintendent Harold 'Spike' Daniels was in charge of Central Division, and he was getting a growing litany of complaints.

It was his concerns about police handling of prostitution at that time that led to a Royal Commission in 1976. I never got the chance to speak to Spike Daniels. He had passed away when I began to investigate Shirley's murder, but his family lent me a copy of the controversial whistleblower's unpublished memoir *With Equal Poise*. He also had plenty of friends who'd sided with the renegade police officer, and they had documents and anecdotes to share with me. At the time, Spike Daniels felt like a one-man band yelling in the wilderness with no-one listening.

A bottle of champagne tossed through a shop owner's window brought the first angry complaint. The startled owner had been sleeping out the back. As he was inspecting the damage, another man had sauntered up to him clutching a brochure for Regency Escorts. The shopkeeper was stunned to find his address on it. When the shop owner rocked up at Central Police Station, he'd asked to speak to the boss. He explained to

Superintendent Daniels he'd been approached by Shirley Finn to rent out the premises, but when he found out the nature of her business, he'd refused. Now here she was advertising his premises. He was outraged, and Spike said he would take it up with the Consorting Squad who dealt with prostitution.

The Consorting Squad detectives had a word to Shirley but did nothing. Spike thought they should have sanctioned Shirley over the advertisement. He was concerned about the growing numbers of brothels in Perth and the lack of police action to stop them.

Worried mothers and fathers also complained to police. A 16-year-old girl had answered a job advertisement offering fun and great money for modelling work. When her mother checked, she found it was a front for an escort business. She had been able to stop her daughter, but she was worried about other girls and wanted police to do something about the aggressive job recruitment advertising in the paper. As a father of five daughters, and having heard stories from the working girls in his younger days on Roe Street (when brothels were confined to a few houses in Perth), Spike understood the parent's dread. He'd taken the address of the brothel the mother had given him to the head of the Criminal Investigation Branch (CIB). The Consorting Squad advised the CIB head that the place wasn't a brothel.

That night Spike drove past, and sure enough, the place was as the mother had described it. He hoped the Consorting Squad were just lazy, but he suspected otherwise. A couple of his officers told him that on another occasion they'd had cause to knock on the door of a Lake Street brothel. They were told if they wanted to talk to the boss they'd need to speak to Senior Sergeant Bernie Johnson at Consorting first. The police being told what they could and couldn't do by prostitutes! Daniels' suspicion and resentment about the Squad was beginning to boil. He met up with some of the old girls from Roe Street who told him there was a powerful new order, highly protected and making huge profits.

At night time the 'Rue de la Roe', or 'The Street of the Pied Piper', as Roe Street was known, was the busiest place in town, up until 1959. Madams opening up outside the area were promptly shut down, confining the problem to a single street in Perth and a few brothels in Fremantle, the city's port area.

Josie De Bray made so much money during World War I that, in 1939, she owned almost half of the Roe Street brothels, adding to her income by leasing out premises to other madams. But the biggest madam in Roe Street was Mary Anne Bergmeyer. During World War II, servicemen queued for metres down the road waiting for their turn and hoardings were erected to protect train passengers from the confronting view. Fremantle was arguably the most important port in the Southern Hemisphere, with 9000 US servicemen visiting Western Australia from 1942 to 1945. The Australian vernacular "overpaid, oversexed and over here" referred to the visiting troops.

When Mary-Anne Bergmeyer (who was married to a German) travelled to Germany during the war on a German passport, she was banned from returning to Australia. Her properties were seized, under the Enemy Property Act, and the Federal Government became landlord to the Roe Street madams. Political pressure forced the closure of all eleven Roe Street brothels in 1958, and the madams moved out—mainly to Francis Street a few streets away. Police later reported that the spread of prostitution was getting out of control. With Roe Street closed, women were opening up all over the place—especially as the mining boom took off in the sixties, and the business became even more lucrative.

The police officer put in charge of getting order back into the North Perth prostitution business was Detective Bernie Johnson. He'd worked Roe Street as a young uniformed cop on the beat, but the old Roe Street madams were not getting any favours from Johnson. He instead gave preference to two eastern states arrivals, Dorrie Flatman and Stella Strong. As their empire grew, Stella Strong was soon replaced by Shirley Finn. The Roe Street madams ousted by the new order began complaining.

They found an ear in Superintendent 'Spike' Daniels. Former Roe Street madam Dot Walsh told Spike Daniels she was forced to sell Francis Street to Stella Strong after Detectives Bernie Johnson and Ron Whitmore repeatedly raided her.

Gladys Harding, a former Roe Street girl, had tried to get in on the 'contained' system without success. She had visited the vice squad but didn't know which man was giving approval. Gladys decided to go ahead and open a brothel but was repeatedly raided and shut down. Two WA Consorting Squad detectives told her not to try to get girls from the Flatman brothel, or she would get pinched. Frustrated at the raids, unable to get girls, and losing money on the premises she had purchased, she had no choice but to close her doors. She took a job as a cleaner for Shirley Finn and worked there on a regular basis, including babysitting for the girls.

Harding said Shirley employed six girls. She regularly saw police officers there, including Ron Whitmore who came in with Detective Johnson. Mrs Harding later gave evidence to the Costigan Royal Commission. Much of it was embargoed except her testimony about Shirley's three envelopes of money and the two detectives:

"Detective Sergeant Bernie Johnson and Ron Whitmore came in and I heard them say to the girls, 'You are going early this evening, have your fines ready and be sure to tell Shirley not to be on the premises.' Next day the place had been pinched."

Harding told Spike that Shirley was paying police. She said anyone who wasn't working for Dorrie and paying police was not able to operate. The police were running the show allowing Eastern Staters to take over the game, according to Harding, who added that Consorting detectives told her the Sydney madams got the go because *"if they do anything wrong, we can just put them on the next plane out of here."* With Shirley, there was no such leeway.

Gladys Harding said Dorrie's Lake Street brothel was known as *"Bernie's Brothel"*, so named by *"the knockabouts at the Newcastle Club hotel"*.

Pandora Young, another madam, who was shut out after the arrival of Flatman, told Spike her premises were demolished to stop her operating. In September 1972, she reported the demolition of the property to police. "I rang him up and said, 'My house is gone.'" Pandora alleged she was subjected to violence and mafia threats, forcing her to leave the trade at this time. She said a black hand painted on her door terrified her. She believed it was a mafia threat. Police identified a black hand at a place she proposed to operate from but dismissed it as a prank. Prank or not, it certainly frightened Pandora. Consorting Squad Detective Arthur Simms said the houses were being demolished anyway. "We found out they were only thinking of buying it and that somebody else had pulled it down."

A standover man, Sam Korcunc, appeared in court after threatening Pandora and ordering she use a mafia network to supply girls. He was charged with soliciting with immoral purpose but absconded on bail.

Gladys Harding expressed her frustration to the Superintendent. The mining boom had brought thousands of single men to WA. There was plenty of business to go round. She didn't understand why the police had only given the green light to two madams.

Frustrated by the lack of action from the Vice Squad detectives, in 1973 Spike Daniels decided to take matters into his hands. Dorrie and Shirley expected the police to notify them when raids were planned, but they were in for a surprise. The first raid was in September 1973.

Lydia, one of Dorrie Flatman's girls, checked in the mirror, adjusted her auburn hair and roughly applied another coat of lipstick. Slumping back on the sofa, she bummed a cigarette off Lisa—a petite blonde with large breasts who'd managed to keep busy all night—and then waited.

Before the cops decided to pay the place attention, punters had been queuing up twelve deep for a turn, and she had longed for a break, but with a marked car parked directly out the front, business had slowed.

Dorrie Flatman marched over to Ray O'Connor's private residence, Mandalay, and demanded Spike be stopped. Spike Daniels was a rogue bull who was not playing the game, and it was affecting her business.

Lydia, a slim American with a diamond in her nose, had been spotted on an overseas holiday and brought to Perth to show some of the local girls how to do the job properly. The girls didn't think she knew any more than them, but Lydia got a 60/40 cut, whereas they had to give up 50% of their money to the madam.

Lisa just wanted enough money to leave her husband. A compulsive gambler and alcoholic he'd threatened to kill their son if she refused to join the game. He'd earned a thousand dollars from the Kalgoorlie madams for depositing his beaten wife through the corrugated gates of the dusty gold town's brothel strip, then gambled and drank it all away.

The first night was hell, and Lisa had cried herself to sleep—although the madam and the girls were quite supportive—and at least she was away from her husband. After a while, it became easy, a job like any other, and the money was a potential path to freedom. After six months living under the rigid rules that bordered on imprisonment in the Goldfields, she was back with her children. Her partner still flared up, and Lisa often copped a beating. It was his nature. However, Lisa's life was about veer sideways into tragedy.

The receptionist pulled back the curtain and gave the cops the finger. They'd have to end their shift soon, and the punters would be back queuing out the door. Finally, the police car moved off.

A tall, clean-cut punter walked through the door and asked the receptionist how things worked. She explained the rules and the punter made his choice. Lisa led him to a cubicle explaining the cost and the options. Lisa left the room, coming back with a plastic douche, a bowl of water with antiseptic, and a small towelling flannel; she told the man to remove his clothes. Most men preferred unprotected sex, but at least she could check for gonorrhoea and syphilis—the plagues of the working girl. She placed the bowl on the side table and smiled at the tall, well-built man.

A moment later uniformed police officers barged through the front. The man in front of her pulled his trousers up as a policeman opened the door. "You're under arrest!" he explained.

In the hallway, she heard the receptionist yelling, "You can't do this!" Dorrie Flatman was furious and determined to make Daniels pay.

Stubbornly, Spike posted a typewritten directive to all personnel under his command to carry out their sworn duty and *report any place where they know or believe prostitution was taking place*. He asked them to write to him in person with any complaints about the directive.

Raiding brothels has always been contentious, often creating more problems than it solves, and potentially driving the industry underground. Spike's campaign was stirring up a hornet's nest. The Consorting Squadand not the uniform branch that Spike headed up—had always handled prostitution. The detectives complained to the head of CIB. He was treading on their turf. He sent communications to the Consorting Squad—detailing his actions and the locations of brothels, inviting them to take on the proper policing of the industry.

Dorrie Flatman's Beaufort Street brothel was raided again in October 1973, a month after the first raid. The girls called Dorrie after they were charged and Dorrie called her lawyer, Ron Cannon, and asked what the hell was going on. Ron Cannon was one of the best criminal lawyers in town, and he looked after both Shirley and Dorrie. His success in the courtroom was legendary. Until this raid, the girls had always pleaded guilty and just copped the twenty-dollar fine. Aside from Shirley's initial arrest in 1969, and until Spike's uniformed police raids, neither Shirley nor Dorrie had ever been present or charged during police raids.

Spike had meant to make a single raid to let the madams know that police were still in charge, expecting the girls to plead guilty as they normally did, but instead, they fought the charge, pleading not guilty.

After each of the two raids, Daniels and officers involved in the raids began receiving harassment calls in the middle of the night, one after another from about four o'clock in the morning. Spike's wife was sick with arthritis.

One of the Roe Street girls asked for an urgent meeting. She warned Spike to watch his back, and he began carrying a revolver.

Spike Daniels wrote to senior officers outlining his concerns. Titled *Manifesto of a concerned cop* he warned that current practices in the administration of prostitution by police would lead to corruption and ultimately murder.

Policing prostitution was tasked to the Consorting Squad, and they were furious Spike Daniels had crossed that line. In December, he met Commissioner of Police Athol Wedd who initially praised Spike for the new level of communication that was operating between the branches, but after the raids, the relationship soured.

"Now it would be a pity if you, one of my most senior Superintendents, should get involved in anything that causes trouble among our branches. I had you in mind for the job of Metropolitan Superintendent, I told you that," the Commissioner told Spike. Spike began keeping records of these conversations and recounted them in his memoir.

Chief Superintendent Owen Leitch met with members of the Consorting Squad involved in administering prostitution. A friend of Spike's was in that group. He reported back to Spike that Leitch had told them to carry on as they had been. *He [Leitch] made unsubstantiated allegations and terminated the speech with words to the effect of 'Do not worry, you will see that I will fix Spike Daniels',* Spike wrote in his memoir.

The Consorting Squad again ignored Spike's request to deal with the two madams. Shirley Finn's William Street brothel was raided the following month in November 1973. Before going on leave, Spike had written out instructions for the raid and passed them on to Inspector Watts. During the raid, one of the men had overstepped the mark, allowing a girl to wash him. As a result, the charges were dropped—not just against Shirley Finn, but also charges stemming from the earlier raids against Dorrie Flatman.

Lisa didn't have to save up enough money to leave her husband. After years of violence, she shot and killed him instead.

She was charged with murder and remanded in custody. Spike Daniels visited her in prison where she told him she had witnessed an exchange of money for the withdrawal of the seventeen charges relating to the three raids on the Finn and Flatman brothels. She named Owen Leitch as the man she saw take the bribe. Lisa later denied the exchange with Daniels. Lisa was in a very vulnerable position.

During her trial for murder, she explained that on the night of the shooting, her husband pointed a gun at her and threatened to shoot her son. *"When I thought he was asleep, I crept over to get the gun and get out of the house,"* she told the court. *"He started to turn around. I pulled the trigger and kept pulling it. I shot him because he would have killed us all."*

In August 1974, she was acquitted of murder but found guilty on the charge of manslaughter.

Spike also opposed Shirley Finn's liquor licence application for her Striparama nightclub in Lake Street, saying she was not of good character. Don Mack, her former boss at the Oasis nightclub also opposed her liquor licence. The licence application failed and at the end of 1974 her nightclub burnt down.

There were several suspicious fires, in businesses owned by Flatman and Finn, which caused Spike concern. Stella Strong also had an unfortunate run with fires in her businesses. Insurance fraud was rife among criminal enterprises in the seventies. As well as Shirley's nightclub burning down in September 1974, a firebomb had destroyed part of Shirley's brothel at 454 William Street four months later, making the front page of the newspaper. Police believed gelignite was used to blow out the back wall of a gun shop—the wall shared with Shirley's brothel. *The West Australian* reported: *Broken glass from the shop's windows covered the width of William Street.*

On the Friday after the blast, *The West Australian* reported: *Detectives have been unable to find a motive for the deliberate blasting of an unoccupied shop in William Street, Perth on Saturday night. They have found pieces of a slow burning fuse believed to have set off the explosion. They estimate that between 5lb and 10lb of gelignite was used. The shop, which adjoins an escort agency, is owned by Mr Tony Yozzi, of William Street, Perth. Several women were at the escort agency when the gelignite exploded at 10:30pm. No-one was hurt.*

The newspaper reported acting chief of CIB Inspector Lloyd Taylor as saying he doubted whether there was any connection between Saturday night's explosion (at Shirley Finn's brothel) and an explosion that destroyed a duplex building in Brisbane Street four years earlier. That explosion, in 1970, had destroyed Stella Strong's brothel. The terrified madam had already been forced to flee Sydney's Kings Cross from a firebombing in 1968 before taking on the Brisbane Street brothel under the police 'containment' system.

Dorrie Flatman recounted the night she received a phone call from Stella after Finn's parlour was blown up. "I remember that because I got the phone call in the early hours of the morning to come and look after her because she was hysterical."

Stella said the Brisbane Street bombing was as a result of rivalry between the protected madams and those who were not included. "The mob who couldn't get an opening started to burn the ones in existence." No-one was charged over the explosion. Stella escaped back to Kings Cross, living for a while in St Kilda in Victoria before ending up in

Kalgoorlie, in the Western Australian goldfields, where she would spend most of her life.

After Stella Strong had left Perth there were only two madams left running the lion's share of the trade—Shirley Finn and Dorrie Flatman.

Dorrie also had an unusual number of fires in her businesses. One fire destroyed her Newcastle Street brothel in October 1973. Dorrie set up an ultraviolet light in the burnt-out ruins. "The place was black, all charcoal. We kept operating. She decked it out with white sheets. She made a fortune," Kim Flatman recalled with a smile. That fire was blamed on an electrical fault in the adjoining home. Other fires caused damage in her Stirling Street and Beaufort Street brothels; electrical faults were deemed responsible there too.

Inspector Lloyd may have been right. Stella Strong had been intimidated and frightened by the blast at her Brisbane Street massage parlour four years earlier, but Shirley Finn didn't seem so worried about the recent explosion at the William Street Escort agency. Shirley's ex-husband, Des Finn, believed the fire in the William Street brothel was deliberately lit, an insurance job. "Shirley rang me up and said she had a job for me. She didn't want to tell me over the phone. She asked me to firebomb her premises. I said, 'You must be joking, with my luck there'd be a copper with a match ready to oblige me, no bloody way.' I told her she was getting into big shit doing things like that. People could die. She said that no-one's going to die, the place is going to be closed. It wasn't an insurance job for her; it was for someone else. Three days later the place was firebombed."

Elsewhere in Australia, extortion rackets forced nightclubs to pay up or be firebombed. The Whiskey Au Go Go nightclub in Brisbane refused to pay the blackmail in 1973. It was firebombed while it was full of patrons, resulting in the deaths of fifteen people and millions of dollars of property damage. Extortion bids on brothels were not uncommon on the East Coast, but there was no evidence of extortion involving fire in the West; attacks from competitors and insurance fraud are a more likely explanation.

Spike expressed concerns about the number of fires in brothels to management.

When Spike returned from a period of leave, he was summoned to the office of the head of CIB, Chief Superintendent Owen Leitch. Spike was offered retirement providing he agreed to admit he was mentally unstable. He refused to do so. Spike took notes, and the following is an edited version of his account of the conversation as described in his unpublished memoirs, *With Equal Poise*.

"*Spike, you can retire just as soon as you like in 1974. Why did you get into that prostitution business and rock the boat? Why didn't you get out and do something about the road toll, about all the burglaries or something like that? You have always been a 'stirrer', but you have stirred a big one now?*" the Chief Superintendent said; to which Spike replied, "What have I done wrong? Everything I did was perfectly lawful."

Leitch told Spike he had damaged relations between Uniform and CIB and involved politicians, which was a breach of police regulations. Spike complained that he had done everything to communicate with the CIB. Leitch then explained how a doctor's report could get Spike early retirement. "*Well, what exactly is your proposition? That I retire on a medical of some sort?*" Spike responded. Mr Leitch told Daniels if he didn't cause a fuss an early retirement would be arranged. "*Well on what grounds Mr Leitch? Are you proposing that I am ill or mentally unstable or something?*"

Leitch replied, "*Yes, of course you are mad and you would have to be mad to do a thing like you did. You know that it is government policy to allow things to operate as they have in the area of prostitution. You also know that it is the department's policy and further you know that CIB has always been in control. Look Spike, why don't you bow out quietly? You are not short of friends, I will grant you that.*"

Spike refused, so the Chief Superintendent threatened to send him to a psychiatrist. Prepared for the onslaught, Spike had already had his sanity assessed and obtained the all clear. Professor Allen German confirmed this despite, as Dr German later testified, daily contact from Owen Leitch attempting to persuade him otherwise.

Daniels claimed the conversation ended with Leitch telling him that he was too dangerous to be put in charge of men and would be sent to a back room or a cell.

Spike was told his room was bugged and a check by a radio technician confirmed his fears. When questioned about whether police were illegally tapping phones, Mr Leitch told a reporter, *"I am not going to confirm or deny it. What we do within our organisation is nobody else's business."*

The nuisance calls to Spike's home continued and were traced back to Flatman's brothels.

Spike had done nothing illegal but was working against the tide, breaching the uniform/CIB divide and applying laws to a trade that many thought unworthy of upholding.

Chief Superintendent Leitch presented Spike with an official report form, saying the latter was applying to be relieved of his command. Spike refused to resign. Leitch said, *"Well, do you want it on your personal file that you got the arse from Central Command?"* Spike said he would serve where he was sent, but that was all he would agree to. Feeling he had done nothing wrong, Spike turned down the $30,000 offered to him in pension payments. On return to duty, he was taken to Commissioner Wedd, who was about to retire. Wedd advised he'd found a suitable job for Spike in the School Lecturing Staff Office at Jaxon House, revising and rewriting Police Routine Orders.

As one of the most senior officers in the police force at the time, he sat outside the Sergeant's office in a small partitioned area with other young constables. Spike had lost his command and, despite medical evidence to the contrary, he was widely mooted to be insane. He wrote in confidence to a colleague about the effect of the move where he stated, *"I am destroyed within myself."* The letter was tendered as evidence at the Royal Commission as further evidence of his 'mental aberration'.

In his unpublished memoir, *With Equal Poise*, he wrote of the indignity he felt: *I had been in charge of Central City Uniformed Police Station with another Superintendent, some six inspectors and about 200 other ranks, and now I was to work in the common room with some half a dozen young constables of the School Lecturing staff, who each had swivel chairs on wheels and who would have impromptu races with them up and down the room. I had a flat table and an old bentwood kitchen chair in their midst. Their Sergeant had a glass-enclosed office and a telephone, which phone I could use until he went on annual leave for a month, but then his office was locked and to use the phone I had to perch on top of the glass partition and stand on a chair to reach it. I knew that I was doing penance and resolved to accept it as cheerfully as I could…I was required by Leitch to submit a written daily diary to him to account for my time, which is a most unusual requirement for one of the department's most senior superintendents.*

Spike added, *if persons are censured for doing their job and placed in 'exile' how different are we from the Communist regime? Is this not the Gulag Peninsula technique of winning by secretly spreading the propaganda that the protestor is mad?*

While visiting headquarters on one occasion, Daniels confronted Commissioner Wedd who asked how he was going. Spike replied, *"You would have to know how I'm going. If I am sane, I should be back at Central, and if I am queer you have no right to have me in a back room rewriting the Routine Orders for every sensible policeman in the job."*

This time Spike was ordered to Northam. After spending ten of the last twelve years in the country, prior to his appointment at Central command, he was again being sent bush. He called on a friend, National Party MLA Matt Stephens, who intervened and put an end to the transfer.

Angered by his experience, Spike broke the most important rule that existed in the police force at that time—the Code of Silence. In a speech to Rotary in 1974, he said the laws concerning prostitution had become *"bent, then broken and finally abolished"*. He began by lamenting the loss of morals of the 'permissive society', including the dramatic rise in the number of prostitutes in Perth and an increase in drug usage. The speech ended with the following warning: *The mafia claim that in four years of illegal activity that they can completely legitimise their activities to be a threat to businessmen like yourselves. It is not sufficient to say, "This kind of thing has always been with us." For so has every other type of crime, it is the increase which is frightening. I have already told you—that all things seen in the East are already heading for the West.*

Take heed from the History of the World. Where all the great crime empires have been built, these same so called 'victimless, non-reportable' type of crimes. And in their wake comes the associated crimes of protection, corruption, coercion and violence. The American experience is that, "where vice rules, fear also reigns" corrupting the very core of our society.

Rotarians, if I shake your complacency, then I am glad. For a Community not only gets the kind of government they deserve, they also get the kind of police service they deserve, which in turn results in the kind of society they deserve, because police action is so firmly affixed to public attitudes.

When we know what is occurring in our society, and fail to protest, it is we who permit the permissive society.

After Spike's Rotary speech, civil libertarian Archie Marshall became involved and, with Spike, began interviewing madams and prostitutes about the brothel scene. Archie Marshall was deeply disturbed about the allegations of protection rackets in prostitution and began calling for a Royal Commission.

It was because of Spike Daniels' campaign that 11-year-old Bridget learnt about her mother's profession. Word of the charges against Shirley Finn hit the newspaper, and the distressed child invented the story of a lolly shop to hide her embarrassment at school.

8

The Lawyer and the Tax Debt

Every difficulty slurred over will be a
ghost to disturb your repose later on.

— Frederic Chopin

Shirley hadn't seen her father for a decade. Jo Shewring told me he was surprised to get the call from her in August 1974, ten months before her murder.

She sounded cultured when she rang him on the phone. He was apprehensive about reconnecting. "So much water under the bridge."

When Shirley told him her address, he was impressed. "Flash area," he remembered saying, interested to know how things had turned out for his wayward daughter who had wanted nothing to do with her parents since she was a teenager. She couldn't wait to show her home to him, he recalled.

The woman who met him at the door of her home in South Perth was well dressed, more refined and well-spoken than he remembered; a far cry from the rough, rebellious teenager who'd taken off with an older man when she was way too young, and he had tried to stop her.

She proudly showed him around her luxurious home, a stone's throw from the Swan River. Antique furniture, monogrammed glassware, chandeliers and a manicured garden. It all seemed so tasteful and upmarket. "I was staggered," Shirley's dad later recounted to me.

They sat down on the deck by her large swimming pool, the gold lettering "SS" embossed on the bottom. She was making idle chat. He says he didn't know how she made her money, nor did he ask. He could tell she wanted something, "Why else would she have asked me there?"

He hadn't told Shirley's mother that she had called. He wasn't sure she would cope. He interrupted her small talk. "I said to her, 'Well honestly, you didn't just bring me here to show me your home. What's the problem?'"

The story he repeated to me was the same as the one he had told civil libertarian Archie Marshall in 1975. Archie went public with that recorded interview.

"I need money!" he recalled Shirley saying. "I haven't asked you for anything since I was a kid, but I'm asking you now. I need $5000, and I need it really quickly." She explained she needed it in the next few days.

It was an extraordinary request. Jo didn't know where his daughter imagined he could find that type of money, but her desperation had taken him aback.

"You reckon I've got a spare $5000 lying around," he'd responded.

He asked what it was for and she said she couldn't say. They continued chatting for a while. She told him she owed a lot of money to the tax department, but that problem was going to be sorted out. "I have a friend, a politician, an MP. I'm flying to Canberra with him shortly, and he will square this taxation away." Jo Shewring said his memory of the conversation with his daughter was vivid and he was certain of the detail.

"Any names?" he remembered asking, wondering just what his daughter had got herself into this time.

"Oh no, we don't deal in names," she had laughed.

"Shirley implied the tax debt would be sorted out in some underhand way—that the politician was going to sort something out, so the debt did not have to be paid. She was quite definite—a Member of Parliament or a politician," he said. A story he has repeated several times over the years, including to police in the days after the murder.

The interest and security offered for the loan were enormous if he could source the money. Shirley's father had a friend he agreed to approach, but wanted an assurance he'd get his money back.

Shirley went inside and returned a short time later tipping a handful of diamonds on the table. One of the diamonds was more than a carat.

"I mean, I'm no expert but I can recognise something that's fairly big and fairly valuable and this thing would have been about I would say $85,000 and she offered them to me," he told Archie Marshall in 1975.

"Why don't you sell some of those?" he asked.

She told him, "I need the cash by Wednesday, Dad, and I can't afford to let anyone know I'm short of a penny. I have to be discreet. That's why I need your help."

Polished cut diamonds and a financial caveat on property held in her name provided security for the loan. The lender's money would be safe.

After Shirley's murder, Jo Shewring told police about the phone call and his meeting with his daughter in 1974. When they did nothing, he told Archie Marshall, who had been helping the besieged Spike Daniels after his speech to Rotary. In 1976, Archie Marshall aired details of Shirley's '74 meeting with her father.

Shirley's father borrowed the money from a friend. "She [Shirley] tied it up through Ron Cannon [her lawyer]," he said. "She rang him and said, 'Well, the money is here for you,' and she went to the office of Cannon and the money was paid out and she did mention that she had, in fact, returned from Sydney. She paid in cash, small denominations." Shirley sent her father a bouquet of flowers in gratitude.

Shewring told Archie Marshall he was frustrated that detectives would not follow this lead but instead chose to follow inane leads. "The thing I was pressing [to detectives], she wasn't kidding me! She gave me the impression that this fellow—this Member of Parliament would fix this deal for her. I came away very convinced, because I said, 'Mother (my wife), she must be mixed up with some very big people because she mentioned this fellow would fix it.'"

Jo Shewring said he had confirmed with CIB that Shirley travelled to Sydney between the 14th of August (when he secured the money for her) and 9th of September when it was repaid.

Shirley's father had less reason to lie than most. He is adamant that Shirley told him on 11 August 1974 that she was travelling with an MP, a politician who would square away her tax debt. It is a story he told to police in 1975, to Archie Marshall in 1975, again in 1982, and to me in

2003. The family, by their own admission, would have preferred to have nothing more to do with Shirley.

I tracked down the man who lent Shirley the money, as his name appeared on one of the titles to Shirley's investment properties. He held a caveat over a block of flats owned by Shirley. The date the caveat was taken out was 14 August 1974 at Cannon & Co., three days after Shirley's meeting with her father.

Edward Spini was working with Shirley Finn's father, Jo Shewring, the day after he had reconnected with his daughter. This is the conversation as he recalled it: "He asked me if I wanted to earn a few easy dollars. He said a close friend of his was desperate for a short-term loan, the interest will be good and that he could vouch for her. He said the money would be secure and I wouldn't lose." He wasn't told "the family friend" was Jo Shewring's daughter.

"I was building a house, so I had a few dollars in the bank to pay for it," Mr Spini explained to me. "He took me round to her house in our lunch break. It had ornaments everywhere, crystal, silver, I suppose they were antiques.

"I lent her the money. I think it was the next day that we went into Ron Cannon's office. Ron Cannon was there, Shirley was there, but [Shirley's father] was not," he recalled. "I signed a caveat against a block of flats. That ensured I'd get my money back. It was a boomerang job. It came back very quickly within a few days." Mr Spini does not know the intended purpose of the money.

I thought perhaps Shirley's lawyer, Ron Cannon, could throw more light on the loan, which was later regarded as a clue to the motivation behind her murder.

Ron Cannon was still practising law in his trendy Subiaco office despite his advanced years, when I caught up with the veteran criminal lawyer in 2004.

"I was a suspect when she was shot. I said, 'I wouldn't be out there shooting my best client,'" he joked.

Ron Cannon was a big man with a low, gravelly but commanding voice. The colourful courtroom performer had represented the Mickelbergs over the gold mint swindle; Barlow and Chambers, Australian drug traffickers sentenced to death in Malaysia in 1986; and international clients like Fiji Coup leader, George Speight, charged with treason in 2001.

On graduation from UWA, the brilliant young lawyer scored the highest marks ever achieved by a student at that time. Admitted to the Bar in WA and the High Court of Australia, he soon travelled abroad, studying African and oriental languages at London University. The British Colonial Office sent him to the British Protectorate of Uganda in 1953 where he became Assistant District Commissioner and then Assistant Registrar of the High Court of the Protectorate of Uganda in the days leading up to Ugandan Independence.

During his time in Africa, the Cold War was at its height. Russia and the USA were vying for control of Africa. Ron Cannon passed on intelligence to London. "Because I spoke the language, and three or four tribal dialects, with the Mau Mau rebellion [against British Rule] in Kenya [1952-59], because you travel around so much, you were asked to pick up information, rivals against each other, tribal differences and conflicts."

Still working for the British Colonial Office, Ron Cannon went to Hong Kong around 1960, where he became magistrate and Crown Counsel. The British colony knew it could not defend itself from China militarily, so it chose diplomacy as its best option for survival. Ron Cannon prosecuted members of the KMT. Headed by Chiang Kai-shek, the KMT had been battling the People's Republic of China in a civil war since 1927.

"There was a lot of sabotage going on from Hong Kong and the Chinese gave a very terse warning to the British colonial government that they needed to stop the sabotage. It was very, very political," Ron told me.

Hong Kong had one of the world's most notoriously corrupt police forces at the time. Corruption was syndicated and systematic. Securing a job in a vice area where the pickings were rich could cost a police staff sergeant as much as A$45,000. Until the arrival of the Independent Commission Against Corruption (ICAC) in 1973, corruption was endemic across the public service. When ICAC arrived, corrupt police officers began shuffling their money offshore and some of it ended up in Australia.

Ron Cannon said his office in Hong Kong was relatively immune to the corrupt practices of the broader public service. Back on his home turf in 1964, Mr Cannon joined legal firm Jackson McDonald, later setting up on his own. As one of a handful of criminal lawyers in town, he represented drug dealers, prostitutes, thieves, murderers and gambling operators. Renowned for his courtroom flair and his ability to win cases, his client base grew quickly.

WA's most high-profile criminal lawyer represented most of the principals of the contained system including, the gambling kings—Vincent Rispoli, Bert and Laurie Tudori, who together ran Il Trovatore; 'Ginger' Antonetti, head of Ginger's Two-Up School and madams Dorrie Flatman and Shirley Finn. He counted Vincent Rispoli as not only a good client but also as a good friend.

"The really powerful one was Vince Rispoli. He was beautifully dressed."

It was 1969 when Mr Cannon represented Shirley over her first conviction at the body painting (escort) business she ran with her husband. "I think it was her first appearance in court, and they were very staged things back then, everybody would know, like with gambling, a group of old age pensioners would be invited the night of the raid," he said. "When I first met her, she'd gone out on her own. She was a very vindictive woman. She was certainly avaricious and had delusions of grandeur."

Back in 1975, he had a kinder view of his former client. *The Sunday Times* reported him as saying: *Her place was always spotlessly clean, as you often find with madams. She would polish everything and I think this fetish with them is associated with their way of life. She was always extremely concerned about her children. I think she was too inadequate to make any in-depth contact with them. She showered gifts on them. She was the most sentimental woman I ever met. I think she would have collected every Christmas and Birthday card ever sent to her. There were hundreds and hundreds of greeting cards and I don't think she ever forgot anybody's birthday.*

While defence lawyers and police officers often have a mutual distrust of each other, Ron Cannon grew up with a healthy respect for the difficulties of policing. His father was a Detective Sergeant in CIB and Bernie Johnson was his father's driver in the 1950s. The lawyer and the detective remained good friends.

Mr Cannon could shed no light on the purpose of the money Shirley needed so urgently. He said he had no idea who the politician might be that Shirley had mentioned to her father, and he could not recall the meeting with Mr Spini and Shirley Finn at his offices.

Despite your promptings, I cannot retrieve any memories of the second loan of $5,000 in August 1974 and repaid a month later, the loan being secured by a caveat over a property described by you as situated in Mill Point Road, he wrote to me some years after our face to face interview. But he did remember helping her with her tax problem.

They did a benefit tax on her and found she had more property than her tax return indicated. Her problems were nothing except she didn't want to pay tax, he said.

In 1973, the tax department conducted what was referred to as a betterment assessment on Shirley Finn. It looked at Shirley's assets, including property, her car, her businesses and her bank accounts and determined that Shirley had spent far more than she claimed to have earned. As well as her home in Riverview Street in South Perth, Shirley owned a block of flats in South Perth and some land in Bunbury. More than $70,000 appeared in two trust accounts in 1971 and 1972, one named Hong Kong Syndicate, the other a trust account held in her name. The tax department gathered a list of her assets and found she had understated her income by more than $150,000.

They asked her to explain the Hong Kong Syndicate. Shirley wrote to The Commissioner for Taxation in December 1973. She said the money in her trust accounts was not income but rather a loan. The Hong Kong Syndicate money, which related to almost half of her tax debt, belonged to someone else and had to be paid back. She would not or could not say whose money it was.

I believe that the first lot of monies were received through the Bank of New South Wales in William Street because I can remember going there and giving them the appropriate authority to forward the same to [name deleted]. They received the money from Hong Kong. The second lot of monies I believe were sent direct to the Perth Building Society in the name of Hong Kong Syndicate. The other member concerned is a person who is involved in the same type of business as myself only in Hong Kong. It represents a capital investment and was paid from Hong Kong to be invested in Western Australia. The person paying the money is a person known to me whose identity I do not wish to divulge. He has received no income and is not liable to pay income tax in the State of Western Australia, Shirley wrote (tax letters obtained under Freedom of Information).

Shirley said she had to make payments to operate but, due to the nature of her business, could not divulge the details of those payments.

Ron Cannon advised Shirley in writing about her tax debt. He wrote:

You will appreciate that if this case goes to Court there will be tremendous publicity because of the nature of the action. You have alleged that you have understated your income by $153,000 [equivalent to more than $1.2 million in 2015]. If this comes out in Court of course they are going to make all sorts of enquiries as to how you were able to operate in the State of Western Australia and make such a large income. We believe that the case will be held against you and of course on this basis never again would you be in a position to carry on in Western Australia because naturally the Police would be suspected of having treated you with favour.

In March 1974, Ron Cannon sought additional advice on the tax debt on her behalf.

The writer saw the leading taxation lawyer in Sydney and had prolonged discussions with him, he wrote.

Cannon told Shirley that she was facing bankruptcy.

We can only see a salvage operation in which you should try and keep the house in South Perth, he wrote in 1973 (letter obtained under FOI).

Shirley Finn's house in Riverview Street was her most prized possession and losing it would have caused her deep distress, but it was not her most valuable piece of real estate. The block of flats she owned at 88 Mill Point Road, also in South Perth, was worth twice as much as her home. Unusually, at no point was consideration given to the sale of these apartments.

The tax department was not satisfied and said unless Shirley provided names, they would treat these funds as income. *"She was too frightened to divulge the [circumstances of the] loan because of the consequences that might follow,"* accountant Edward Dymock later told police, *"This was what she told me and I believed her."*

Ron Cannon advised the tax department in writing that Shirley admitted understating her income but insisted the Hong Kong monies were not income. *Quite frankly Mrs Finn is terrified of the consequences of revealing anything further to the taxation department.*

She states she can make certain revelations to the income tax department but she is terrified. Recently gelignite was put in the back of her premises but fortunately it blew up the premises next door rather than her premises. This happened about six to seven weeks ago and no doubt you read about it in the paper. She states that she is in fear of her life. The writer knows that she is a complete nervous wreck as a result of this whole business and obviously she is going to have to make up her mind what she intends to do.

The story of the gelignite appears to have been a ruse. Des Finn said Shirley had rung him up and asked him to blow up her William Street brothel, but he had refused. Whether the event was for insurance purposes, to create the illusion of threat for the tax department, or both is not known.

Ron Cannon advised Shirley that he couldn't help her further with her tax dispute in August 1974 and she sought the help of an accountant, Edward Dymock. Police later interviewed Mr Dymock who said Shirley had explained the Hong Kong trust accounts were loans used for investing in Western Australian property.

At that time, elaborate financial schemes were being run in Perth to avoid tax and to launder money. Commercial lawyer Jim Kenneison said Shirley Finn was one of his clients between 1970 and 1972. He said she used his services to move significant amounts of cash offshore. However, he said it wasn't Finn's money—it was other people's money.

For most small illegal operations, cash is the standard exchange. Criminal associates and suppliers expect cash, and they pay cash for most living expenses. Typically, they avoid bank accounts, which can be scrutinised.

"I remember when she was buying a house she brought a sackful of money. She was short about $5000—next time she was over $5000. She brought around sackfuls of money to buy houses," Mr Cannon recalled.

It wasn't just property that Shirley acquired for other people. Ron Cannon said. "She told me once she needed money to buy a helicopter for someone up north. She paid for everything in cash. Everything was sold for cash; it was never put through the books."

Shirley owned other assets that the taxman didn't find, including a racehorse called 'Shirley's Boy'.

At a meeting with the tax department, accountant Edward Dymock together with Shirley outlined their objection explaining that she would not be disputing the rest of the betterment assessment, only the Hong Kong syndicate portion of her income. She paid a deposit of $5000 against the agreed taxation debt and arranged to pay $1000 a month, which she continued to pay until her death. Ron Cannon said the money was paid from trust accounts held by Cannon & Co. The remainder of her tax debt was still in dispute at the time of her death.

Mr Dymock felt they had a 50/50 chance of having the money disregarded by the tax department. *I told her to maintain the story which she had been telling all along, that it was a capital loan from Hong Kong and she was too frightened to divulge the name because of the consequences which might follow. This was what she told me and I believed her. In my opinion, had the appeal at the Taxation Department failed, she would not have been able to raise the necessary money from the sale of her assets, after payment of liabilities. She impressed upon me that the house in Riverview Street was the last thing with which she would part and she would have to endeavour to raise the money by other means, and she gave me the impression she could do this,* he told police shortly after her death. There was no mention of the block of flats, which may have been held in Shirley's name for someone else.

That appeal against the tax assessment was due to be heard on Tuesday, 24 June 1975. She was killed on Sunday night, two days earlier.

The timing of her death and statements from witnesses that Shirley had threatened to name names as a result of the disputed tax debt led police to believe the tax debt was the primary motivation for her murder. The $5,000 loan she sought from her father to pay off an MP failed to resolve her financial troubles.

9

Stella's Secret

Repeated trauma in childhood forms and deforms the personality. The child trapped in an abusive environment is faced with formidable tasks of adaptation. She must find a way to preserve a sense of trust in people who are untrustworthy, safety in a situation that is unsafe, control in a situation that is terrifyingly unpredictable, power in a situation of helplessness.

— Judith Lewis Herman

Stella Strong retreated to Kalgoorlie in the early seventies after her brothel in Perth was firebombed. "I thought I was in Siberia; I felt like I was in jail. Dirt roads, all red dust, the washing was always dirty. There were bars on the windows. We (prostitutes) were allowed into town to go shopping for two hours. We couldn't go to the racetrack or the public pool, and we had to tell CIB where we were."

Stella was in Kalgoorlie when Shirley got shot. "Shirley was a working girl, with a greedy husband, trying to support three kids. She did not deserve what she got."

Sitting back in her big chair with two white poodles by her side, Stella's accent reminded me of Zsa Zsa Gabor. "They hurt something in me. The people I knew before, they were thieves and con merchants but not killers and liars. To run a monopoly in anything was shit. Shirley didn't deserve what happened to her. She was only a day late."

"With her protection payments?" I asked.

"Yes."

"Do you know who did it?"

She paused and sighed, taking a long drag on her cigarette. "It was someone in charge. I can't afford to tell you. I hope some day someone will tell it, but I want to live. If a criminal speaks [out], they can't win."

Had it not been for my search for Bridget, Shirley's daughter, I would not have made the seven-hour trip to the Goldfields town from Perth in 2003 to meet Stella Strong.

Intrigued by the death of Shirley Finn, I had visited her grave at Karrakatta Cemetery. Buried with Finn just behind the cemetery chapel and rose garden was a 15-year-old girl named Angela. She could not have been her daughter, as her death occurred in 1996—almost twenty years after the death of Finn. Inquiries at the cemetery revealed the dead girl's mother was Bridget, Shirley's daughter. I wondered what cruel twist of fate could rob a woman of her mother and her daughter. It became very important to me to find Bridget, and the grave gave me a clue to her new identity.

A search through the electoral roll gave me an address in a small country town in the Wheatbelt called Cunderdin, not too far from the Kalgoorlie Goldfields. Knowing my search may prove fruitless, and the distances required for me to check out the address enormous, I decided I would also track down a madam who was operating at the time of Finn. She had left Perth for Kalgoorlie in 1972, three years before the murder happened.

I knocked on many doors in Cunderdin, but Bridget had long moved on. I wrote a long and emotional letter to a woman that I thought could be Bridget and left it at the Cunderdin post office. The woman who rang me back from Queensland a week later was intrigued but was not the Bridget I was after; her maiden name was not Finn.

I had failed to find Bridget, so I drove on, not knowing if Stella Strong was going to add anything more to the story, but Stella's story would make an indelible impression on me.

The long road to Kalgoorlie ran alongside a water pipeline that had provided life to the goldfields town for more than a century. Burdened with public criticism, C.Y. O'Connor, the visionary who built it, committed suicide before its completion. Without him, Kalgoorlie would never have grown to be what it is today—the largest gold producing area in Australia.

It was nighttime as I made my way down the main street of Kalgoorlie, past well-kept, turn of the century buildings. Hard-bitten men battled heat, thirst, dust and disease hoping to strike gold here—and some did. The miners drowned hope, failure and fortune in the pubs, two-up rings and brothels of the remote mining town.

Before I checked into my hotel, I couldn't resist taking a peek at Hay Street. The images of the street I had glimpsed through the window of my friend's car twenty years earlier with a combination of fascination and guilt, remained etched in my mind.

Standing or sitting in doorways were girls: tight tops, big breasts, high heel shoes and short skirts. Row upon row of what looked to me like corrugated tin toilet cubicles—some doors open, others closed. A glimpse into one room revealed insects clinging to lights, a whirring overhead fan to ease the drenching heat, and a double bed. Nowhere else in Australia were brothels so openly tolerated, a rough and wild 'throw together' version of Amsterdam.

The biggest of the bordellos on the corner of Hay and Lionel streets was gone, replaced by the six-million-dollar working brothel museum called Langtrees 181. Among the luxurious theme rooms, 'The Madam's Room' was decorated with a royal purple and gold décor. The circular revolving bed with satin sheets was overlooked by a portrait of Shirley Finn in her cinnamon-coloured pleated gown. The room was a shrine to the murdered madam who was remembered for her courage, kindness and the high professional standards she demanded of her working girls.

Other brothels had been converted to youth hostels. Stella's Red House was one of only two working 'starting gate' brothels that remained, and both were heritage listed. The last of the old-fashioned brothel madams, Stella Strong was still running The Red House in 2003. I had read she was regarded as something of a cultural icon in Kalgoorlie, where she was known for her generosity.

My appointment wasn't until the next day, but my curiosity got the better of me, so I stopped out the front of The Red House. Business was quiet. There were bars on the windows and glass doors. Air conditioning, fresh carpet, fresh paint and, out the back, I caught a glimpse of a pool; the Red House was a far cry from the miserable conditions that would have greeted Stella Strong back in 1972. Back then, rigid rules meant the girls were often virtual prisoners in the brothel.

Irene—said to be the wife of notorious Sydney gunman and brothel owner Joe Borg—worked for Stella and Dorrie in Perth after escaping Sydney violence back in the sixties. She moved to Kalgoorlie and ran brothels in the remote mining town. She said to the author of *On The Game*, Arthur Bingley, "*You also had to lead a life of solitude. You had to stay on the premises. The police used to threaten me. Sometimes they were going to lock me up. I told them it wouldn't make any difference, they could lock me up because it wouldn't be any different to living in Hay Street.*"

Stella wasn't in, so I retreated to my hotel room.

The next morning I drove out to suburban Kalgoorlie, to Stella's brick and tile home in a quiet residential street. The tiny elderly woman greeted me in polka-dot pyjamas at the gate.

"Sorry, I've been speaking to my daughter in America and didn't have time to change. Estelita Roma Strong—the Roma is because I was born in Rome." She had a pronounced but flamboyant Eastern European accent. She beckoned me inside, enthusiastically pointing to a sign on her bedroom door. *I am not a bitch, I am the bitch and to you I am Mrs Bitch.* "This is where I spend nearly all my time."

Inside, the bedroom was cluttered, her king size bed covered with fake leopard skin and a large crystal chandelier overhead. Mirror wardrobes lined the right hand side of the room. She opened them to reveal clothes packed in tightly. On the left, a walk in robe, also overflowing with clothes. She showed me another four wardrobes in other rooms. All full.

"I buy these from all the women who have dress shops in town. See! Most of them still have the labels on. I have to support the local businesses. After all, their husbands support me," she laughed—a throaty smoker's laugh.

Although she does not drink or play pool, she has a billiard room, complete with bar, which she said was for the KGB—her nickname for the police. "If they call me, I have to leave everything and come to the KGB, no matter what I am doing. They say, 'Stella it's CIB.' I say, 'Bullshit, it's the bloody KGB.' They're the same to me."

Like Shirley Finn, she had her name embossed on everything. There are Stella towels, a Stella telephone and Stella crockery. "She got the idea from me."

There were no living plants in Stella's garden, only plastic ones. "I hate anything that dies. Don't ever buy me flowers." A statement that at the time meant little but would come to mean so much.

We sat down in her lounge, and her two poodles came and sat beside her. "Do you mind if I have a cigarette? I've been smoking for 40 years, starting with a very long cigarette holder. You couldn't smoke properly through one anyhow. You had to have one for the look." She lit up and began to tell me about her life. "Being the last madam is not the most exciting. But you know, the mayor said 'everyone who knows you, Stella, likes you for *you*.' Those that don't know you ignore you because they wouldn't ignore you, if they knew you. I just ignore them back. I do a lot of charity work. I like to help people."

What follows is Stella's story, as she told it to me.

"I was a very naughty child. If my mother told me to be home, I would be home an hour later. My mother's family had something like a Malvern Star bicycle factory, and my dad had a travelling Luna Park that went all over Europe. I was dragged all over Rome, that's my middle name Roma because I was born there."

Perhaps Stella was a gypsy but I didn't ask her then, one of many small regrets.

"He had so many women in this Luna Park. All of a sudden I have so many brothers and sisters. With my mum he had only three, me and my two brothers, the Galeas, but maybe there's about twenty others around. When I came here [to Australia], I didn't speak any English. I didn't know what land I was in. I didn't know anyone. It was very hard for me."

She pulled out an album and opened it up. "Look how innocent I was," she said pointing to picture of herself as a young woman with no make-up and long frizzy hair. She was resting on her elbow looking up. "I'm not photogenic, but it's a normal person isn't it?" She looked me in the eye, seeking my reassurance. "Very innocent," I replied, and she smiled.

"When I came here, I learnt all the colourful language. No-one could understand me and I spoke like I had chewing gum in my mouth."

On the next page of Stella's album, she is standing with some of the girls at her Sydney brothel, all dressed in high-heel shoes, white coats—her black hair teased up high on her head in the beehive style of the 1960s. She wore heavy black makeup and held a long black cigarette holder in her hand. She pointed at the white coats. "I was a nurse, a chiropractor. I spent ten months in Osaka learning massage," she said. "My original surname was Galea. Have you seen this book?" she said, pulling out David Hickie's exposé on crime and corruption in NSW in the 1970s, entitled *The Prince and the Premier*. The Prince was Perce Galea, the affable uncrowned king of Sydney's gambling world, a pillar of the Catholic Church and a flamboyant racetrack punter who enjoyed entry into the most privileged of circles.

"My father, he sold me for a racehorse. I was so stupid, so naïve. It was my decision. You should have seen the dollars. I didn't speak English. He was a benefactor. Look, he's given me this tip, a handful of money. The tips, you should have seen the tips. He was my father. My benefactor."

Galea maintained a façade of honesty and respectability despite his extensive links to organised crime. Journalist David Hickie quoted an 'impeccable' source from the Galea empire as saying that NSW Commissioner of Police, Fred Hanson, and NSW Premier Askin each got $100,000 a year from Galea's gambling operations.

"He had a travelling Luna Park show all over Europe. He stopped in Rome—that's where he met my mother." From the lounge room, she pulled a small bronze cast of a horse from the shelf—a memory, she said, of the day her dad sold her to get the money for a racehorse. "It was his favourite, Eskimo Prince. He made a fortune from this horse. He sold me for this horse."

Galea was notorious for fixing races and doping horses.

"He set me up at the Lotus Blossom with my husband." She said she had received overseas training to set up her massage parlour, the first "properly trained" madam in Sydney.

"They liked my style in Sydney, but I had too many relations and being a ding [foreigner of Italian descent] is not always the best. Through my cousin Vince, a Yugoslav, I cannot tell you his last name because he could hurt me. He knew the vice squad. He had a book and knew who to protect, who to collect and who to leave out."

Stella loved to tell stories about her Sydney underworld connections. She had relied on and had been abused by many of Sydney's toughest men.

"The worst of the lot was Lennie McPherson. He tells you, 'Go and shoot him. Right knee, left knee…between the eyes.' Two of my husband's friends, big businessmen from America, 'Mafiosi'—I seen them with Lennie McPherson. I said, 'Who is going to get knocked off?' Next day, Johnnie Regan."

Regan was one the heads of the Sydney underworld in the late sixties. He was known as The Magician, as people closely associated with him had a habit of disappearing—permanently. Ruthless and cruel, Regan was executed in a hail of bullets in Marrickville in 1974.

At the murder trial of Joe Borg, a suspect, painter and docker Robert Lawrence Steele, admitted he'd been brutally beaten outside the Rex Hotel in Kings Cross a couple of days after the Lotus Blossom massage parlour was destroyed by fire, but he denied he knew the proprietors of the parlour.

Aside from gambling clubs, racehorses, and brothels in Sydney, Stella said Perce Galea had business interests in Kalgoorlie.

"My father was a contrabandist, a smuggler. From here he smuggled gold. If Perce was still alive, Kalgoorlie would not be on the map anymore. He was a big shot for being a little shit," she paused and sighed. "I think I have worked out most things, but there is one thing I have not worked out and never will. For what purpose are we alive? Why are we born and where are we going? There must be an after something?" She looked back at the photo. "See, I wore stilettos. I was very provocative, and I talked like I fucked the world."

As well as the Lotus Blossom, Stella owned brothels in St Kilda in Melbourne and one in Mt Isa, Queensland, in the late sixties. She said nothing of police involvement at Mt Isa, but Kalgoorlie madam Irene told the author of *On The Game*, Albert Bingley, she left because the police there were too involved in the business.

We found out that the girl who had sent us had written to the coppers and they were waiting for us. It was a set-up. The coppers wanted to set us up in Mt Isa, get us a flat, and work for them. After all is said and done, if you don't listen to the police rules and you are in trouble, well, they are the only ones who can help you.

Stella said she left Sydney due to the spiralling violence and because of the offer to move west.

"Bernie Johnson was a vice squad inspector. They had three detectives from here. They charged them to look around what's in Sydney, and they ended up in my health studio. He came over with Ray O'Connor, too."

"The politician? The former Premier?" I asked, and she nodded.

Ray O'Connor became Premier of Western Australia in 1982.

"When bloody Bernie Johnson, head of Vice Squad, and Ray O'Connor came down, they said, 'We just closed Roe Street and we got hookers everywhere. Ladies, you would do us a tremendous favour if you open something up.'"

Bernie Johnson says he may have gone to the Lotus Blossom, but never with Ray O'Connor. Frustrated by the crackdown on prostitution in Sydney and wanting to escape the violence, Stella moved west in 1968 for a fresh start. Stella Strong said Dorrie Flatman had a business in the same building as her Lotus Blossom brothel in Sydney, and they knew each other from there, but Dorrie says she never met Stella in Sydney. "I didn't know her before she came here. I was here first. She opened up in North Perth and got in touch with me to introduce herself."

While Dorrie and Stella disagree on who came first, they both agree they teamed up and were friends and business partners when starting up their brothel businesses; that they required approval from Bernie Johnson; and that, in 1970, with Shirley, they were the three women who dominated the sex trade in Perth.

Stella had brothels in Norfolk Street, Francis Street, William Street and Brisbane Street, Northbridge. A dispute, with former Roe Street madam Dot Walsh over the payment for the Francis Street brothel, caused antagonism amongst the madams at the time.

Stella said she paid police in Sydney and the same thing happened in Perth. "Back then we did have to pay police. If we had ten girls, it was $1,000."

That same amount, $100 per girl per week, would be quoted by other madams both in WA and in other states. It seemed to be the going rate throughout Australia.

"I don't want to be the one to say it. I could get in trouble, but I trust you. There was a park in Perth. We had to bring money there every Friday night. We could never go together to pay the money," Stella recalled to me in 2003. "In Perth, it was Bernie [Detective Johnson] who collected money. They take you for a drive in the car. After you paid, your receipt was a Kit Kat. I thought, 'Why do we have to go for a drive in a little Mini-Minor and you give me a Kit Kat when I give you a thousand bucks?' I got nothing much to lose, and I don't lie. From the politicians to the coppers to the girls, you don't last forty years if you didn't do something good."

Like Dorrie and Shirley, Stella frequented the Zanzibar in Northbridge, owned by the colourful Tudori brothers, Laurie and Bert. She alleges Detective Johnson and Bert Tudori were in business together at the Zanzibar. "Bert and Bernie were best of friends, but they didn't trust each other. When one left the Zanzibar, the other had to be there because their money was there. They would never leave it unattended."

Stella was never charged with keeping a house for the purpose of prostitution in Perth, but if the public made a fuss, she said that a few girls with fake names would take the fall. "We used to take turns for the raids. You could laugh. The magistrate would laugh. The girls would all sit there, but they never took me, not the madam. I went there [court] once on foot."

Ongoing violence, with firebombings of her businesses in both Sydney and Perth, forced Stella to escape to Kalgoorlie.

With the government crackdown after Shirley Finn's death and the drop in the price of gold, business in 1975 started to fall off. The Liberal

Government threatened to shut down the brothels on Hay Street in Kalgoorlie.

Stella Strong lost a second brothel in 1975 when a major fire destroyed the Kalgoorlie Starting Stalls to which she had retreated. The fire was recorded as an electrical fault. Stella said she lost a million dollars in a suitcase. She headed to the Pilbara mining town of Tom Price to wash dishes until she could afford to rebuild her brothel and business improved.

Returning a few years later, she continued running The Red House—though the revenues never matched those of the early seventies. "Forty years in this infamous street. You see a lot," she said. "There might be more women now, but Kalgoorlie is a miners' town, and miners are still mostly men. Men cannot survive in the bush without sex. They will always have the urge."

In 1994, her life in the Kalgoorlie brothels was made into a play called *The Starting Stalls* by Cate Smith. Smith told a reporter that the hardest thing about getting to know Stella was her chameleon-like character.

"Do you know what they did when I went away for a while?" Stella told me. "They painted my red house lilac. I was so mad. Red is the right colour for a hooker. If you're a madam, be a truthful one. If you're a reporter be a truthful one. Don't make it bigger or smaller than it is. It's all sad enough as it is."

Another long pause.

"I wish I could forget things but no chance. It stays with you. Then I worked it out. There must be something. An after. I'm sure, because there couldn't be another rotten thing like this Earth."

While I think I understood then that Stella had seen the ugly side of human nature I didn't know that she had witnessed firsthand one of the most horrific crimes in recorded history, losing every member of her immediate family.

I checked back in with Dorrie Flatman to try and iron out some of the anomalies in their stories.

"She's a liar!" Dorrie declared. "Estelita Roma Strong! She's not even Italian, can't speak a word of it. She's not related to Perce Galea."

Stella had no photos of herself with her infamous 'father', just stories. I asked for anything to show the link so that I could publish it, but Stella never sent them to me. I obtained Galea's death certificate, and Stella's name was not on it. If she was not from Rome and was not related to Perce Galea, I wondered what other parts of her story might not be true and considered leaving her out of the book but, after her death, I would learn the terrible truth and why she rewrote her past.

In a death notice in the newspaper in 2008, from the administrator of her will, I learnt Stella's real name was Zdena Strunc. Tracing back through her marriage and immigration records, which after 50 years had become public, I learnt that she had arrived in Australia in 1950 from an Austrian refugee camp.

Born in Pardubice, Czechoslovakia, in 1928, Stella was just thirteen when she was sent to the Bergen Belsen concentration camp during Nazi Germany's occupation of Czechoslovakia. She was the same age as Anne Frank, the most famous victim of the Holocaust, who had hidden in Amsterdam diarising her days before being captured and sent to Bergen-Belsen. Like Anne, Stella would contract typhus at the concentration camp, a disease that killed 35,000 inmates, including Anne Frank. Stella survived, but the scars of those years would stay with her for the rest of her life.

The BBC's Richard Dimbleby accompanied troops that liberated the camp on April 15, 1945. He reported: *"Here, over an acre of ground, lay dead and dying people. You could not see which was which... The living lay with their heads against the corpses and around them moved the awful, ghostly procession of emaciated, aimless people, with nothing to do and with no hope of life, unable to move out of your way, unable to look at the terrible sights around them... Babies had been born here, tiny wizened things that could not live... A mother, driven mad, screamed at a British sentry to give her milk for her child, and thrust the tiny mite into his arms, then ran off, crying terribly. He opened the bundle and found the baby had been dead for days. This day at Belsen was the most horrible of my life..."*

Stella had spent four years living in the horror of Bergen-Belsen. Her father died there, her mother's whereabouts were unknown. The Communists occupied Czechoslovakia and, in 1949, Stella fled across the border to Austria to the protection of the International Refugee Organisation. She was resettled in Australia in 1950 where she had no relatives and spoke no English. Stella married in 1951—her marriage certificates revealing her first husband's address was, for a time, at 105 Palmer Street, the heart of Sydney's notorious Doors district in Kings Cross. He was Czechoslovakian, not American as she had told me. Her second husband was also Czechoslovakian.

The photos of her at the Lotus Blossom in Kings Cross show a woman who looks Italian, but her thick brown hair is a wig and the eyes that look dark, due to the heavy make-up, are grey; they were masks to conceal her past.

With her high school years chiselled away inside a concentration camp, where some of the worst horrors inflicted by humanity took place, Stella arrived in Australia as a refugee with no family and no English. That she came to regard her 'benefactor' as her 'father', is hardly surprising. If, as she says, she was sold into the game for a horse, the living hell and abuses Stella endured as a child continued in Australia where she had sought refuge.

By saying she was Italian, Stella would never have to say why she fled or from where. Surrounding herself with strong, ruthless people, who looked out for her, even if they exploited her, was a matter of survival. The people of the Cross became Stella's family, and the violence and abuses against women in the sex trade were nothing compared to those she had witnessed as a child. She never told a single person, not even her daughter, Kim. In an emotional phone call to Kim, I was able to explain so much about her mother's strange and self-destructive behaviour.

The Red House still stands, though Estelita Roma Strong has moved on, hopefully to a better place. It survives more like a museum than as a working brothel. Today, its few working girls are allowed to mix with the rest of the small community. They are no longer imprisoned in tiny cells, isolated from the town, existing only to serve the sexual needs of the men who worked there.

Still, there were greater hells on Earth.

10

The King of Vice

He struck me as not only intelligent but frank.
In the witness box his attitude to Superintendent Daniels,
whom he had at one time considered suing for defamation,
was admirably restrained and fair.

— Judge John Gerald Norris, 1976

There has never been a man with more control over crime in the state of Western Australia before or since Detective Bernard Bromilow Johnson wielded his stick on Perth's mean streets in the early 1970s. He was said to be unstoppable—a law unto himself.

Newspapers dubbed him the 'King of Vice', though four enquiries would clear him of any wrongdoing. He built a reputation that scared Perth's toughest villains. Bad, brilliant or misunderstood, depending on who you are speaking to, Detective Johnson had extensive contacts with organised crime and police both in WA and interstate and wasn't afraid to use them. Locally he held dirt on lawyers, politicians and other police officers.

Shirley Finn was a 'fizz', an informant who told him who was doing what. It was also Johnson who gave her the go-ahead to operate.

Together with Detective Ron Whitmore, Johnson first arrested Shirley in 1969. "I mainly worked with Ron Whitmore. Geez, he was a funny bloke, a real character. We're still mates," the retired detective told me in 2009. "I call him Ron Titmore," he said as he grabbed a black and white photo. "This is him." Mr Johnson pointed at the picture showing the pair of smiling, shirtless friends in the 1960s, standing next to a dinghy and proudly holding up a large pink snapper they had caught. Mr Johnson's daughter is standing nearby.

"He was in the Navy. He had colourful vocabulary. Always full of funny sayings. He used to say: 'Mate. I'm going to tell you, if we get out of this one, I'm never going to do it again.'"

Humour was an important part of surviving a tough job.

"He reckoned when a person's made an officer they get part of their body chopped out and put on their shoulder. So when I got made an officer, an inspector, this cadet comes in, and I asked him to page Detective Shitmore. So over the PA comes, 'Detective Shitmore to contact Inspector Johnson', right throughout the whole building," he said, smiling about one of the lighter moments in his career.

It was 2009 before I got around to interviewing the detective. For years, no journalist had been able to interview him or lay hands on a photo of him. I had received many warnings about approaching him.

While I was working at Channel Nine on a Western Australian version of *A Current Affair* in 2008, journalist Paula Hudson did a story backgrounding WA prostitution laws, which were in the press at the time. I was the producer on the story. The policy of 'containment', still in operation in WA, had been outlined and made official by Detective Bernie Johnson at the Norris Royal Commission in 1975-76. If anyone knew how it worked, it was him. Paula rang him and asked for an interview and, to my surprise, he agreed. She baked him Rocky Road to sweeten him up. He appreciated the gesture.

Paula built up quite a rapport with Mr Johnson and ventured into some of the more controversial aspects of his career, including the murder of Shirley Finn. I watched the tape when she brought it back to the office. She looked him in the eye and asked: "Did you kill Shirley Finn?" The camera cut to an extreme close up of Bernie, his lined face still alert and on the ball. No sign of discomfort. He stared right back at her, and answered with a smile and a single word, "No."

"Have you got any idea who may have killed Shirley Finn?" Paula asked.

"Not the slightest. No," Bernie replied.

The question in itself is potentially defamatory, but Bernie Johnson agreed to allow Channel Nine to air it. Bernie Johnson had motive, and he acknowledges that fact, but he was one of several people who did, and there was no evidence to show he pulled the trigger.

Emboldened by Paula's efforts, about a year later I rang Bernie, and he agreed to meet me for an interview. I met him in the car park of the Gidgegannup petrol station, in the Swan Valley, north of Perth, then followed him along winding rural roads, through a farm gate, past paddocks of sheep and rolling hills to his timber home set on forty hectares, with sweeping views across the valley. It was a peaceful setting. Dishes sat unwashed in the sink and piles of paperwork lay on the floor.

We sat down at the breakfast bar, and I began recording. "It was easy to manage because we were the power," the retired detective said of the policing system he oversaw in the years leading up to Shirley Finn's death. "The way we ran it, there was only five or six brothels, and if anyone opened, they needed permission from me. We had strict rules, there was no men, no drugs, they had to subject themselves to a medical examination and they had to behave."

Raiding brothels had always been fraught with problems. Police officers battled with laws that made the industry illegal, and fears that upholding those laws would drive the industry underground, leaving it to organised crime and men who were willing to kill to ensure they got the biggest share of the profits. With no legislative guidelines, police officers were often forced to draw their own lines.

The WA Police chose to keep the industry in check through a policy that would later be known as 'containment', though such a policy was never written down. Bernie Johnson said the WA formula was the best in the country. The oldest profession was heavily controlled; there were no streetwalkers, no male pimps and less violence than elsewhere.

Control over the brothels was beneficial to both parties. The police got valuable intelligence, and for the madams, the detectives helped keep violent criminals out and stopped new operators opening up. Police charges could make life impossible for any opposition. Security for the girls was also an issue, and it helped if you could call on police.

"If they wanted to open a brothel they had to come to the Consorting Squad. It was my job to run the prostitution side, and I interviewed them. I laid down the rules. We had a good relationship with the madams. They knew if they didn't do the job they were out," Johnson said.

It was Johnson who gave Dorrie and Stella approval to open up in Perth. "I was there when both of them started." He said the two of them ran a clean game and that is why they got the go-ahead. It was his word that gave Dorrie, Stella and Shirley the power that so annoyed Johnson's colleague, Spike Daniels. "Shame what happened to Spike. He used to give me veggies from his vegetable patch."

The line about the veggies irritated me. I believe it was a rehearsed line to make the officers seem kinder than they were. It was rolled out at the Royal Commission in 1975, and repeated in numerous interviews since. Former Police Commissioner Owen Leitch had said the same thing about Spike to me a few years earlier. Johnson didn't deny he approached Stella Strong at her Kings Cross brothel. "I may have. I went on a number of enquiries to Sydney, and I know prostitutes in Sydney."

But by his account, Stella came over on her own accord. "If they wanted to open they had to come to the Consorting Squad. It was my job, and I interviewed them."

"How did Stella know to come to you?" I asked.

"Maybe she was going for a job," he said. "She ran a clean house and played by the rules."

"But she knew the Sydney rules," I replied. The detectives worked closely with their NSW counterparts, no doubt sharing ideas on how to manage prostitution; perhaps this extended to a uniform set of fees, charges and regulations, and even knowledge of who was in on the racket; information the girls received before their arrival.

"I thought our rules were unique and didn't require honing."

He said the former Premier Ray O'Connor was never with him. "I have never been to Sydney with Ray O'Connor! If Stella was still alive, I'd grab her by the left ear and poke her eyes out, from through her nostrils, because she's telling a naughty lie," he replied.

Shirley also sought approval from Johnson. The retired detective appeared to remember her fondly. "She was quite a character. She was good company. I did not have any knowledge of her being involved with criminals."

He said he had no idea who would want her dead, but he remembered the day her body was found. "I went to work early that day as usual. I was in the office and Peter McGras, the duty inspector, said, 'Can you get down to the Esplanade in South Perth. It looks like there's been a murder.' I went down there. I knew it was Shirley Finn's car as soon as I saw it. I knew it was Shirley Finn."

"You knew Shirley. What went through your head?" I asked.

"Not the same as went through hers," he replied, smiling.

Bernard Bromilow Johnson joined the police force in 1951 as a cadet, becoming a detective seven years later, prior to the closure of Roe Street. Boxer and safe-breaker Arthur 'Scotty' Bishop trained Bernie to box in premises above a bookmaker's shop, not far from the police station on Beaufort Street. SP betting was illegal, but police mostly turned a blind eye. Bernie earned a reputation as a fearless fighter. He was known to criminals as a tough and ruthless detective. They knew not to cross him.

Johnson was seconded to the Consorting Squad in 1962 in the lead-up to the Commonwealth Games in Perth. Considered the eyes and ears of the police force, the Western Australian Consorting Squad was set up in 1955 to stop racketeering and organised crime. Their duty was to obtain information and carry out investigations into serious crimes. No convicted criminal was allowed to consort with another convicted criminal; if caught three times they were charged under the Vagrancy Act, declared habitual criminals and put inside for three months.

In 1975, there were 180 officers in CIB covering the whole of Western Australia. The Criminal Investigations Branch was the division of the WA service responsible for investigating crimes. These detectives were responsible for solving at least some of the sixty to seventy thousand crime reports the police received each year. Nine officers were assigned to the Consorting Squad, and two of these were responsible for prostitution control.

Only experienced detectives were included in the Consorting Squad and they were grossly undermanned. Their workload covered everything from armed robbery and serious assault to prostitution and murder.

Sometimes, the Consorting Act was used to put pressure on criminals. The 'Rugby Room' at police headquarters was the name given to the interrogation room where criminals were beaten up to obtain information or 'loaded up' with a charge. Magistrates in the police courts usually supported the cops.

What went on in the Rugby Room was not talked about. "As long as I am alive I would never speak disparagingly of situations that occurred in the pursuit of criminals. It was sacrosanct," Johnson said.

"Were interviewing techniques heavy-handed?" I asked.

"I would say successful. If your name is Kickett then…," he smiled, appearing to imply he meant the surname literally. Kickett is a well-known aboriginal surname in Perth. I wondered if some members of the family had been on the receiving end of Johnson's boot.

Bernie was good at getting confessions. He arrested one of the Croatian men said to be a member of the Croatian Revolutionary Army, wanted for the detonation of a series of bombings in central Sydney in 1972. Lawyer Ron Cannon wrote inside the cover of a book to Johnson: *To Detective Sergeant Bernie Johnson, the only police officer in WA who can obtain a confession from a non-English speaking Yugoslav whose jaw is broken, and teeth wired up and clamped shut.* The man Johnson arrested was later acquitted.

Johnson got results when results were what mattered. Former Police Commissioner Owen Leitch said Johnson was one of the best detectives around at the time. "Bernie knew more criminals, so he got more evidence," he said. His close associations with the madams, gambling lords and sly-grog operators, as well as interstate consorting squads and criminals, ensured that Johnson knew when crooks were trying to move in from other states. Bernie was the gatekeeper.

Detective Kerry Tangney joined the Consorting Squad under Johnson's wing in the early seventies. He was an intelligent and ambitious detective, though, like Johnson, his career would be marred by controversy and allegations of corruption.

When a security guard was shot during an armed hold-up of David Jones department store in the city in 1974, Robin Holt was soon arrested in Perth, and co-offender Archie Butterly was arrested in Sydney. Christopher Dale Flannery had been working in David Jones collecting information about the movement of payroll money. He was in Sydney when the robbery took place.

Immortalised on the hit television series *Underbelly*, Christopher ('Mr Rent-A-Kill') Flannery would become known as one of Australia's most ruthless hitmen. Flannery already had a string of convictions behind him when the David Jones robbery took place.

The David Jones robbery in Perth would be the first sniff that something was foul with one of Australia's most notoriously crooked police officers, Roger Rogerson. Rogerson's arrogance and ruthless disregard for the law he had sworn to uphold, as well as his ability to escape conviction for the vilest of deeds, would become folklore. He was charged and escaped conviction for trying to murder a police officer who wouldn't take a bribe from him. He killed drug dealer Warren Lanfranchini, who was probably unarmed; and when Lanfranchini's girlfriend, Sally-Anne Huckstepp, went on television saying so, she ended up dead too. Rogerson was pure evil.

WA detectives Tangney and Johnson travelled to New South Wales to extradite Flannery to the West. NSW Detective Rogerson was the officer that dealt with this case on the east coast. The now infamous New South Wales detective arrested Flannery in Sydney. At the time, Rogerson was the most decorated officer in the NSW Police Force, with thirteen awards for bravery and devotion to duty. He was touted as the next commissioner.

The charges against Flannery were robbery with violence and possession of an unlicensed pistol and a sawn-off shotgun, allegedly sent to him by Robin Holt from Perth. Police had a written confession, but Flannery always insisted it was fabricated. A newspaper report at the time said NSW police were forced to quieten an outraged Flannery who was shouting out that he'd been verballed, claiming he never made admissions to police. Though tendered at trial, his confession was unsigned.

Roger Rogerson and Bernie Johnson had worked together on a number of cases over the years. "I worked with him, and I liked him very much. He was a top cop with huge potential," Johnson said of Rogerson.

Bernie Johnson liked spending time at Kings Cross. It was a chance to gather more intelligence and get to know the Sydney detectives and how they worked. Bernie would meet some of the Cross's most notorious and colourful operators including casino operator and organised crime figure Perce Galea. "I know Perce Galea, but not through Stella. I'm not a gambler, but I don't mind a bet. I went to one of the clubs in the Cross that was run by Ronny Lee and Perce Galea. I was winning quite a bit of money. Ronny knew me, or he knew of me, and he introduced me to Perce and said, 'This is a copper from Perth.' The favour I was getting was they weren't taking a commission from me," Bernie recalled to me in 2010. Perce came up and said: 'You'd be pretty much in front wouldn't you.' I'd won as much as a house cost. It was about nine grand then, might have been fifteen. I knew Perce through Ronny Lee. His wife Norma used to run the book. They had a son in Perth."

Ronny Lee was revealed by the Moffitt Royal Commission of 1973-74 to be a leading figure in organised crime.

Butterly, Holt and Flannery were violent criminals. Some say they went on to do the bidding of corrupt police, but back in 1974 they were rounded up and brought back to Perth for trial. *"We knew it was going to be difficult to get them onto aeroplanes because the plane people don't like dangerous criminals on board. I put a strong belt around each of their waists, handcuffs on their arms and legs, and a chain around their feet—and they were handcuffed together,"* Johnson told Perth journalist Louise Momber in 2009. *"He [Flannery] was a mad screaming killer who delighted in his illicit trade. He loved to kill. A good looking bloke but a very nasty criminal."*

Christopher "Mr Rent-A-Kill" Flannery stood trial in Western Australia in October 1974. He was found not guilty of armed robbery. Convicted criminal Neddy Smith alleged Flannery paid a bribe to Rogerson to escape conviction. If true, this is evidence of further corrupt dealings in the West. As Flannery walked from the court, detectives arrested him with a provisional warrant on a charge of conspiracy to commit an armed robbery in Victoria.

Detective Johnson entertained NSW Detective Rogerson while he was in town for the trial, taking him to the Zanzibar where Rogerson would occasionally take to the floor, playing the piano.

Archie Butterly and Robin Holt were both convicted of the David Jones armed robbery and of rendering a person incapable of resisting, by shooting the security guard in the stomach. They were sentenced to four-and-a-half years jail at Fremantle Prison and were then to be detained as habitual criminals. Holt and Butterly spent most of the rest of their lives in and out of jail for violent crimes.

Journalist Adam Shand reported that Flannery later planned to break his friends out of Fremantle Prison using a helicopter. He said two Perth detectives met up with Flannery at a gambling club in Perth. *"You should be aware that you'll be flying in Swanbourne Army Barracks airspace, where the SAS are based," they warned. "If they spot you, they'll shoot you out of the fucking sky. So I'd think twice about it, if I were you,"* Shand wrote.

The plans were put to rest. Archie Butterly later escaped from a Melbourne remand centre with two other assailants, Peter Gibb and prison guard Heather Parker, in 1993. Butterly was shot dead while on the run after a shoot-out with police. The Coroner cleared police of any wrong-doing reporting: *Whether Butterly took his own life after firing a limited number of rounds at police or he was shot by Gibb or Parker essentially will remain unanswered.*

During his time with the NSW Police Force, Rogerson was implicated in bribery, assault, drug dealing and murders, but not convicted of anything until after his dismissal in 1986. Flannery was at the centre of a number of Rogerson's alleged crimes over the years. Most notably the shooting of NSW detective, Mick Drury, who had refused to take a bribe from Rogerson. It was alleged in court that Rogerson drove Flannery to his home, where Drury was shot through the kitchen window while feeding his infant daughter. Rogerson was acquitted.

Christopher Flannery went on to commit up to ten murders. He disappeared on 9 May 1985. Neither he nor his killers have ever been found. He is presumed dead, with Rogerson the key suspect. Rogerson's life of crime caught up with him in 2016. The 75-year-old disgraced former cop was convicted of the murder of student drug dealer Jamie Gao.

Johnson stands firm that he was not involved in the murder of Shirley Finn in any way and has no idea who was. "Spike Daniels made me the main suspect, and everyone hopped on the bandwagon."

With Bernie Johnson holding power over who could and couldn't operate in WA, the claim that containment came at a cost was inevitable. Over the years it's an allegation that's been put to Bernie a number of times. "To admit would be foolish, to deny it would be fruitless. Spike did not have the slightest iota of evidence. His accusations came from a demented mind. So to answer your question, 'Did I ever cop a quid?' No, never, ever. Never and, if I did, it would be a foolish question, and even if I knew someone who did, I can't remember one."

He denies he was a partner in the Zanzibar, or that he offered gambling kings the Tudori brothers any favours, though he admits owning a gold mining lease in the goldfields with Bert Tudori in the eighties.

While still a member of the Force, Bernie Johnson took out a prospecting licence for a ten-hectare property in Marvel Loch, Yilgarn, south of Southern Cross with Bert Tudori. According to Mines Department records, Johnson and Tudori filed production records indicating they found gold worth $70,000 in 1987. *The West Australian* reported in 1989 that several sources confided little work was done on the tenement and the gold purportedly found there was of dubious origin. *The venture is highly questionable, especially as it began at a time when the former policeman was still a serving member of the force*, Robyn Cash wrote in 1989. She went on to detail Tudori's links with a convicted heroin dealer. *Sources say the gambling man consulted the former police officer before asking Sui—a convicted heroin dealer—to come to Perth. The apparent reason for the visit was to settle a power struggle within the gambling fraternity.*

Mr Johnson also had a prospecting licence for a North Coolgardie tenement from December 1986 until March 1988.

As head of the Consorting Squad, Bernie Johnson said it was necessary to have a close relationship with well-run nightclubs for the purpose of intelligence gathering. "I knew them [the Tudoris] from the day they started. I had the run of the place. If I wanted a drink, I got a drink. It was sly-grog. If your job is to collect intelligence, standing there with a glass of water isn't going to work. It was well run. Cops frequented the joint. Everyone went there. They might go to the FW William dance hall then they'd call in at the Zanzibar. It had good bands, hotel bar meals and the Japanese seaman could buy a Seiko watch."

Detective Johnson also demanded subtlety when the Tudori brothers were breaking the law. "Bert used to park his sly-grog van out the back of the Zanzibar. I told him it was only semi-tolerated and he shouldn't make it so obvious. He kept parking it there, so I knocked it off. He came to me and demanded it back. I told him: 'I don't know who's got it. Maybe Jesus is punishing you.' Laurie said: 'There's a bottle of whisky in it for you if you get it back.' I tell you Bert didn't like seeing the whisky going across."

As to the identity of Shirley's killer, "If I knew who killed Shirley Finn, I would affect a citizen's arrest because of all the harm they've done to my reputation, putting me in the frame. Then again, it hasn't done me any harm. Any publicity is good publicity. I know it's a sloppy investigation and I'm one of the suspects."

It had been suggested to me that a professional hitman had been used. I ran it by him. "If it was a professional hit, whoever organised the murder would have sent to Sydney and paid. If I want you rubbed out," he said looking at me, "I ring up Roger [Rogerson], and say: 'Have you got any good hitman at the moment?' He'd say: 'Christopher Dale Flannery.' I'd say: 'Hitman, not somebody you want to hit.'"

11

The Ace of Clubs

Casinos and prostitutes have the same thing in common; they are both trying to screw you out of your money and send you home with a smile on your face.

— VP Pappy

Before Burswood sealed the multimillion-dollar gambling trade in WA in the eighties, a handful of Italian gambling operators made a vast fortune running illegal gambling dens in Perth. Their ability to grow and prosper relied on police turning a blind eye. Their power remained virtually unchecked as they gathered dirt on powerful people, applied their street brand of rough justice and corrupted enough people to ensure they got their way. The illegal gambling lords were at their zenith in the days when Shirley Finn was running brothels and nightclubs.

As miners poured into the West to provide labour for the burgeoning iron-ore trade in the 1960s, they looked for somewhere to play. North Perth, later renamed Northbridge after a radio competition in 1979 was where they headed. Known to locals as Little Italy, it was a place where stiletto heels, tight trousers, slicked-back hairstyles, spaghetti houses and card games added colour and life to the city.

Women, sly-grog and gambling were in hot demand. They were big business in the mining boomtown in the early 1970s. No operators were more powerful than the Tudori brothers, Bert and Laurie, and Bert's father-in-law, Vincent Rispoli.

They moved onwards and upwards. They never had to face the level of scrutiny that their east coast counterparts endured. Isolation and enormous wealth have their advantages.

As long as they had the police on their side, and politicians chose not to focus on their illegal businesses, they could continue to profit without interruption.

Perth's notorious sly-grogging, loan-sharking, casino king and thug, Bert Tudori, held one of the top civic roles in the state when I caught up with him in 2003.

Born above a barbershop, he'd made his fortune from his criminal enterprises and bought up property all over Perth. When he couldn't get developments through, he got into council and loaded it up with his mates. Bert Tudori was Deputy Mayor of the city. His timber-panelled Council office suite had sweeping views across the Swan River.

He leant back in his leather chair, oozing confidence and bravado.

"Perth was like a wild west town because the big projects were opening up north. Very primitive. The people would get up there. No women, red dust, living in tents and they'd work for six months at a time with no alcohol. They were all single, and they'd come down to Perth, and all they wanted to do was play: women, gambling and grog, everything went. There were illegal gambling dens, illegal brothels, sly-grog places where you could drink to all hours and authorities turned a blind eye to it. Containment and toleration. Perth was a very lively place," Bert explained, of the time when he was casino king in the 1970s.

Bert and his brother Laurie rose to prominence as the proprietors of the Zanzibar. Sly-grogging made the brothers a fortune. Known as the six o'clock swill, in the early sixties it was illegal to serve alcohol in pubs past 6pm. The Tudoris saw an opportunity. "We could charge $80 for a bottle of scotch that cost $6," Bert recalled. On the black market, there was huge money to be made. "We'd have doctors, lawyers, magistrates, shoplifters, professional burglars. In those days you could put in an order. If you wanted a shed, 42 inches with stripes down it, before you know it, a shoplifter would supply you with one. Everything went. It was a strange era."

To say people either loved or hated him may be a cliché, but it was certainly true of Bert. He elicits a passionate unquestioning loyalty from his friends while creating deep animosity among his enemies. Wily, quick and clever, Bert Tudori was known to have a short fuse. An ace at card games, he was once dubbed The Ace of Clubs.

"If you want to know what Perth was like in the 1960s, go see *A Bronx Tale* with Robert De Niro. It was just like that," he smiled, remembering his youth.

The Zanzibar was one of the contained nightclubs and gambling dens overseen by Johnson. A curtained room at the back of the club was said to be for police only.

Detective Bernie Johnson was a regular, and some say a partner. Bert Tudori said, "We were in the army together. Bernie was one of the toughest coppers this town has ever seen. Frightened of nothing and strong as a bull and didn't care about anything. And just as well the police force had a copper like him because he attended to a lot of things that a lot of coppers were too frightened to do. There wasn't criminal gangs running around, and by jeez, the bikies, they were frightened of him. He had everything under control."

The Tudori brothers also looked after law and order issues in their own style. "There were no drugs. Couple we caught selling the stuff. We'd take them out the back, threaten to break their legs and tell them to piss off and don't ever ever... We had Northbridge under control my brother and I." Thuggery and beatings could be easily arranged at a Tudori establishment.

Shirley got to know people at the club, and it's most likely this is where she met Dorrie Murray (Flatman). As Deputy Lord Mayor, Bert said he had no time for madams. "I knew Shirley Finn well. She was no good. She was a terrible woman. Anyone dealing with prostitutes (whether women or men) are lowlifes. We've got principles!"

Gambling went upmarket in Perth in 1971. The Tudori brothers convinced their brother-in-law, Vincent Rispoli, often referred to as 'the godfather', to turn his Italian gambling club, Il Trovatore, into a Las Vegas-style casino. After linking up with Italian gambling operators in Vegas and the Cross, new gaming tables were added. Blackjack dice and roulette were introduced, and croupiers were recruited from overseas. The expanded and refurbished casino opened to the wider community in the early seventies. Women were allowed in, and the crowds followed.

On a busy night, more than 500 people could pass through the doors and, over the course of a month, more than a million dollars would change hands. Unlike the early two-up rings and baccarat schools, which could easily be packed-up, police patronage was vital to their success.

Australia-wide, the early seventies saw an expansion of illegal casinos, with the explosion and entrenchment of organised crime and its subsequent corrupting influences. A photo with a prostitute, a great win and celebration at a casino, donations to political parties, outing a homosexual, tax evasion, fixing a debt, there was enough human vulnerability to ensure the business of crime succeeded.

In 1972, an American FBI agent visited Australia. John Cusack warned mafia connections in the United States were channelling money into Australia for illegitimate as well as legitimate business activities. He said the Calabrian L'Onorato Society (Honorable Society) was well entrenched in Australia, Western Australia included.

Mr Cusack said the mafia was *already engaged in extortion, prostitution, counterfeiting, sly grog, breaking and entering, illegal gambling and the smuggling of aliens, and small arms.* He warned that within 25 years, if unchecked, the Society was capable of diversification into all facets of organised crime and legitimate business.

A Royal Commission into Gambling heard of the difficulties of policing illegal casinos in 1974. *Perth's gaming houses were generally built like fortresses. Installed with two-way mirrors, speaking appliances, electrically controlled doors, and with other locked doors instructed to obstruct the entrance of police. The windows are barred and bolted and the whole place is blocked from outside view. Air conditioning is installed in most places in order to keep the place completely locked off.*

Police protection was vital to limit competition and to ensure illegal businesses could operate with minimum disruption. However, the police would need help up the line, and a compliant media was necessary to ensure unwanted attention could be curbed.

"We were the biggest at Il Trovatore. We had fifty-two—mainly girl— dealers," Bert recalled. "It used to be for Italians. It wasn't that we wanted to keep others out, it was we wanted to keep all the information inside."

The club became famous Australia-wide for its no-limit dice game. At some tables, bets started at $5,000. As with the Zanzibar, Bernie was a regular, the liaison point for the club, the police and government. In the Police Force, Bernie answered directly to Owen Leitch. The Chief Superintendent had his back.

Stella Strong said Bernie was a partner in the club; and so did Ginger Antonetti.

Rocco 'Ginger' Antonetti ran Ginger's Two-Up School just down the street from Shirley's William Street brothel. Ginger's Two-Up School was in on the containment system.

I found Ginger's address through the electoral role and went to visit. When I entered his property, his Rottweiler ran at me, baring its teeth and barking. I froze. Inside, I was terrified, but I tried to settle the hostile dog by talking to him calmly.

Ginger emerged, calling the dog off. Instant relief, coupled with concern about how I might be received.

Once as strong as an ox, his famed red hair had gone, and he walked with a frame. I explained I was writing a book and hoped he could share some stories with me. He invited me inside to his small suburban unit. He later said he spoke with me because he thought I was brave when confronted by his dog. I must have masked my fear well.

Ginger told me about the partners involved in Il Trovatore.

"There's a lawyer Ron Cannon. He was lawyer for all the clubs. Everyone. He had to play the cards the way he wanted, for 38 years," Ginger told me in 2003. "He was partner to Bernie Johnson in Il Trovatore. Without Bernie Johnson Il Trovatore couldn't survive," Ginger said. "Ron Cannon is the boss of the clubs."

A former Italian soldier, Ginger arrived from Italy in 1952 under the government migration scheme, without even shoes on his feet. He used his fists to survive. "I had a nightclub in the sixties; then I borrowed some money from a bookmaker. When it started to be real good—*boom*—they busted me! Wouldn't take the doorman. Straight away they give me four weeks in jail," Mr Antonetti said.

Ginger hired thugs to remove any opposition. "There was two or three different clubs offering two-up. After this bloke came and met me, I said, 'I want you to go around and smash everything.' Couple of weeks, he smash the two-up ring, everything."

Mr Antonetti's business was a roaring success, but he said it paled when compared to the Tudori's gambling club. "Bert [Tudori] had the police onside. He had everything. He had Bernie Johnson onside."

"The only one was me and Il Trovatore. They couldn't play two-up. We had a rule. Made a deal. I play two-up, they play whatever, doesn't worry me." Mr Antonetti was in on the containment system, but he denied paying the police.

Italian principals often met to outline business operations in Northbridge. No-one dared step on another's business. Bert had the casino and Ginger had two-up. A line was drawn, and crossing it could have dire consequences.

Ginger liked Shirley and hated Bert Tudori. "She was nice person. She had a nightclub in Lake Street. She helped women, stray women on the street. Picked them up. Everyone tried to get blood off her."

"Someone went to see her at South Perth. It was Bert that arranged it. She knew too much. She knew a lot of things. She was very nice. She worked the politics to get the money. All in it for something. She was working for nothing. When things went bad, she said, 'I'm broke after all these years, leave me alone for a little while. I got no more money.' They say to her, 'you want to finish, then finish.' It was about a week after—that was the end of her," Ginger recalled.

"She was honest. She helped everybody. She should not finish like this. She never did nothing wrong. Police, politics—there was never enough. Everyone wants a piece of her blood. A lot of people knew. There was more than one person – lots of people – they got rid of her. They love her money. Took her blood; quite a few of them, not one or two."

"It was Bert that arranged it. She knew too much."

"She never made trouble. Never drunk. She loved what she was doing. She was successful. Someone come, brought over, somebody set her up."

"They never found out who it was. They don't want to find them. Everyone makes jokes. Not me, I love the person... After time passes. Everything went quiet. They never find because they never look. More than one person. A lot of people got rid of her."

It didn't seem possible that no one had seriously looked into the murder; but the more I travelled down this path, the more I realised Ginger was right. No one had tried to get to the bottom of this complex, multi-layered murder and cover-up.

Bert denied the claim. *"I was supposed to be the getaway bloke with the car, and a mate of mine who was a cop was supposed to have shot her. Well, that's not true. I can tell you that, right here and now, that's bullshit. I still believe today it was Rose, her girlfriend that did it over jealousy. But I got questioned day after day after day. It was nothing to do with us at all. I even barred her from the club,"* he told the Northbridge History Project.

Bert seemed content to point the finger at Rose. He had done the same in his interview with me, giving no thought as to who else might have been involved in the elaborate charade that played out on the night of Shirley's murder.

Playing with other people's lives may have been just a game to the Deputy Lord Mayor. A game he was used to winning.

Following the 1974 Royal Commission into gambling, Lawrence Tudori toured Europe, the USA and Asia. He carried a letter of recommendation from his friend, Police Minister Ray O'Connor, stating: *As a Royal Commission has been held into gambling, and as there is a possibility of a casino licence being granted, Mr Tudori is exploring this venue with a view to bringing back information on its merits and operational advantages to Western Australia.*

The Sunday Independent reported two months after Tudori's trip that an American syndicate with mafia or underworld connections was negotiating the establishment of a company to run gambling casinos in Australia.

Former Premier, and suspect in the murder of Shirley Finn, Ray O'Connor said he knew Laurie Tudori well, as their children attended the same school. I asked him if the Tudoris ever contributed to his campaign or to the Liberal Party's. "Myself, personally, they didn't, but the Liberal Party, I don't know the funds to see whether they contributed or not."

Bernie Johnson said he attended a Ray O'Connor fundraiser with Northbridge identities and Bert Tudori said looking after politicians was part of his business and that he regularly contributed to campaign funds.

In Parliament in 1975, Labor leader John Tonkin said: *"Many members know the big baccarat schools that are operating in the city, and we know that whenever any other person attempts to start up a similar school, it is closed down. Why, some of these people associated with big baccarat schools are quite wealthy. How is it they continue to operate with impunity?"*

Some police officers warned the containment system came at a price. Like Spike Daniels, Superintendent Graham Lee also went public with his concerns but waited until he retired. *"There are all the signs that organised crime is at work here, and by organised crime I mean criminals paying money to people in authority for regular protection—to police or politicians or both,"* he told Jan Mayman of *The Western Mail*. *"I don't know who is being paid off, but it is clear to me from what is happening that some people are paying for protection."*

Bert Tudori was paying a lot of people to ensure his business could operate with as little trouble as possible. When I asked about this, he denied paying money for protection. "No-one made money from our casinos except us," he said.

Bert also said there were corrupt police officers who tried to "cop a quid", but he couldn't remember their names. But, in an interview he gave for the Northbridge History Project in 2006 while he was still vague on police, he admitted paying politicians and newspaper editors after some bad press about Il Trovatore. *"We were actually paying off* The West Australian *and* The Sunday Times *and* The Daily News. *We were paying the editors off, only $200 a week, but that was good money in those days. We had the green light—if you know what I mean by the green light—with the police and state governments. Don't worry about that. You couldn't operate without the politicians. It was a wild west town, that's what it was. And the police were a bit like that too and others. Members of Parliament. I'd say Australia is one of the most corrupt countries in the world or is equal to any in those years. They were wonderful years. They were wild years, fights, but we had it under control. And to us, after a while, it became part of a game. It wasn't making money. We had all the money we wanted. It meant nothing, the money. It was the game. It was the game to us and to the police. That's what it was: the game; the excitement. I couldn't do it now. Everything was wide open. There were brothels going everywhere."*

Honest cops and investigative journalists had nowhere to go. The Tudori brothers and their henchmen had the town sewn up. Organised crime flourished amid a virtual monopoly.

Author and journalist David Williams traced back Italian principals behind the drug traffickers Kevin Barlow and Brian Chambers, who were executed for their part in trafficking 140 grams of heroin in Malaysia in 1986. In his book, *This Little Piggy Stayed Home: Barlow, Chambers and the Mafia*; he said Perth's gambling clubs harboured and supplied a valuable meeting place for the principals of Perth's Italian underworld, many of them compulsive gamblers. *In suitably darkened corners deals can be made without fear of interference, and in the true nature of Omerta [the Mafia code of silence] the dealers are protected by their fellow gamblers.*

Many senior members of the heroin ring laundered their illegal money by sitting at the card tables for a while, then leaving. If police were to attempt to follow the paper trail left by the sale of heroin, the owners and organisers of clubs would testify the money was won gambling.

Gold, drugs, gambling, organised thefts, beatings, prostitution, money laundering, tax evasion, prostitution, gambling—Il Trovatore was crime central in Perth.

Il Trovatore flourished for a decade but steadily died when the Burswood Casino opened its doors in 1985 becoming, at the time, the biggest casino in Australia and the third largest in the world. Gambling was a popular pastime in WA, and when Burswood opened its profit exceeded a million dollars a day, far exceeding expectations. Before Burswood, most of Perth's gambling profits rested with the Rispoli and Tudori families.

Bert says his profits weren't nearly as high, and he was still bitter that his local consortium missed out on the casino deal when the Burke Labor Government took over from the Tudori's friend in politics, Ray O'Connor.

Bert had felt confident that Ray O'Connor would ensure he would get the licence when casinos were legalised. In the lead up to Charles Court's resignation, colleagues within the Liberal Party said the casinos had become the dominant issue, and Ray was pushing for legalisation. Ray O'Connor didn't hold onto the Premiership long enough. When it was clear Brian Burke would win the election in 1983, Bert Tudori tried to do a deal with him. Bert didn't win the casino licence, which instead was given to Dallas Dempster and Genting Berhad. "At the end, our biggest problem was the casino." (Burswood casino opened on 30 December 1985). "When the casino opened up, they all went their way, and the casino got the money, and I never got my money."

While illegal gambling was on the wane, there was still enough money rolling in for a little loansharking. Debts were racked up all over town. A lot of people owed the Tudoris and Rispolis lots of money, and those debts could be called in at any time.

Even after Burswood opened its doors, the Northbridge casino operators continued to offer generous finance to friends in need. A District Court jury heard in 1996 how people involved in a $2.7 million cannabis conspiracy were able to get loans from $5,000 to $100,000 with no documentation, no interest and no pressure to repay. A co-proprietor of Il Trovatore, Carlo Rispoli, generously handed over $100,000 to fruit and vegetable merchant Sam Scaffidi in September 1993. The only condition was, "repay me when you can."

The police had raided Scaffidi's Bickley orchard in May 1993, seizing $1 million worth of cannabis and $755,000 in cash. Scaffidi was sick with mesothelioma and didn't repay the loan before he died.

"When things were going OK, we were doing it every week. I was lending money and money was coming back," Mr Rispoli told the court.

Bert Tudori had already accumulated considerable wealth and continued to be a formidable businessman. Frustrated by red tape at the Perth City Council and desperate to get property developments through, he joined the Council in 1995 and filled it with loyal supporters. He was Deputy Lord Mayor from 2003 to 2005.

It was 2004 when I spoke to the casino ace, early on in my search for answers. The city had been good to him, and he continued to milk it from the civic centre. No one stopped Bert Tudori. Sitting up in his grand council offices, overlooking the town, the man seemed to own it. I wish I'd known then what I know now. There are many more questions I would have asked the former Deputy Lord Mayor.

Bert passed away in January 2009, aged seventy-two. Bikie bosses, former police officers, politicians, businesspeople, councillors and organised crime figures stood side by side at his funeral to farewell the controversial—but larger than life—figure.

12

Dress to Impress

Here it comes sparkling,
And there it lies darkling;
Now smoking and frothing,
Its tumult and wrath in,
Till, in this rapid race,
On which it is bent,
It reaches the place,
Of its steep descent.

— Robert Southey

The economy was in meltdown in June 1975. Inflation was skyrocketing, and the stock market slid to a three-week low with 12,000 job losses reported in Victoria alone. The oil shock a few years earlier had hit hard.

Western Australia's spiralling economy, spurred on by the burgeoning mining industry, had come to a standstill. The gamblers—who binged on the stock market with shares like Poseidon, which was listed at 80 cents and soared to $280—were waking up with a terrible hangover. In 1975, those shares were worth nothing.

Nationally, the last Australian combat troops had left Vietnam, and Gough Whitlam was battling for survival and about to suffer the most controversial blow ever swung in Australian Federal politics.

It was the second year in office for the conservative state government of Sir Charles Court, who blamed Canberra for the economic woes in the West. State exports were damaged by a revaluation of the Australian dollar, and federal government requirements that foreign investment companies deposit one-third of capital investment in the Reserve Bank had dampened investment. A growing number called for the state to go it alone and secede from the rest of the country.

In Western Australia, the party had come to an end, and people were calling in their debts.

The tax man was knocking at Shirley's door, and Shirley was worried. It was 19 June—three days before the execution. A visit to her accountant, Edward Dymock, left her fearing that all she had worked for was in jeopardy. Her home was the security she had long sought, and she was fighting to keep it. Mr Dymock said she had a fifty-fifty chance of losing her upcoming appeal with the Tax Department on Tuesday—a meeting she would never make.

A police statement from Dymock read: *She impressed upon me that her home in Riverview Street was the last thing with which she would part. She would have to raise the money by other means and she gave the impression she could do this.* Handwritten at the bottom of the typewritten statement—*Declined to sign.*

Shirley did not tell her accountant who she planned to lean on for the money, but two events in the coming days provide clues.

It took Jacqueline forty years to reveal details of the day a distressed Shirley Finn arrived at her front door. It was Friday, 20 June—two days before the execution. Jacqueline was watching her favourite TV program, *Days of our Lives.* She'd had special headphones made so she wouldn't be interrupted when the show was on, but she heard the knock on the door. She didn't get up. Jacqueline's partner—SP bookmaker, Don Mack—was preparing the books for the races the next day. He knew not to interrupt her during the program; besides, the visitor was almost certainly for him.

The woman at the door was agitated.

"I have to talk to you. It's serious!" Jacqueline heard the woman say, and caught a glimpse of Shirley Finn. She'd seen Shirley at the Oasis

Nightclub. Don owned the club, and Jacqueline helped out sometimes. Don had known Shirley for years, but Jacqueline hardly knew her, and she didn't have much time for her anyway. She continued to watch her favourite show, but she turned the volume down on her headphones.

Shirley glanced over at Jacqueline, but Jacqueline kept her eyes on the television while listening intently to the drama off-screen. The conversation she heard that day would remain etched in her memory. Her partner reassured Shirley that, as long as that show was on, it was safe to speak, and Jacqueline wouldn't listen. He was wrong.

"This time I'm gone!" Shirley told him fearfully.

Don reprimanded Shirley, "Don't be such a drama queen!"

Shirley continued, "It's serious! I told Owen [Leitch] I am meeting with the tax office soon and I won't muck around. I will give all the names. He [Owen] said, 'Watch your mouth or bang.'" Jacqueline saw Shirley lift her left index finger to her temple and mimic pulling a trigger.

Shirley told Don she was going to dinner on Sunday with someone that was going to help her. She had a dress, which she'd picked up from the dry cleaners, hanging over her arm.

Don asked Shirley what she had said to Owen. "I told Leitchy if I go down, so will you with your boys."

Don looked out the window and asked where Shirley's car was. Shirley explained she'd caught a taxi and asked Don for a lift. Jacqueline went with them both.

Shirley thought they were being followed and asked them to go down a few side streets to check. When Shirley was confident it was safe, they dropped her near her car, which she had left in Mt Lawley.

Articles I generated in the newspaper led Jacqueline to contact me in 2016 and finally to reveal her story. She wanted Bridget to know, despite ongoing warnings not to get involved.

Recalling the event forty years on still caused her deep distress. "On Monday morning, the news came on. A body had been found on the golf course in a Dodge. I connected straight away. It was her."

"She was in my lounge! I could have asked her to stay over, but I wasn't supposed to be listening."

Jacqueline was a young mother and concerned for her safety at the time. She was relieved, at last, to tell Bridget what she knew.

TV and newspaper reports in August 1975 said Shirley Finn was in the police canteen two days before her murder.

In 2014, I wrote to retired police officers inviting them to correct any wrong information in my book before its publication. I had striven for truth and fairness and was concerned about litigation. A retired police officer, Brian, made contact. He eventually revealed he had seen Shirley Finn at the police canteen.

A road traffic constable, Brian said he had finished his shift around 11pm; he thought it was the night of the murder, but it could have been earlier. He headed up to the police canteen to play pool. He was one of only two policemen in the bar when Shirley and a younger woman entered in the company of two detectives. The barman, called Huntley, was the only other person in the room.

"We were having a game of pool. I'd had one or two beers. I was playing the shot when Huntley called out, 'Dennis, get that woman out of here,' and, 'we don't want that sort in here.'"

I queried Brian on the name Dennis, as I'd never heard it before. He said he wasn't sure of the name. It may have been Bernie, but Dennis was the first name that came into his head.

"He [the detective] said, 'we're just having a quick drink and getting a bottle of something.' He [Huntley] said, 'Well, sign them in the book.' I saw him write something in the book. Later the pages were gone," Brian explained. "There were four people: two plain-clothes detectives and two well-dressed women. He signs her in the book and then went and ordered something off the top shelf. They had a drink, and then all four left together," Brian recalled. "The one who was with the younger lady, he was about six foot one, the other about five foot ten or eleven. Medium build, brown hair—older than me, probably in his thirties."

I asked Brian if he was the source behind the media reports in 1975. He said it wasn't him. The report had said Shirley Finn was signed into the police canteen, but the pages in the visitor's book had been ripped out. The newspapers had followed up on this story. The police replied it was '*blown up out of all proportion.*'

Superintendent Bruce Brennan said, "*The inference that Shirley Finn was drinking in the police canteen is a slur on the whole police force.*

"*My enquiries have found that three young women were there on the night in question, but none were Mrs Finn or had anything to do with her calling. They were three decent young women.*

"*They had been invited by a young officer,*" Mr Brennan told *The West Australian.*

"*The page had been removed by a 'misguided young man' who was worried about a senior officer's investigation of suspected unauthorized guests in the police canteen.*"

Three days later, Minister for Police Ray O'Connor told *The West Australian*, "*The Chief of CIB has investigated the allegations about Mrs Finn being in the canteen and has found she definitely was not there.*"

The report went on to say it would be several months before the inquiry into the missing page would be complete because one of the people involved was overseas.

Coincidentally, in mid-August, at the time of the report, Bernie Johnson had just set sail for several months on the 42-metre ketch, 'Ebb Tide'.

I am yet to see a copy of the police report. I do not know what their investigation uncovered.

The same day that Shirley visited Don Mack, Detective Bernie Johnson was seen entering the office of Police Minister Ray O'Connor at Dumas House. The Minister had advised Acting Private Secretary Mick Healey to go home early, but Mick had work he needed to finish off, so he stayed back late. Several prominent businessmen, some of the wealthiest in Perth, entered the Minister's office along with Bernie Johnson. Mr Healey knew some of the businessmen and Bernie Johnson but had never seen the detective at the government offices before. Mr Healey does not think it was a coincidence. Most Friday afternoons were pretty relaxed at the Minister's office—a few drinks, girls dropping in, gambling on penny up (the winner was the player whose coin would land closest to the wall), but that Friday the mood was serious. This meeting was exceptional.

Rose mentioned nothing to police of her partner Shirley's agitation in the days leading up to her death. Either Rose didn't know, or she was involved, or she was too scared to say. According to her statement on police records, regarding the day before the murder, the couple prepared a meal at home with Shirley's daughter and Bridget's boyfriend Kim.

Earlier on Saturday, a friend, Glenn Properjohn, had rung wanting to have dinner with them. He had two friends in town from Sydney, Kandy and Spice, a cross-dressing duo who were performing at Dorrie Flatman's nightclub, Tramps. They wanted to open a massage parlour in town, and Glenn believed Shirley could tell them who was giving the nod.

Saturday night was not possible, as Shirley had agreed to allow Bridget's boyfriend over for a roast dinner. Neither Rose nor Shirley felt like catching up on Sunday evening either, and they had agreed to make excuses. Shirley told Glenn she was short-staffed at the brothel on Sunday night, and she and Rose couldn't join them.

Shirley was anxious to go when she dropped Rose at the William Street brothel before her shift, on Saturday, the night before the murder. *"She told me that she was going to go straight home as she was expecting a telephone call from someone to arrange a business meeting,"* Rose told police.

A former working girl, a friend of Shirley's, said Shirley dropped into the Raffles Hotel in Applecross. "I am very willing to swear that Roger Rogerson [NSW detective] was at the Raffles Hotel, with Bernie Johnson, Abe Saffron and a Chinese guy with a puggy face. I said 'hello' to the group; I believe that day to be Saturday 21 June," she told Bridget and me in an interview in 2016.

A man with an English accent told *The West Australian*, in 1989, he went to Finn's house the day of the murder with a business partner to sell her a 1974 Ford LTD in exchange for her Dodge and $4,000. He said she was worried about the tax debt and told him, *"It looks like I'll get something done on it tonight,"* and, *"Them bastards can pay their part towards it."* Arrangements were made to return the Ford to Finn's home for an exchange the following day, but by then she was dead.

Rose got up late on Sunday. Late night work ensured that mornings were a time for catching up on sleep. Shirley prepared some lunch for her.

The two women were always working on the home they loved and needed some things for the garden.

After lunch, they went for a drive in the hills, stopping to buy three canaries in a cage and some gardening supplies on the way to Lesmurdie waterfall. They walked around, admiring the scenery, and then drove back via Kenwick where Shirley stopped at her ex-husband's house, Rose's statement explained. Des Finn said his ex-wife called in hoping to pick up two outdoor benches to put in the garden, but the boys had smashed them up. He said she seemed in good spirits.

She'd had an almighty row with the boys two weeks earlier after they'd stolen money from her. Shirley felt they were out of control. Shane had always been the black sheep of the family. Diagnosed with behavioural problems from a young age, he'd been in and out of the care of Welfare, but for Steve she was optimistic. He had some focus, and she hoped he was destined for naval cadets. Shane was fourteen, and back in Hillston (a home for boys said to be delinquent), and Steve, who was sixteen, had moved out with some friends.

During that day, Shirley had not mentioned anything about the meeting she was to have that night, she was quite natural and did not appear worried at all, Rose's statement to police read.

A friend of Shirley's, who asked not to be named in the book, said that Shirley called him on the day she was killed. Their friendship dated back to the fairground days with George Stewart. He provided security for her, and she knew she could call him at any time.

He said Shirley was apprehensive about the meeting that night.

"She told me it was Bernie. She said, 'I'm meeting him tonight', and because he wanted more money from her." He confirmed the Bernie he was speaking about was Detective Bernard Bromilow Johnson.

He says he knew of the power Johnson wielded and that is why he never went to the police. He has since agreed to speak to police, and they have been advised he is willing to testify. At the time of writing, they had not taken a statement nor made any approach to collect the evidence.

Johnson denies he met up with Shirley that night, but another witness would put him metres from the Royal Perth Golf Course just moments before the crime was committed.

Rose and Shirley returned home from their Sunday outing and began preparing for the barbeque.

Around 5pm, Shirley phoned a babysitting service. The service operator later confirmed to police that she had received the call, but she hadn't had anyone available.

Bridget joined her mum and Rose. The rain stayed away long enough for them to enjoy a pleasant family meal around the pool, after which Bridget headed upstairs to watch television.

What follows is Rose's version of the night as recorded in her police statements. Shirley sent Bridget to bed, then asked Rose to go out as she had an important business meeting. In all the time they'd been together, Shirley had never asked Rose to leave their home so she could hold a business meeting. It was very unusual, and Rose wasn't quite sure where to go.

Rose says she thought about heading into work or maybe dropping in on Louise's flat—Louise was one of the girls she worked with at the brothel.

"She [Shirley] said Louise's place is best, as she could pick me up from there. It was on the way," Rose later recounted to police.

Rose was undecided, so Shirley told her to ring and say where she had gone. *"Let me know where you are. I'll pick you up after the meeting,"* Shirley had said.

Shirley sent Bridget to bed and, soon after, Rose left in a taxi at about 8pm. Shirley was still dressed in jeans and a T-shirt with a brown fur jacket for warmth. Louise was surprised by the visit as Rose hadn't visited before, but then again Rose had never had to vacate her home at short notice.

Rose says she called Shirley at 9:40pm. The TV show she had been watching with Louise had finished, and Rose was hoping the business meeting was over too. Shirley told her to stay away a bit longer.

"I'm expecting him to knock at the door any minute," Shirley supposedly told Rose. These may have been the last words she ever spoke to Rose.

Rose couldn't tell detectives who he was. *"I have no idea whatsoever who Shirley was going to meet for the business meeting. In the two-and-a-half years I've known her, she's never asked me to leave because she has a meeting,"* she told police investigating the murder.

Louise McLaughlin confirmed to detectives that Rose came over to her place around 8.30pm. She said Rose rang Shirley three times.

"The conversation relating to Shirley, by Rose, during the telephone calls she made, was that Shirley had possibly left and was on her way to pick her up," Louise told detectives investigating the case.

A neighbour, Lorretta-Anne Kerr, told police they saw Shirley dressed in a long glittering gown in the driveway of her home searching through a purse at exactly the same time—9:40pm. The purse also glittered and matched the outfit she was wearing. With her was a young woman dressed in jeans.

Bridget is adamant this young woman was not her. Rose was 25-years-old at the time of the murder and may have been the young woman Lorretta-Anne saw.

I haven't been able to find Lorretta-Anne Kerr, who spotted Shirley in the driveway that night, but I spoke with other neighbours in the street. They recalled Lorretta was unhappy with the time written on the statement. It was not her true recollection, and she felt coerced to record it as 9:40pm.

The taxi driver who picked Rose up between 7:50pm and 8pm saw two women standing in the door.

If Shirley's business meeting was at home, Shirley didn't need a babysitter and if the person did not want to be seen, Shirley would not be bringing her home with her teenage daughter in the house.

Rose's statement, as recorded by the police, does not add up.

Whoever she was meeting asked Shirley to get dressed up for a special event—not just 'after five' wear or a cocktail dress but a ball gown—her very finest. Shirley must have believed her night out to be a very special occasion. Why else would you wear a ball gown unless you had an invitation to a ball?

She chose a full-length cinnamon-coloured pleated satin gown worth thousands. It was her favourite. She'd had cosmetic surgery on her breasts, and the low-cut dress showed off the surgeon's handiwork beautifully.

She placed two large gold rings set with big black stones on her fingers, a weighty gold necklace around her neck and a gold, diamond-studded watch around her wrist. She carefully applied her make-up and then added the piece-de-resistance, a tooth cap containing a diamond valued at more than $15,000. Her Italian imitation snakeskin shoes matched her gown. Shirley liked things to match. She was a perfectionist in her home and her dress. Decades later, builders would comment on the exceptional attention to detail in her beautifully designed home. On the night of her murder, she had applied the same attention to her dress and accessories.

She had dressed to impress.

13

The Execution Ball

Dying is not romantic, and death is not a game which will soon be over... It's the absence of presence, nothing more...a gap you can't see, and when the wind blows through it, it makes no sound.
— Tom Stoppard

Along the West Australian coast, the rain is accompanied—all too often—by a ferocious, gusting wind. So it was on 22 June 1975. Shirley was terrified of the dark on still nights—let alone stormy nights. However, her destination was the golf club at the end of her street—less than a kilometre from home.

Minutes after a neighbour saw Shirley in the driveway of her Riverview Street home, a white Dodge Phoenix was sighted at the edge of the golf course. The location was a known meeting spot for police and their informants.

Stella Strong said the golf course was where she often met detectives to pay bribes. She would get into a car, and they would drive her around. She said she and Shirley didn't like going alone. "We went together to the park sometimes, but we were not allowed. We would have to pay the money, but we couldn't go together to pay the cops."

Consorting Squad Detective Kerry Tangney later confirmed that detectives regularly met informants at the golf course location.

The police report recorded no sightings before10:30pm, but two witnesses claimed to have reported seeing the Dodge on the golf course between 9:45pm and 10pm. Both saw a white van and one claims to have heard gunshots. They reported these sightings to police.

There was no sign of a struggle. The killer pushed the muzzle of the gun so hard against Shirley's head it left an imprint. The mother of three was shot four times at point-blank range. One shot fired from the passenger's side hit the left side of her head; the other three were fired from the right—most likely from the back seat. The bullets lodged in her brain. She died instantly. It was quick, and it was clean; detectives later described it as a 'professional hit'. Her purse, which she had rifled through as she left Riverview Street, was later found back at her home, complete with her cigarettes without which she never went anywhere.

The police report to the coroner attempted to explain the absence of the purse at the murder scene: *A possible explanation regarding the purse could be that the deceased, realising that she had not transferred the contents of her handbag, returned to the house for her car keys and then left the evening bag behind. The other possible explanation is that someone had taken it from the crime scene and had entered Shirley's home, perhaps searching for something, and left the purse on the bed.*

A luxury Dodge Phoenix with a black vinyl roof sat parked near the ninth fairway of the Royal Perth Golf Course, alongside the busy Kwinana Freeway, just before the Freeway crossed the Narrows Bridge into town. It was the type of car people noticed.

Three different cars were seen next to or near the Dodge that night, though none of these witness reports appear on police files.

'Joe' said it was about 9.45pm when he saw the Dodge on the golf course, just five minutes after Shirley was seen leaving her home a short distance away. He was road testing his vehicle after fitting new brakes. Heading south on the freeway, Joe noticed a Dodge parked on the lawn at the Golf Club. He was into American cars, so he slowed down to take a better look.

"When I was almost stationary, I noticed a white van coming towards me, down the golf course road. When it got closer, I could see it was being driven by a policeman and noticed the blue government plates. I said to my sister, 'she's gonna get busted'. A lady was clearly visible in the driver's seat of the Dodge," Joe told me in an interview in 2015.

A white HQ Holden, with no police markings, pulled up alongside the Dodge.

"The policeman got out and took a step toward her car. Realising he still had his hat on, he stopped and turned half a step—looking directly at me—and removed his hat and put it on the dash of his van. He then stepped over to her car and surprisingly got into the front passenger seat alongside her.

"The policeman was in a full dark blue uniform, including a jacket, the rank insignia of a crown above three chevrons, but the most notable thing was his white hair. He did not look old and had black eyebrows.

"I proceeded down to Canning Bridge to turn around and come back [without any further testing]. When I was about 500-metres away from the Dodge [now heading north on the freeway], I saw the van reverse out and head north along the Golf Course road. There were no other vehicles or people in the area.

"As I came alongside the Dodge, I could see the interior light on, and the driver's door slightly open, but no lady. I thought he must have arrested her and taken her away in the van. The van turned right at the first street on the north end of the Golf course and went up to the main street.

"It had its left indicator on, and I was expecting to see it as I came out the Mill Point Road exit to turn left into Mill Point Road and go home. I was nearly going to go back to the Dodge and close the door so the battery wouldn't go flat, but it was way past my little sister's bedtime so I went straight home instead.

"I saw the paper the next day and spoke to my father about what I had seen. Later in the day, I went to a phone box in another suburb and reported it [the sighting of the Dodge, the woman believed to be the victim, the van and the police officer including their movements and descriptions] to the phone number in the paper. They didn't seem interested in what I had to say and didn't even ask my name. They just said they already had that, thanks, and hung up.

"I have since reported what I saw every time I've seen it [the story] in the paper," Joe told me in 2015.

'Dave' also reported seeing a white van. He first told his story to Torrance Mendez at *The West Australian* in 1994 and repeated it to me years later.

He said the time was about 10pm. He and his girlfriend drove down Melville Parade when he noticed a big white 'yank tank' (Australian slang term for a large American-style car] parked at right angles to the road. At least one other car was parked next to it, and possibly a third. One was a police panel van, and the other a dark car. He was with his girlfriend, now his wife. They pulled up about 50 to 100 metres away from the Dodge. They needed quiet time to talk before he dropped her home around the corner. The radio was on. About fifteen minutes later, he heard people arguing, a motor revving and shots fired.

"I heard two or three quick shots, and then another shot after that. I said to my girlfriend, *'That sounds like a .22.' I'm off a farm and happened to know what the report of a .22 sounds like,*" he told Torrance Mendez at *The West Australian.*

He asked his girlfriend if she had heard the shot and she said she hadn't. He thought he must have been mistaken. About ten minutes later, as they were planning to leave, he heard a thump on the roof and was startled to see two men standing either side of his car. They shone a torch in, and he couldn't see their faces.

"*It gave us a hell of a fright because they were shining these torches and we couldn't actually see their faces, and they had no distinguishing badge numbers on their tunic. I believed that the police who did it would know who I was and if I divulged this information they would be able to track me down pretty quick. The first thing I was worried about was what would happen to me—I was frightened.*"

One of the men asked if they had heard anything, and Dave explained he'd had the radio on. They were warned to say nothing.

Dave caught a glimpse of them as they drove away in a large black car, which he described as a limo and a yank tank.

A private investigator by the name of Terry McLernon, a former cop with a fist-up attitude to fighting corruption in the West, uncovered another witness in 2009. The witness, Max, had contacted McLernon and claimed he saw Detective Bernie Johnson on the night of the murder.

Max 'Rodgers' frequented the Zanzibar nightclub. Bernie Johnson had helped him out in the past, and it was through Bernie that he received free entry into the popular nightclub. He said Bernie determined who could come and who could go at the nightclub. Max knew him well, as did all regular patrons. Two weeks before the murder, Max was at the bar when he saw Shirley Finn arguing with Bernie Johnson and then slapping him.

On the night of the murder, Max said he was driving past the Pagoda Restaurant at about 10 o'clock at night in South Perth, a few metres away from the Royal Perth Golf Club.

"Johnson was standing outside a large dark car talking to the driver and stood up and looked towards my car as I approached. I didn't see the faces of the two people inside the car. A few weeks later, I saw him at the Zanzibar and innocently asked him why he was there in front of the Pagoda that night; and he angrily denied it and said I was mistaken, and warned me to never state that to anyone again. A few months later at the Zanzibar, I was lured out the back by Bert Tudori and jumped by Johnson and some big thug, and they beat me savagely until they thought I was unconscious, and one of them (I think it may have been Laurie Tudori who came out after they had started to beat me) said, 'Don't kill him here, go and get the car and put him in the boot.' When they left to get the car I managed to get to my car and drive home somehow."

None of these three witness reports appears in the police records. The police records indicate first sightings on the golf course begin half-an-hour later. Between 10:30pm and 10:45pm, three separate people who passed by the golf course reported seeing the car parked with its tail-lights on. Five minutes later, a passerby reported seeing two people in the vehicle facing each other. At 11:30pm and 11:35pm, passersby stated the lights were out. There were no further sightings of Shirley's car until after 6am the following morning.

Don Sutherland was driving to night shift at the Swan Brewery, on the banks of the Swan River, less than a ten-minute drive from his home in Labouchere Road, Como. It was about 11pm at night on 22 June 1975.

Heading towards the Narrows Bridge, road works diverted him from his usual route down Labouchere Road to Melville Parade. He passed the white Dodge Phoenix, admiring the car and noticing it was parked unusually, then continued on. The road swept down under the Narrows

Bridge, then took him up onto the Freeway, which would carry him across the Swan River to the Brewery.

As he rounded the bend under the bridge, he noticed a few fishermen to his right on the banks of the river; their lights lit up the area under the bridge. Mr Sutherland slowed down due to the bend in the road. As he drove through, two people came walking briskly down the left side of the bridge, past the limestone tailings that supported it. "I thought maybe they'd come from the car and that it had broken down, but they did not stop at the pay phones they passed," Mr Sutherland told me.

"I thought they were heading for a car park under the bridge."

The first man he saw was tall—about six foot two inches or 188 centimetres tall—wearing a dark blue suit, tie and hat. He had a badge on the left lapel of his coat, possibly an RSL badge. He was of slim build with a dark complexion, but Don couldn't see the colour of his hair under the hat. The other man was shorter—a little under 180 centimetres—with a fairish complexion and goldy-gingery hair, but not a redhead. He was stocky and wore a patterned sports jacket that Don thinks was grey. He said, "They looked like cops."

Don Sutherland said he attended the South Perth police station the day after the murder, wanting to give a detailed description. "They didn't seem very interested," he told me.

He spoke with Torrance Mendez at *The West Australian* in 1994, and again he passed the information on to police. He later asked police for a copy of his statement. They told him they didn't have it.

The detailed description of the two men at the scene that night was a key piece of evidence. Sutherland was never asked to help with an identikit picture. The information is not in Read's final report, and police will not confirm whether his evidence was ever recorded—despite it appearing in the newspaper. An FOI application, to find out if and when Sutherland's evidence was recorded, was met with the standard reply. *The case is under investigation and cannot be released.*

Sutherland's evidence was vital, yet it wasn't recorded when he offered it the day after the murder. Constable Brian's description of the two detectives he saw in the police canteen with Shirley Finn (and a younger woman) on the night she died was similar to the shift worker's.

The coroner put the time of death at around midnight, though her car would not be spotted on the golf course again until morning.

Rose returned home around 4am but had barely slept worrying about Shirley. The taxi driver who dropped her said she had a musty smell and was wearing a blue pantsuit.

When she entered their bedroom, she was surprised to see her ring tree on the dressing table. *"I usually keep my rings and the ring tree in the safe,"* she told police. She noticed one of her rings was missing.

After dropping off Rose, the taxi driver headed back towards the city. Passing under the freeway, he saw a green Hillman that had hit a pole. He stopped to investigate. No one was hurt, and the car was empty. The Hillman was near the same location where Don Sutherland had seen two men pass by the telephone box.

The taxi driver recorded the number plate, and it is in the police file. I couldn't believe I had missed that detail for years. When Bridget and I inquired in 2016, neither the Motor Vehicle Registry nor the Police were willing to divulge who owned the Hillman in 1975.

The green Hillman was gone when the police attended the scene in the morning.

14

The Dodge

There is not a crime, there is not a dodge, there is not a trick, there is not a swindle, there is not a vice, that does not live by secrecy."
— Joseph Pulitzer

The news on the radio was dismal—and so was the weather—on the morning of 23 June, as frustrated drivers made the slow crawl to work along the Narrows Bridge. Police Constable Geoffrey McMurray was patrolling the freeway, the police report says he was in a *marked police vehicle*, but his recollection was that he was on a motorcycle. The rain had stopped, but the wind was still howling when Constable McMurray noticed the upmarket Dodge seemingly abandoned on the edge of the golf course. He thought it might have been stolen.

Turning off the next exit, he drove down Melville Parade towards the car. As he approached, a silver-green Holden pulled alongside him. Its driver asked the Constable how to get to Cottesloe. McMurray gave him directions but recalled thinking a local would know the way. Noting the WA plates, and concerned the man had something to do with the 'stolen' car, he took down his number plate details and later passed these on to detectives.

"I thought he'd dumped a stolen car [the Dodge] so I took his number. I gave it to Bill Read and the guys who turned up at the scene. They told me it was checked out and it was alright," McMurray told me in an interview in 2015.

"In reflection, I wouldn't have thought he was a suspect at that time in the morning because people said they saw that car there at 10 o'clock at night."

McMurray continued to the parked Dodge. A sticker on the back window read *Mafia Staff Car*. There was someone in the driver's seat. The woman slumped behind the wheel seemed to be sleeping. The shimmer of her gown caught his eye. He peered through the window but did not try to open the door. Her short styled hair and cinnamon, silk-pleated ball gown were stained red with blood. There was no sign of life.

McMurray radioed for assistance and waited for CIB. It began to rain heavily, moments before the detectives arrived. Detective Bernie Johnson was one of two detectives first on the scene. Detective Johnson knew the car and the woman whose lifeless body lay inside.

Back at the station, a police officer thumped hard on Superintendent Spike Daniels' office door. Daniels had returned from his exile at Jaxon House, where he'd been forced to rewrite police standing orders, and sent to a new posting in the Firearms Branch. His public speech to Rotary—about concerns the police force had lost its integrity in dealing with prostitution – had been met with hostility and resentment. He had few friends left in the police force but knew that speaking out was the right thing to do. It felt good to have an office again. He beckoned the officer to enter.

"Spike, your predictions are true. They've just found Shirley Finn over at Royal Perth Golf Club, shot in the head," the officer said. In 1973, Spike had written to senior officers in a document titled *Manifesto of a Concerned Cop*. He warned that the administration of prostitution would lead to corruption, and ultimately to murder.

The Superintendent stood up and walked to the window and looked out towards the car park. Below, detectives, including some Consorting officers he no longer trusted, were scurrying into vehicles.

Rose was up when Bridget came downstairs for breakfast. They didn't speak, and Bridget headed off to school. Bridget thought her mum must be sleeping, and Rose said nothing of her concerns.

Detective Johnson arrived soon after to give Rose the news: Shirley had been murdered and Rose was a suspect.

Detective Johnson returned to the office and advised his Senior Sergeant of the situation. Johnson was confident, with his inside knowledge of the brothel trade, that he would be tasked to head the investigation; but, to his surprise, CIB chief Bruce (Brickie) Brennan appointed Detective Senior Sergeant Bill Read instead.

The buzz was on well before Detective Read walked into the office. Bill Read said he got the job because he was in the right place at the right time. Honest, religious and dedicated, he had worked on various significant cases, including serial killer Edgar Cooke—the last man hanged in WA. He counts the Finn case as one of his most frustrating.

Read was as straight as a die and always looked uncomfortable dealing with the saucy conversation of madams and criminals, whereas Johnson enjoyed the banter. Detective Johnson's arrest rate far exceeded Read's and the girls favoured by Johnson had provided him with valuable intelligence over the years. Johnson was unhappy with the decision but accepted his boss's choice.

Read travelled to the scene—it was a shocking day for gathering evidence. He asked his men to rig a tarpaulin over the crime scene, to keep out the driving rain. The wild winds were hampering the rigging of the tarp, but, eventually, enough hands grabbed hold of the flapping plastic to secure a cover over the crime scene. Unfortunately, important forensics like footprints had already been lost.

Before long the scene was swarming with police wearing raincoats and carrying umbrellas, trampling the ground. Photographers, the scientific branch, ballistics section and detectives all scoured the car for clues.

Read inspected the body. There was no sign of a struggle and robbery did not appear to be a motive. Shirley's expensive jewellery, including a diamond watch and two heavyset rings, had not been touched. She looked surprisingly calm.

If he could solve it, it would be a career maker.

Shirley Finn's unsolved murder still weighed heavily on retired Detective Bill Read when I interviewed him in 2004. "We followed every possible lead. I'd love to solve it. I wish to God someone would come up with something now."

He recounted the day back in 1975 when he arrived at the crime scene. "By the time I got there, there were eight or ten detectives there. Back in those days, a murder was a big thing," Detective Read recalled. "It was raining. Wet. We were trying to get tarpaulins up. It was not good, as far as evidence was concerned. The scientific guys hadn't arrived. We could see it was a gunshot wound."

Traffic police were keeping people away, but other detectives had also come to have a look. As soon as they formed, tracks were washed away by the driving rain, hampering the gathering of evidence.

When a big murder happened, everyone pitched in including the traffic policeman, who assisted in the search for a weapon. The army was called in, using metal detectors; and police divers trawled the river, also yielding no results.

Photographs were taken of the body before removing it to the mortuary.

The autopsy revealed four entry wounds, three shot at close range from the right. Another shot was fired into the left side of Shirley's head from the passenger seat. All the bullets were recovered. The ammunition was said to be very old, possibly fifteen years or more. Ballistics revealed the weapon used was a sawn off Anschutz .22 calibre rifle.

"Somebody found a .22 cartridge case in the back," Read explained.

The cartridge case found in the Dodge was identified as a .22 calibre short 'Civic' make, with 'ICI' stamped on an arrowhead at the base (last manufactured in 1959). The casing was considered rare.

"To use a gun of that calibre—.22—more of a professional hitman-type execution, because of the calibre. They [the bullets] were .22 shorts, which means they don't go right through; they rattle around in your brain and make sure you die. We assumed that if an ordinary person was going to shoot someone, they'd use the best bullet—a .22 long. I would say he flew over from interstate. Somebody said, 'She's dangerous, and we need to get rid of her.' Somebody said, 'How are we going to do it? We'll get someone from the eastern states to come over and do the job for us,'" Detective Read told me in 2004.

Subsequent checks found that only 3500 Anschutz rifles were licensed in Western Australia at that time—200 of those were unaccounted for. Read said they checked hundreds of rifles in the year following the murder.

Vicky was standing alongside her brother and his friend, Craig, on the banks of the Swan River in South Perth near the Narrows Bridge, when Craig hooked a muddy-brown, terry towelling car seat cover. They were taking part in an annual fishing event that involved trying to catch a tagged fish. Craig cast again, this time pulling up a rifle. She's not certain of the timing, but she knows it was around the time of the murder because they all thought the rifle must be the weapon. This fishing event typically runs in February.

Vicky was 10-years-old at the time. She told me they had handed the weapon and seat cover to police and never heard from them again.

In Parliamentary Hansard, in May 1976, Ray O'Connor is asked whether a rifle pulled from the Swan River was the murder weapon. He said it was not.

Detective Read stated that no rifle was pulled out of the river that year.

A car seat cover from the Dodge is noted in the police crime file as an exhibit. A large number of short brown and darker coloured hairs were found on the seat cover, mostly near the top section of the bloodstain. The car seat cover was brown terry towelling.

Heavy rain forced police to move the Dodge to cover, at Police Headquarters, to allow a detailed examination.

Hair from the driver's door and vacuumed debris from the front and rear floors were sent to the Government Chemical Laboratories. Fingerprint impressions were taken from six positions within the vehicle. All fingerprint impressions, except two that were unsuitable for identification, were matched from a list provided by the investigating officers.

Before Read was appointed to head up the case, Detectives Read, Clarke, Johnson and Kiernan travelled to Shirley's home in Riverview Street.

Detectives searched the home for clues. Rose pointed out Shirley's two safes.

"Prior to Christmas 1974, Shirley had one wall safe situated in the dressing room behind her clothing. She used to have amounts of money up to $18,000 in a red beauty case. I talked her into getting the safe put in

because her children were taking some money out of the beauty case," Rose Black told police. *"After Christmas, she had another combination wall safe installed in a closet in the entrance hall. I have seen Shirley put money into both safes. She kept all her jewellery in the closet safe. I am aware that an amount of about $8,500 was taken from the closet safe by police and Mr Cannon,"* Rose Black said.

As executor of Shirley's estate, Ron Cannon had also attended her South Perth home after the murder. He took control of her assets and valuables to pass on to the Public Trustee. Ron Cannon never pretended to be a friend of Shirley's. I was surprised he was so readily available to secure her assets, ahead of police completing their investigation. I do not know if this was normal protocol at that time.

Rose was stunned to see her missing ring back at CIB headquarters. She'd noticed its absence from her ring tree when she arrived home at 4am the night before. The ring tree was out on the bench, though she usually stored it in the safe. *"Detectives told me it [the ring] had been recovered from Shirley's body. It was unusual for Shirley to wear my rings."* She wrote in a complaint to police.

The diary that numerous people reported Shirley keeping was either found and destroyed or—according to the police account—it was not located. A lot of people had a lot to lose should its contents have been disclosed. Shirley had counted it as her insurance against anyone who might want to harm her.

Des Finn said his wife kept a detailed diary; and Shirley's friend, Scherry, said Finn had shown her the diary. "I didn't see inside it, but she showed it to me and patted it and said, 'This is my bible, and this will keep me alive.' She kept it since she was busted in '69 at the first place—that's when all the trouble started," Scherry told me.

I asked Detective Read whether the diary held any clues. He said police never found a diary, just a book with phone numbers: "More or less like a phone book ... Not a diary as I know a diary to be."

The book that Detective Read described as a phone book did not name anyone particularly controversial. "Nothing that would point the finger at police or anyone political. Talk of the memoirs was Shirley's way of stirring people up," Detective Read said.

Rose was a suspect and required to hand over the clothes she had been wearing that night. Grief and fear must have swept over this woman who had survived the mean streets of St Kilda and, for a while, found a sanctuary of sorts with Shirley.

Bernie Johnson wrote up Rose's version of events. According to this account, she said that, after her conversation with Shirley, she went back to watching television with Louise until all programs went off the air. It was midnight, and Louise wanted to go to bed. Rose rang the house, but no-one answered. Fifteen minutes later she tried again. Aware she was imposing on Louise by staying late but worried that she would disturb Shirley's important business meeting if she went home too soon, Rose booked into Park Towers Motel nearby for the night and booked a taxi. In case Shirley was on her way, she left a note on the door so Shirley wouldn't knock and disturb Louise. Louise's statement matches Rose's account. The taxi driver confirmed he picked Rose up at 12:30pm taking her five minutes down the road from the Park Lane Apartments to the Park Towers Motel. His statement is unsigned. Rose booked into the Park Towers in the name of Sandra Williams.

Later, when Rose took Detective Johnson to Louise's flat, a note she wrote for Shirley was still pinned to the door: *Shirley, have gone to Park Towers to visit a friend from Melbourne. I didn't want to keep Louise awake all night. Her name is Sandy Williams. Love Rose.*

Rose had been at a loss as to why Shirley didn't pick her up. Unable to sleep for worry, she had tried the home phone again at 1am. This time Bridget answered and went to check if her mum was in bed but found she wasn't.

After hanging up, Rose managed to fall asleep, but it was a restless sleep, and by 4am she was wide awake and worried. She decided to catch a cab home from the hotel. The taxi driver said she was in no mood to talk. He said Rose had a dry, musty smell and was wearing a blue-coloured slack suit (which conflicted with other evidence). There is no mention in the police files of why Rose might have changed outfits. It's possible the taxi driver simply remembered the colour wrongly.

There was no sign of Shirley when Rose returned home, but Rose made no further calls. After discovering the ring tree and her missing ring, she lay in bed but didn't sleep. She heard Bridget getting ready for school and decided to get up. Rose said nothing that would alarm Bridget, so the 13-year-old headed off to Kent Street High.

There was no gunshot residue on Rose's clothing though police did find a small bloodstain, on the right hip pocket of her suit trousers, that Rose couldn't explain. *"I cannot explain these stains. I have not been injured at all,"* Black stated. It was a brown suit that was tested, and not the blue slack suit the taxi driver said he remembered.

In the days following Shirley's murder, a death notice in the newspaper read: *A loved one goes, yet she stays. To wait beside me, all the way. I loved her in life and she is living yet. In the hearts of those who will never forget. I miss you darling. Rose.*

I tried to find Rose, having been told she was out of town. I left numbers for her to call, and she did call me back twice. She offered little information, other than that she was scared. She wouldn't leave her number. The calls were cut short with a promise she would call me again soon, but she never did. Shane (Shirley's son) told me Rose said Shirley was murdered at a flat nearby and her body placed in the Dodge, but there was no forensic evidence to suggest the body had been moved. He also said Rose lived in constant fear.

However—if traffic constable Brian's account is accurate—then Rose is most likely the "younger woman" seen in the driveway of their South Perth home and later by him at the police club just before midnight. Rose's statement to police on her movements that night may be a fabrication, with Rose either a terrified witness to the murder of her partner or an accomplice to murder.

The police gave Des Finn the unpleasant task of identifying his ex-wife's body. "They called me in when she was shot. I was a major suspect. We had an alibi." Des was doing shift work at Chamberlain John Deere in Welshpool, working in the machinery shop. "We had the dust on us... They said, 'Bingo' when they did a test." What was first thought to be gunpowder turned out to be cast iron dust from Des' workplace.

About seven hundred people were quizzed in the two weeks following Shirley's death, and twenty-four senior detectives would file reports on the case.

"Bridget was home when it happened. I thought if anyone knows anything it was her, but she didn't seem to know what was going on," Detective Read said. "Shirley was a closed business person. She didn't give much information to Rose or anyone."

Shirley must have been planning to leave the house. Why else would she try to book a babysitter? Given she had failed to find a babysitter, and if Rose wasn't going with her, couldn't Rose have minded Bridget while Shirley went out?

"She [Shirley] wasn't going to go very far because her daughter was home alone and there was no-one to look after her," Detective Read explained.

Bridget was taken out of school and questioned by police. The frightened teenager said she knew nothing of her mother's activities.

Shirley's dressmaker, Glenn Properjohn, who had hoped to catch up with Shirley and introduce her to two visiting entertainers the night she died, went to police hoping he could help. Shirley had been a close friend of his. I tracked him down and spoke to him through a screen door. He was busy and did not have time to speak. I told him I believed many witnesses were still worried about speaking even after thirty years. He said, "If I saw a murder across the road, I would not report it—not after what I went through." He didn't elaborate.

Years later we spoke again.

"On about the third time they spoke to me, they took me into a room and started punching me—blows to the stomach. They wanted to rough me up a bit because I was a suspect," Properjohn explained. "I'd gone to them. I'd wanted to help."

The night of Shirley's murder he had picked up Kandy and Spice and taken them to the Sunday session at the Paddington Hotel. Shirley had told him she had to work, so couldn't meet his friends. The trio went back to a friend's flat for a few drinks, and, at about 10:30pm, Glenn dropped in to Shirley's William Street brothel hoping to introduce his friends to her. Shirley wasn't there, so they went to the Coffee Pot for a meal. Glenn said Shirley was a good friend, but she never talked business with him. He said she wasn't showy and flamboyant but rather down-to-earth. She was cheerful by nature.

"She always used to say, 'I Love Life.' That was her. That summed her up. I still think of Shirley just about every day," Glenn Properjohn told me, thirty-nine years after her murder.

Some statements—given at that time by certain witnesses—did not appear in police reports. The missing reports included descriptions of people near the murder scene that night, the gun and seat cover hauled from the river by three children in South Perth, a white van spotted next to the Dodge around 10pm on the night of the murder, the number plate recorded by Constable Geoff McMurray, and details of a green car seen next to Shirley's white Dodge hours before her car's first official reported sighting the next morning.

15

The Game

It wasn't making money. We had all the money we wanted. It meant nothing, the money. It was the game. It was the game to us and to the police. That's what it was: the game; the excitement.

— Bert Tudori

Fear swamped the sex trade in the wake of the murder, and many girls fled interstate. "Girls were scattered all over Australia since then," Detective Read recalled.

Detective Sergeant Donald Leslie Hancock interviewed the four women working at Shirley's brothel on the night of the murder. Dubbed 'the Grey Fox', he was the detective who was alleged to have fitted up the Mickelbergs (with a fabricated confession) in the gold heist. Hancock was later killed in a car bombing in 2001, after clashing with bikies.

All four women said Shirley hadn't been into the brothel on the night she was killed. They hadn't seen her since Friday. She'd seemed happy and relaxed. They spoke fondly of their late boss. "If ever the girls were in any trouble, they told me, she'd fix it for them, help them out, lend them money. I don't think I spoke to any of the girls that had a bad word to say against her," Detective Read recalled.

These statements were taken in October and November, three months after the murder. Police said none revealed clues that helped with the murder investigation.

In the five months following Shirley's death, forty-six charges were laid against working girls, resulting in many single operators being jailed—a situation unheard before Finn's death. The fear that workers or their managers might end up like Shirley Finn was strong in the minds of all in the trade at this time. Believing police and the government were involved they felt they had nowhere to go.

Sydney's *Daily Telegraph* suggested mobsters had ordered the 'contract' because Finn stood in the way of Sydney prostitute operators who wanted in on the business in Perth. However, taking over a brothel in Perth was not up to Shirley Finn. It was police who provided the means or the obstruction to operating in prostitution in Western Australia. The police decided who was in.

The Daily Telegraph report also claimed that Finn's girls were recruited and supplied by a vice ring operation out of Sydney.

A national supply chain was in operation. Finn did get girls from Sydney, as did Dorrie and Stella. "The girls that they employed, they'd swap between Dorrie and Shirley. And they'd go east. They'd bring girls back, and send girls over. They were moving all the time. Most of the girls spoke very, very highly of her. They said she was like a mother to them," Detective Read said.

The Costigan Royal Commission into the Painters and Dockers in 1982 revealed the girls were a commodity, moved around the country to meet supply and demand. They found the prices and even the décor of the brothels throughout the country were remarkably similar. Senior Counsel assisting Costigan, Douglas Meagher reported to a 1983 conference on organised crime: *The rates for the services of the "girls" seem to be fixed Australia-wide and although there is an appearance of competition, in truth it would appear the industry is well regulated.*

The price paid for police protection based on the information that has emerged since, also appears to be uniform, $100 per girl per week seemed to be the going rate a madam had to pay corrupt police officers in Australia in the 1970s.

The Daily Telegraph article also quoted police as saying that Mrs Finn was linked with one of two major rivals (in prostitution) in Perth; and that they had been bitterly opposed to each other for the last six months. Dorrie Flatman was at the helm of the Sydney infiltration of Perth's brothel industry in 1968, and their relationship had soured in the lead-up to Shirley's death.

"When she turned lesbian it changed her completely. I couldn't understand Shirley taking off with Rose. Rose was a junkie. Not Shirley," Dorrie told me.

"We had difficulty with her," Kim Flatman explained. I asked him to elaborate on what the problem was with Shirley.

"We started to receive these calls. We traced the call back to Shirley. We heard sirens. There was a fireman at the door with an axe to cut the door down...Then five police cars turned up to a murder. There wasn't one. The police told her to behave herself. She was trouble. She threw lavish parties, so people hung around her."

Mr Flatman explained that Dorrie had Shirley dealt with. "She got the detectives to sort her out. They were going to do something to close her business down because she was getting out of control. She was the kind of woman who kept tabs on the customers," Kim Flatman said. "Records. Notation. When they came, what they did—to use that, to have that as a leverage when she needed it. She was leaning on somebody and had information to expose them."

Dorrie owned Tramps nightclub in Murray Street. A staff member working at Tramps that night told me Dorrie Flatman had known about Shirley's death even before her body had been discovered.

He shared the information with me on condition the source was kept anonymous. He said he was working on the door at Tramps and overheard a conversation between Dorrie and a family member. "She walked down and said, 'Well, we got rid of her.' I didn't know who she meant. Then the next day I heard it on the news." He does not know who the 'we' might be.

Later testimony from Gladys Harding, who cleaned for Shirley, revealed she'd seen envelopes of cash left by the madam—one for rent, one for the police marked B.J., and one for Dorrie.

Dorrie had been set up in Perth to run the monopoly that was evolving Australia-wide on behalf of Sydney gangsters; a system set up by Abe Saffron in NSW after his visit to US crime figures in the sixties. If police stopped the opposition, there was no need for violence. To run a hugely lucrative crime business unimpeded, you needed crooked cops on your side, backed up by financial benefits to political allies, ensuring the protection and operation of less violent criminal enterprises. It all worked, there was great money to be made; so long as no-one exposed the corrupt system.

I asked Dorrie if she knew who killed Shirley Finn. "I got no idea."

As for Spike Daniels, "Spike Daniels was a crazy person. He picked a fight when he picked on me. He didn't expect anyone to fight him back."

A year after my interview with her, Dorrie sold up her William Street brothel and retired. She said prostitution in Perth had got out of control.

In 2013, she passed away taking her secrets to her grave.

Two days after the murder, Minister for Police Ray O'Connor said that it would be prejudging the matter to infer it was a gangland crime connected with prostitution. *"We don't know it was connected in any way with prostitution. It might have been the result of a domestic argument. If it is proved that prostitution is involved we will have a look at the question of an inquiry at that time. If there is a gangland war we will take the necessary action. But at this stage, on the information available, a royal commission is not warranted,"* Ray O'Connor was reported to have told *The West Australian*.

Chief of CIB, Superintendent Bruce Brennan said the Consorting Squad had no knowledge of any dangerous rivalry among Perth prostitutes or escort agencies.

Given that police had the situation 'contained', and that by their definition they knew all the operators, the greater question is: was it police that organised crime? Were politicians also complicit in maintaining control over prostitution and gambling? Were they, too, party to the organisation of criminal networks?

Were the organisations responsible for countering crime in Australian society, by their power and knowledge, placed at the helm of criminal business enterprise?

16

Shut Your Mouth or Die

Throughout history, it has been the inaction of those who could have acted; the indifference of those who should have known better; the silence of the voice of justice when it mattered most; that has made it possible for evil to triumph.

— Haile Selassie

Shirley Finn's photo flashed across the television screen as news of the murder broke. Brian, the young constable who had been playing pool in the police canteen, saw the bulletin and was alarmed. "I thought, 'Strewth, that was the lady in the canteen last night,' and I said so. About two days later, I'm on day shift. I started really early as I was on freeway duty. Hit the freeway at six in the morning. It was dark. I come out of Koondoola Avenue on Mirrabooka Avenue. No traffic around at all. I'm at a stop sign—nothing to my right, nothing behind me, nothing to the front of me. Turned left and, all of a sudden, I heard this screech of tyres, and a car comes in on my right-hand side and hits the front of my motorbike and sends me off into the sand on the side of the road. I thought, 'What the hell's going on?' I didn't know because I didn't see it. I'm assuming he has no lights on. I'm laying there, then I jumped up, as I wasn't injured.

"Next thing I know four guys get out of the car. One of them had a gun. One said, 'Shut your mouth! If you want to live or see your children again—shut your mouth! You know nothing!' It frightened the shit out of me," Brian recalled. "I went and saw my father and told him what happened." Brian's father had also been a police officer. "He told me to see Dick Larsen. He's a good bloke. He (Larsen) said, 'You gotta be joking—the bastards can't get away with this.' He said he'd have a word with the head of CIB, which he must have done because the following day I go to get on my bike and there was a car parked in my driveway. A khaki-coloured HQ Holden.

"The back door [of the car] opens up, and out gets someone who I thought was a friend of mine, and he said to me, 'Brian if you want to see your wife and two kids again—shut your mouth—or you'll get killed or something worse.' I'm shitting myself. What could I do? I couldn't even trust my colleagues. Kept thinking, 'what am I going to do? What am I going to do?'

"We had a meeting at traffic control, and I give my case. Dick Larsen was there. As a result of our meeting, there was about forty or fifty of us. I felt good. I had all these cops standing behind me. We thought, 'Let's get these bastards.' We were knocking them off for pissy-driving. We were getting them. There was a hatred between CIB and Traffic. There was a war.

"Over the years—I thought someone would contact me but the only contact I've had on the matter is to be threatened. I thought, 'This doesn't go on, surely to God!'"

A career cop, Brian took forty years to break his silence. He is still concerned about the influence of those involved in the crime on today's police force.

Several witnesses reported seeing a green car at the murder scene next to the Dodge just before daylight on the night of the murder. An MTT bus driver reported a green car parked behind the white Dodge at about 6:20am and noticed two men were standing near the Dodge. Returning thirty minutes later, the bus driver saw the two men moving off down Canning Highway, in the green sedan, towards the port suburb of Fremantle. His description of one of the men matched that given by Don, the shift worker.

John and Jenny Mearns reported seeing the green car parked alongside the Dodge on the morning of June 23. The couple set off just before dawn to begin their family holiday in the south-west. John noticed the big American car parked with its doors wide open. "It was raining heavily and what was of immediate concern was that such a flash car was parked on a golf course with the doors wide open," Mr Mearns recalled. "We reversed back, and if it wasn't for the rain and the fact it was on the golf course, we would have gone over." A small green sedan was parked about two metres away. "My wife mentioned that perhaps someone had lost something whilst playing golf and was looking for it. Something didn't seem right, and it was raining so we did not—thankfully—hop out. I asked my wife to take down the number of the cars which she did."

As soon as they heard of the murder, they informed police of the sighting. Mr Mearns said the sergeant at the central police station in Perth told him they had enough information and to forget it.

Seven years later the story was again being aired, and John Mearns rang the media saying he had reported the number plates of Shirley Finn's car and the green car to police at Central. He was certain he had offered that information—the number plate he had written down and stored in his glovebox—and was surprised they took little interest. *The West Australian* published his concerns and police were forced to investigate.

A detective flew up from Perth to interview Mearns and his wife separately.

"All diligence was used to discredit our stories...which incidentally matched," Mr Mearns said. He said police were more interested in trying to pull their evidence apart, and in discrediting them, than in the information they offered. A Carnarvon detective told him to watch his back and check his car for bombs.

Torrance Mendez from *The West Australian* applied for Mr Mearns' witness statement and complaints, under Freedom of Information legislation in 1994. The government office responsible for FOI reported to the newspaper that there were no records whatsoever of Mr Mearns' reports or complaints. The Information Commissioner stated: *If Mr Mearns did provide information to the agency following the murder and again in 1982, I am of the view that it is reasonable to expect some record to be made of those contacts with the agency. In fact it would be surprising if this had not been done. However, the searches undertaken by the agency have failed to locate any records of this nature. Nevertheless, I am satisfied that the searches undertaken by the agency to locate documents have been reason-*

able in all the circumstances. Therefore, I am not satisfied that the documents exist, although I consider there are reasonable grounds for believing that they did.

The articles in *The West Australian* resulted in police taking another look. Sergeant David Caporn and Detective Paul Greenshaw limited further investigation to the new witness quoted in the paper as seeing two uniform police officers at the scene. They eliminated his evidence claiming the man had the wrong time and place. Mearns' evidence could not be found. Apparently, he too had placed the vehicle in a different location.

The first police officer at the scene on the day of the murder, Constable Geoff McMurray, also recorded a number plate (for the silver-green Holden that pulled up alongside him on Melville Parade seconds before he discovered Shirley's body) and gave those details to CIB. That was two hours after the initial sighting of the green car by Mearns and the bus driver. The details of the number plate noted by McMurray are also not on the police record.

These details were absolutely vital, and on this fact alone, the police have sufficient evidence to show the investigation was compromised. They have failed to acknowledge this fact in a timely manner despite being repeatedly called to do so; they have failed to conduct a thorough investigation.

Brian, who saw Shirley Finn and the "younger woman" with two detectives in the police canteen, is still frightened of the repercussions of talking. Not for himself but for his family.

The tactics used by outlaw criminal gangs and the mafia were also being used by members of the WA Police Force to silence their own. The WA Police Force, possibly complicit in the crime of murder and needing to cover its tracks, may have become the most dangerous gang in town. The murder of Shirley Finn brought the seedy world of prostitution into the public eye in Western Australia, and politicians and police were eager to distance themselves from the trade.

The Officer in Charge of CIB at the time of Finn's death, Superintendent Brennan, said the tax debt was at the heart of the matter. *"We think she expected to raise some of that money from the person she met on the night she was killed. The inquiry narrowed down to associates who were able to raise at least $50,000 to satisfy her demands."*

Long since retired, Detective Bill Read concurred with earlier public statements made by the late Superintendent Brennan. "My thoughts were: she was under pressure from the taxation department. She got dressed up to impress this person. Somebody she thought could use their influence, hence the thought politician, or something like that. Someone she thought could go and say, 'Ease off this woman, she'll pay the money, but give her more time.' Whether that was true or not, I don't know. Either someone with influence or someone with money," he explained.

Frustrated at the many brick walls that blocked his road to a conclusion, he is still convinced a hitman did the job.

Interstate inquiries were made, but nothing came up. "If it's a professional, he doesn't leave a trail for us to follow like sheepdogs."

If a person or group conspires to commit murder, and there is no scientific evidence to tie them to the scene of the crime, then the only evidence is motive and witnesses to the conversation. Organised hits are the toughest murders to crack and rarely result in prosecution.

Police advised they knew of no hitmen in Perth at the time. But, coincidentally, a known hitman did arrive in Perth onboard the Iron Yampi. Charles Chicka Reeves was a murderer, safe-breaker, gunman and thief, with a thirty-year history of violent crimes. He claimed he had killed ten people before he was shot dead in Wollongong in 1979. He arrived in Perth from the eastern states onboard the BHP steamship, Iron Yampi, on 6 June 1975—two weeks before the murder. The ship left port a month later on 6 July with Reeves onboard. A crewmember said Chicka secreted a "ringbolt" in his cabin, and all were warned to steer clear of the man. But neither Chicka nor the ringbolt matched the descriptions given by witnesses of people seen at or near the Dodge that night.

In 2016, I would hear of another known killer, in town at that time, who had a direct relationship with the key suspect—a man who did match the description given by witnesses: NSW Detective Roger Rogerson.

Less than two weeks after Shirley's death in 1975, property heiress and journalist, Juanita Nielsen, disappeared without a trace from Kings Cross in Sydney.

Nielsen, the publisher of *Now* magazine, was campaigning against property development at Kings Cross. Her body has never been found. Two years later, anti-drugs campaigner and politician, Donald McKay, also disappeared without a trace. Both were believed to be victims of professional killers associated with organised crime.

Shirley's hit was different—unlike any other hit in Australia before or since. There was no attempt to conceal her body, nor the manner of her execution. Shirley would not disappear like Juanita Nielsen or Donald Mackay, nor would her death appear a suicide like madam Shirley Brifman's in Queensland. Instead, Shirley was killed next to the busiest road in Western Australia, near the centre of the CBD in a standout vehicle, and wearing standout clothes. It showed a blatant disregard for the law. It seemed as if the killers didn't fear being caught, that they were above the law—a murderous announcement warning others not to tread in Shirley's path.

Vitally important reports by witnesses from the night of the murder— the description of men seen running from the car, a rifle and car seat cover pulled from the river, and a number plate—were simply not recorded. These witnesses would not know until decades later that their evidence had been ignored and lost. If police played no part in the cover-up, then it is hard to imagine how this could have been possible.

If the police were involved, and the destruction of evidence and failure to investigate has robbed the Finns of any chance of justice, then surely the family is at least owed an apology. However, no apology, explanation or admission has ever been offered, compounding the trauma the three children suffered after their mother's death.

17

The Skeleton on the Beach

No man really becomes a fool until he stops asking questions.
— Charles P. Steinmetz

After receiving a tape recording of Police Superintendent Spike Daniels' speech to the Rotary Club in 1974, from fellow member Jim Kane, former president of the Civil Liberties Association, Archie Marshall was alarmed by Spike's serious allegations of organised crime and alleged corruption in Perth. Marshall met with the whistleblower and became his ally when Spike most needed a friend.

Shirley's murder compounded Spike's view that the prostitution protection racket was out of control and that he was in danger. Chief Superintendent Leitch wanted Spike out of the way. Archie's friendship proved invaluable.

As Spike had passed away when I began my investigation, I tracked Archie down. Archie was retired, spending his days gardening and fixing up his vintage Mercedes and a 1936 Sunbeam 30 Cabriolet. It took some time to gain his trust. He gave me documents that he and Spike had gathered over the years.

"He [Spike] struck me as extremely genuine and open," Mr Marshall explained. "[Spike] believed there was a highly dangerous police protection racket operating. He had tried to point it out and was getting no support."

Archie had put his life and his business on the line to help the besieged Superintendent. An intense Englishman, he had once tried to import retired defence vehicles from Britain for sale into Australia, but a last minute change to the law had left him with a mass of unsaleable cars and a huge debt. He was angered by the government's turnaround but felt powerless to change the rules. The Civil Liberties Association was an organisation pushing for the rights of the citizen against bureaucracy and corruption. They took on causes lobbying government for change, so Marshall joined. He was contemptuous of authorities and passionate about the rights of the little man. Aside from vintage cars, fighting for the underdog against government red tape and corruption was Marshall's passion. He saw in Spike another victim of Big Brother.

Archie met with Spike and agreed to set up a phone line to receive allegations of corruption and impropriety about the prostitution industry. Lobbying for a Royal Commission, Archie publicised the phone line at his car yard. He says he received calls from people in the medical profession, the motor trade, solicitors and prostitutes.

Most callers preferred to stay anonymous. *"People are afraid of what may happen to them,"* he told *The West Australian* in the weeks before the Royal Commission. *"Fear has been one of the common features of the calls I have received."*

With Spike, Mr Marshall began taking statements from people. Mr Marshall received harassment phone calls, and pressure was placed on his secretary who resigned. He received allegations of police protection rackets, and that police acted as debt collectors. It was Archie Marshall who recorded the interview with Shirley's father that alleged she was heading to Sydney with an MP to fix up her tax problem. He took the recording to the television stations, airing it on Channel Seven.

In August 1975, two months after the murder of Shirley Finn, Mr Marshall received a phone call on his hotline from a distraught woman. Archie can't remember the exact time of the call but says he still believes the call was genuine. A woman who claimed to be a middle-aged nurse, but who sounded younger, said she was nursing a prostitute who was dying. The prostitute had claimed that a friend of hers, another prostitute, was thrown overboard from a yacht between Rottnest Island and Fremantle and drowned. He said she described the boat and its location. She said she would come forward if a Royal Commission were held. "I believed the woman. It was second-hand information, but I didn't doubt what she was telling me, she believed to be true," Archie told me. If the middle-aged nurse existed she did not ring again, nor did she come forward after the Royal Commission was called.

Mr Marshall reported the conversation to some members of the Civil Liberties Association including a reporter from *The Sunday Times.*

Two days after Mr Marshall received the phone call from the nurse, the remains of a female washed up on Cottesloe Beach. A young man walking along the beach noticed the body floating in the water twenty metres from the shore, being carried in on the tide, and alerted police.

On the same day as the body washed up on the beach, but before anyone knew about it, newspapers were being delivered around Perth with the headlines *Prostitution – New Murder Alleged.* The report stated allegations of a new murder in Perth's prostitution racket would be made if a Royal Commission were held. The witness would only speak to a Royal Commission because she feared she would be murdered.

"It could be nothing more than a sheer coincidence that within forty-eight hours after me receiving that phone call a female body appears on the beach. I haven't seen all the evidence, but if there is the slightest shadow of a doubt, they should check it out," Archie Marshall said.

In the sex trade, the story was used to terrorise others. Thirty years on, former working girls recounted the tale. Linda Watson, who now runs the House of Hope, a support group for former prostitutes, insists a woman was thrown off the back of a boat by a policeman; though no-one has a name or can identify the woman involved. The story became folklore for the working girl.

Another former prostitute who worked at Theodore's brothel, within a stone's throw of Parliament House, said she heard a police officer, soon after the Finn murder, threatening the madam who ran Theodore's. "There was an argument, and he said to Gloria she'd end up in the sea like others."

When I met with Archie in 2003, the question of the identity of the skeleton that washed up on Cottesloe Beach in 1975 still plagued Marshall. I decided to investigate.

In the State Archives, I dug out a file revealing conflicting autopsy reports on the age and background of the skeleton. The enormous disparity between the reports added weight to Marshall's concerns that the Cottesloe corpse may have been the victim of a crime.

Police suspected the remains were those of 48-year-old Violet Walker. Violet lived on her own in John Street, about 100 metres from Cottesloe Beach. Violet used to walk and swim on Cottesloe Beach almost every day and was known to sit on the groyne for hours. She was reported missing by her landlady on August 4, a month before the body washed up on the beach.

Violet worked at the flour mill and had not collected her wages or touched her bank account. She had paid a fortnight's rent on 27 July to her landlady, Mrs Kelly. A week later, Mrs Kelly was surprised to find Violet's key left in the door to her flat and her cat unfed, so she reported her missing to police. All that was missing from her flat was her purse, her bathers and a long fawn wool jacket.

A newspaper report calling for any information on the whereabouts of the missing woman at the time attracted no sightings. She had vanished.

The report in State Archives revealed the Coroner, Dr Derek Pocock placed the age of the Cottesloe corpse at between 25 and 35 years old, much younger than Walker. A second autopsy was requested. This time City Coroner, Professor David Allbrook concluded the bones belonged to a woman aged approximately 30 - 40, still too young to be Walker. A third autopsy by State Coroner Dr John Hilton said that he believed the skeleton could be an older woman.

An examination of bone marrow found none of the minute organisms found in water that would indicate drowning and therefore the coroner could not confirm death was due to drowning. Police concluded the remains must be that of 48-year-old Violet Walker and closed their investigation book into the Cottesloe corpse. The coroner refused to rule the body was that of Violet Walker due to the wild variations in the autopsy reports.

More than a year after Ms Walker was last seen, the remains of the Cottesloe corpse were buried in an unmarked grave at Karrakatta Cemetery on 5 August 1976. Violet's daughter, Pat Holmes, was left to wonder the fate of her mother for almost thirty years.

Set amongst the tranquil gardens of Karrakatta cemetery in Perth, past rows of marble pillars, tall crosses, carved headstones and sculptured angels, I found the bare patch of lawn which marked the grave of the mystery skeleton that washed up on Cottesloe Beach, three months after Shirley Finn was murdered. On either side, headstones spoke of love and peace and relatives who had the chance to say goodbye. But at gravesite 53, in lawn area 2, there was no headstone, no small plaque, no flowers, nothing.

Finding the gravesite was not easy. I had obtained the missing person file on Violet Walker through Freedom of Information as well as the autopsy reports from the State Records Office. I searched cemetery records and found a Jane Doe buried on the date that matched a record in the missing person file of Violet Walker, where the coroner had refused to sign it.

As I stared at the grave, I knew that whether she was Violet Walker or the victim of foul play, as Archie believed, this person might have family who had probably long anguished over her fate. DNA had come a long way and science could now possibly resolve the mystery.

In 2003, I put an ad in the *Can You Help?* section of *The West Australian* calling for relatives of Violet Walker to contact me. For Pat Holmes, who responded, her mother's whereabouts had been a long-held mystery. I carefully explained why the body in the grave could be her mother, and I asked if she was interested in applying to the Coroner to have the body exhumed and DNA tested. I explained details of the conflicting coroners' reports.

"It would finish the unknown. It's always been on my mind," she said. "When you don't have a funeral, you don't have a memorial, you can't say goodbye. It's very important to me. I remember one time when she thought the water was calling her, drawing her to it. I don't want to put a big monument there. I just would like to know if it's my mum, to say my goodbyes."

Getting a body exhumed is no minor feat. Senior Coronial Investigator, Peter Harbison explained that in his twenty-five years in the State Coroner's office he had known of only one other. Pat lodged her application and waited.

An article on the mystery grave appeared in *Woman's Day*, which was picked up by Channel Seven's *Today Tonight*. Later I was told that on that same day in April 2004, when I appeared on television speaking of the mystery, a police officer in the Tactical Investigation Group (TIG) accessed my vehicle registration details. The TIG is, a group of detectives tasked to follow minor inquiries. I had no traffic infringements. The interview had been pre-recorded, and I was overseas at the time. I had interviewed senior police officers involved in the Norris Royal Commission using the vehicle that was checked. Following a complaint lodged with the Anti-Corruption Commission, the police officer who had checked my registration on the police computer was asked to explain. He explained that while conducting routine surveillance at a shopping centre, he had written down the wrong registration number.

The unmarked grave had remained undisturbed for nearly thirty years. It was opened early in the morning. Pat Holmes had provided her DNA to the coroner, and it was hoped there would be sufficient DNA left on the remains in gravesite 53 to give a definitive answer. If it was Violet Walker, then Pat could have closure; if not, then Archie Marshall could well be vindicated and the missing person files opened—but Pat would have gone through a lot of pain and hope for nothing.

I was present when the remains of the unknown woman were removed from their resting place. It was strange when it happened, and I felt a little guilty for disturbing her. The Coroner took away the skeleton to a laboratory for testing.

In October 2004, after months of anguishing over whether I had created false hope for Pat Holmes, the coroner deemed that the skeleton washed up on the beach in September 1975 belonged to Violet Walker. Mrs Holmes asked for her mother's remains to be buried near her home overlooking the lake at Dumbleyung.

18

A Playboy Version of *Blue Hills*

Beware lest you lose the substance by grasping at the shadow.

— Aesop

The Opposition pressured the Government in Parliament to hold an inquiry into the brothel trade in the wake of the murder, but Sir Charles Court refused, claiming it would be a waste of time and money. *"It would probably degenerate into something like a Playboy version of Blue Hills,"* he said.

The Court Government agreed to a limited inquiry, appointing Peter Brinsden QC to examine the available evidence to see if a Royal Commission was warranted. Brinsden's eighteen-page report found no credible evidence of any liaison between police and brothel keepers.

When civil libertarian Archie Marshall went public with the tape-recorded interview with Shirley's father saying she had sought an urgent loan from him to get assistance from a politician to deal with her tax debt, the growing public pressure forced the government to acquiesce. The opposition demanded wide-ranging terms of reference including identifying people and organisations who directly or indirectly financed or managed prostitution; whether the brothel industry had been policed consistently; whether prostitution was linked to other illegal vices such as gambling; and whether these, in turn, were linked to vice operations in other states.

Court and O'Connor met often in an attempt to draw up terms of reference which wouldn't be *shooting arrows in the air* and, on 30 September 1975, the government yielded, announcing the vice probe would go ahead.

The terms of reference were watered down so that none of the points raised by the opposition would be investigated: not the tangled web behind the trade, nor whether the brothel industry was being policed consistently, nor whether the trade was linked to organised crime in other states.

Instead, the Royal Commission would investigate whether Spike Daniels made any allegations of impropriety and whether his allegations had substance. It also would look at what the Labour Tonkin Government had done about Daniels' allegations.

In the weeks leading up to the Royal Commission, the Police Union unanimously passed a motion calling for the expulsion of any policeman who made allegations to an outsider about other members of the force. The warning, demanding officers uphold the wall of silence or face expulsion, was published in the newspaper to make sure the message was widely received.

John Gerald Norris, the 73-year-old former judge of the Victorian Supreme Court, headed the Royal Commission *to inquire and report as to a number of matters relating to allegations of impropriety in the administration of the law relating to prostitution and to make such recommendations in respect to the subject matter of the aforesaid inquiry as might be thought fit.*

Judge Norris' relationship with Sir Charles Court went way back. He'd served in the same army division with Court in World War II. Norris achieved the rank of Lt Colonel in the 1st Armoured Division in March 1942, the same month Sir Charles was promoted to Captain.

Daniel O'Dea was appointed Counsel assisting the Commissioner.

Within a month of appointing Judge Norris, the Royal Commission was up and running.

In the week before it began, Ray O'Connor appointed George Owen Leitch, Commissioner of Police, to replace Athol Wedd, who took early retirement. On his appointment, Owen Leitch was quoted in *The West*

Australian newspaper as saying, "*The police force was suffering from the presence of a radical in its midst ... The police force must be a team.*"

Spike didn't want a Royal Commission, a feeling that would prove justified when the Royal Commission opened on 7 November 1975. "He never expected to get a fair hearing. I had more faith in the honesty of government," Archie Marshall explained.

On the opening day of the inquiry, the Senior Counsel assisting the Royal Commission, Daniel O'Dea, said that senior police officers would show Spike Daniels was suffering from a mental aberration, and that Daniels had committed a serious indiscretion that bore upon his motives.

The conservative state media joined the government in focusing the inquiry on the state of mind of battle-weary Superintendent Harold E. Daniels.

THE WEST AUSTRALIAN November 1975

PROSTITUTION INQUIRY OPENS

The royal commission into the administration of the law on prostitution was told yesterday that Supt H. E. Daniels would make thirty-seven specific allegations of police impropriety in connection with vice.

The commission was also told that senior policemen would testify that Supt Daniels had shown signs of mental aberration.

Mr D. J. O'Dea, Counsel assisting the Commissioner, said there would be evidence that Supt Daniels had committed a serious indiscretion which bore upon his motives in the case.

There would be evidence that Supt Daniels had listed his complaints in a document headed "Manifesto of a Concerned Cop" which he gave to his senior officers in 1973.

In the document he warned that the administration of the prostitution law would lead to corruption and ultimately murder.

Supt Daniels would say that some brothels had virtual immunity from prosecution. These had included the Kalgoorlie brothels and those run in Perth by the "principal operators", Mrs Dorothea Flatman and the late Shirley Finn.

Other allegations by Supt Daniels would include:

Toleration of prostitution had led to criminal exploitation of some women.

Some women, including girls who were under age, had been recruited through advertisements in a Sunday newspaper. The police had not acted against people who had underage girls in their brothels.

Policemen were indoctrinated that their careers would be jeopardised if they intruded outside their own areas. Uniformed police were expected to turn a blind eye to prostitution.

Two women were often selected to be charged after a raid on a brothel.

The West Australian

The Royal Commission had no independent investigative resources and relied almost entirely on evidence gathered by the poorly resourced Spike Daniels.

Police, who had never defined a policy for dealing with prostitution, came up with the 'containment' policy. It had never been written down nor mentioned publicly before its first official mention at the Norris Royal Commission. The unofficial policy involved the Consorting Squad regulating the industry, by determining who could operate. To the public and Judge Norris, it made sense. Sex work, while illegal, was best semi-regulated, rather than being forced underground. By allowing a few known good operators to administer the operation of brothels, police could keep the industry in check and keep out the gangsters.

A rookie journalist named Paul Murray, who went on to head-up *The West Australian*, reported on the Norris Royal Commission for the newspaper. "My perception of Judge Norris is he was very intent on not uncovering much at all. He was intolerant of anyone in the game," he told me in 2006.

"Politicians often say don't call a commission of inquiry unless you know what it is going to find. I think it was a predetermined outcome. I'm pretty sure the counsel assisting and the investigators were hand-picked for that task."

Daniels' conversations were monitored by other police officers in the lead-up to the Royal Commission. Defending the Commissioner's decision to use phone taps to keep Daniels in check, Judge Norris said, *"This was done because of information he heard that Daniels was neglecting his work at the Firearms Branch and still concerning himself with prostitution, newspaper people and the Civil Liberties Association."*

Judge Norris said dismantling the bug would have been illegal. He did not balance his argument by advising that bugging Daniels was illegal in the first place. Despite earlier implying Owen Leitch was entitled to bug Spike's phone, Norris then said the bug never existed. *"In my opinion the whole business was again a case of paranoid thinking on Daniels' part."* The judge did concede Spike received nuisance calls, which were traced to a Flatman brothel.

Four days after the opening of the Royal Commission, national attention was diverted to the single most significant event in Australian political history, the sacking of Prime Minister Gough Whitlam. Protests broke out in the streets of Perth. The Premier, Sir Charles Court, responded by banning public meetings.

The Royal charade continued drawing marginal attention. This Commission was supposed to be investigating prostitution, yet Norris dismissed the evidence of the very people at the centre of the trade, describing the prostitutes' evidence as "gossip", "embroidery", "hearsay", "tittle tale" or simply "unreliable".

On Friday 16 January 1976, a tall, thickset prostitute named Ingrid, who had worked for both Dorrie and Shirley, delivered frank evidence to the Norris Royal Commission on organised police raids and the protection of certain madams. She had wanted to set up on her own and said that Shirley and Dorrie had both told her she needed to pay protection money. The woman was due to give further evidence the next Monday, but she did not appear as she had been assaulted.

The Royal Commission threatened to issue a warrant and force the frightened witness back to court. Terrified of further repercussions she reluctantly turned up on Tuesday. The Royal Commission reprimanded the prostitute for not turning up to give evidence, even though they acknowledged she had received a bashing. No-one bothered to ask from whom.

On the day she was forced to attend, she explained she had not turned up due to fear of further intimidation. *"I didn't like to have anything happen to me again because I do think it was set up somewhere in the line. You don't have to laugh down there!"* Someone found it amusing that the woman was too frightened to turn up to the Royal Commission. Commissioner Norris told the woman she was lucky she was not arrested, prosecuted and punished for not turning up on the previous day.

She stated she believed the police were behind her attack. The allegation of witness intimidation was ignored.

Police officers who would later leave the force under a cloud would be lauded and described as "good types", "impressive", "intelligent", "effective"; while Daniels was "mad", "sick", "obsessed", "round the bend" and "paranoid".

Witnesses who did not support the police line were derided. Judge Norris dismissed one male witness's evidence, saying, *"He admitted convictions for homosexual offences and his general association with the brothels and their inmates [he made dresses for the prostitutes] does not commend him to me."* (Homosexuality was only decriminalised in Western Australia in 1989.)

Another male witness said Shirley had named three detectives to whom she periodically paid sums of money. He delivered an anonymous letter about the matter to the Commissioner but detectives were able to track him down. Again, Norris dismissed the man's evidence, branding him untrustworthy and a "sexual pervert".

In August 1975, three months before the start of the Royal Commission, Dorrie Flatman, the biggest single brothel operator in Perth, took a trip to

Jamaica and the UK. The man who administered the containment policy in the police force, Bernie Johnson, was also headed for the UK.

The 'Ebb Tide' was commissioned for the first time in August of 1975, leaving Perth around the time the remains of Violet Walker washed up on Cottesloe Beach—a coincidence perhaps.

Bernie joined businessman Ron Brown, who owned the boat, and a boatie named Tony for the voyage. They sailed to Reunion Island, Mauritius, then spent six weeks holidaying in the Seychelles. When the boat moored in Cairo, Bernie left the rest of the crew and flew to London.

The detective returned in time to testify at the Royal Commission.

The Judge liked what Johnson had to say about the running of prostitution. Judge Norris remarked in his final report: *There had been so many pieces of hearsay involving him [Johnson] in various improprieties that I was for a long time extremely suspicious of his conduct. As a witness however, he did impress me. He struck me as not only intelligent but frank. In the witness box his attitude to Superintendent Daniels, whom he had at one time considered suing for defamation—was admirably restrained and fair, giving proper weight to Daniels' unusual personality and his personal troubles...I regard [Johnson] as a truthful and reliable witness.*

Police said Dorrie Flatman received the preferred treatment because she was a good operator and the quietly spoken Englishwoman confirmed the police line. Her husband, Kimberley (Kim) Flatman, declined to appear because, he claimed, *"He had been called to Christ and was entering an Anglican Seminary in the eastern states to become a priest."* It didn't last—he was soon back running Flatman's thriving group of companies.

A close friend of the Flatmans' testified that the NSW police had sent Dorrie, that she received advanced notice of raids, and that he overheard a telephone conversation between Flatman and her daughter, Irene Anson. Dorrie phoned Irene from Jamaica a few months after the murder of Shirley Finn. *He [the witness] said that in the course of that conversation Anson asked her mother how important it was that she put $900 in the bank every week. The suggestion was that this was a bribe to someone in authority.* Flatman and Anson denied the allegation. Norris dismissed the man's allegations because he had convictions for homosexuality.

Funded by the Civil Liberties group, Spike Daniels was represented for part of the Royal Commission by Peter Dowding, who would later become Premier; and then by Robert French who, in 2017, is the Chief Justice of the High Court of Australia. "Spike Daniels was an old fashioned, honest cop. He had some very real concerns about the way the police administered the law of prostitution. He didn't have hard evidence of corruption," Justice French recalled.

"He believed the policy was undesirable and improper and without external accountability, it created the appearance and opportunity for corruption. Spike was poorly resourced. The attacks on Spike were coming hard and fast," Justice French said to me in 2004.

Spike Daniels' private life was laid bare. Letters to old friends talking about depression years earlier were submitted as evidence of his mental aberration. An allegation that he had sexually harassed a female officer was raised; and officers complained of his excessive attention on the prostitution trade. The main intent of the inquiry was to prove Daniels' disturbed state of mind; while allegations of payoffs, corruption and organised crime were glossed over and dismissed.

Despite the murder of Shirley Finn being the catalyst for the Royal Commission, it was given no attention. Daniels mental health was the inquiry's primary focus.

In Parliament, John Tonkin said Ray O'Connor had advised Mrs Flatman to get out of town, *"until all this blows over"*. O'Connor denied the allegation and said the only time that Mrs Flatman had visited him at home was to complain that Police Superintendent Spike Daniels was harassing her. He said Daniels had become a thorn in the side of the police force. *"I have never met Mrs Flatman on any previous occasion to my knowledge,"* he said.

Detective Bernie Johnson said his relationship with Ray O'Connor was purely professional. He dealt with him only in his capacity as Minister of Police. In 2009, Bernie Johnson told me the only time he saw Ray O'Connor in the company of a madam was at a Liberal Party fundraiser run by Ray O'Connor at his house. Dorrie Flatman was also there. "No, I didn't happen to be there. She was invited, and so was I. That's the only time I've seen Dorrie with Ray. I said, 'If you're going to have a fund-raising affair, she'll probably throw an extra few quid on the strength of me being there.' I don't know if she contributed. It was a fundraiser run by Ray. There were lots of gamblers there—anyone who was anyone in Northbridge."

Another prostitute would allege she was to meet with Police Minister Ray O'Connor, who wanted to set up a brothel with a man named Ng, but Mr O'Connor didn't show. The allegation was dismissed. Judge Norris said, *"I have no hesitation in saying that there is no truth whatsoever in the whole story."*

When the Police Union withdrew legal representation for Spike at the Royal Commission, it was the Civil Liberties group that raised the money to cover his legal fees. Archie Marshall used his own money to support the whistleblower, as well as storing information at his Maddington offices.

Marshall's offices were broken into during the Norris Royal Commission. Commission officers remained unconcerned. Such were the times that Marshall was anticipating a visit. The burglar alarm was on an outside wall in a steel cabinet five metres above the ground. Someone scaled the walls, cut the casing and carefully cut wires to disarm the high-tech alarm unit. Knowledge of which wires needed to be disconnected implied a professional job. The intruders proceeded to enter the building but were startled by a former British police officer and his partner, friends of Archie's living upstairs. The two men dropped a black bag they were carrying and took off. Inside were big black plastic sheets weighted at the bottom, tape for the windows and two-way radio equipment.

Police made no progress on the case. Judge Norris dismissed Archie Marshall's information saying that Marshall agreed he had nothing directly to support his allegations of graft and corruption. He also said that all the persons who told him they had evidence to give but were too scared to talk were anonymous telephone informants. *These things, and his behaviour in relation to the fable of the girl who was pushed off a boat, and in relation to the allegations regarding Mr O'Connor which I have just considered, satisfy me that he can at times present a very real danger to the reputation of decent people,* Judge Norris stated.

Detective Read describes the mood towards the Royal Commission in the CIB. "Most of us thought it was a load of hogwash, nonsense. I mean, let's face it, human beings—some get tempted. In those days, we weren't well paid; it was just a living. My way of thinking, 99.5 percent of the guys, were all straight. If there was a crooked bunch there, I didn't know anything about it. It would have been very upsetting if we knew someone was taking money or drugs or whatever. In those days you knew everyone. It was hard to realise there was graft or dishonesty because we were pretty happy with our jobs. We like to think we were on top of the crims."

The Royal Commission wound up on 24 February 1976 and Norris submitted his findings in May 1976, concluding there had been no impropriety in administering the law. The Police Force was exonerated. *The discretionary but not capricious manner of enforcement adopted has kept the State of Western Australia relatively free from the evils which may be associated with prostitution.*

The attacks weren't over for Spike Daniels. A madam had told Spike that lawyer Ron Cannon was arranging to re-open Shirley's brothel, and was seeking staff considered suitable by the government and by top police officers. She said it was to provide "cheap rent" for "slow learners" and would be "something for Shirley's kids". Spike Daniels received the information on speakerphone in the office of a politician—with the politician present. He repeated the madam's allegation to a newspaper. Lawyer Ron Cannon sued Daniels for defamation and won.

Soon after the Royal Commission and six weeks short of his sixtieth birthday, Spike Daniels picked up his typewriter, put on his hat and, with no farewell tidings from the half-dozen men above him, left the police department that he had faithfully served for thirty-nine years. He walked down the stairs like a leper but with the fortitude of an honest man.

That year, three Royal Commissions were held into police activities. The Royal Commission into the arrest of Baymis Ugle, at Narrogin in 1974, was held as a result of claims police officers had perjured themselves. The Royal Commission report found senior officers had used "obstructive tactics" to stop conflicting versions (of what happened during the arrest of Baymis Ugle) from coming to light.

A Royal Commission into the arrests of several Aboriginal people at Skull Creek near Laverton found some officers had colluded to prepare a false story about the actions of the individuals involved. Briefs on the incident provided by police were found to be contradictory. The Royal Commission found officers intentionally frustrated their inquiries and it criticised a Senior Inspector for trying to cover up discrepancies by altering the face sheets.

A code of silence permeated the WA police service in the 1970s, whereby creating negative publicity was considered a far greater crime than breaking the law. The Mollen Commission in New York explained the effect of the police code of silence:... *The most devastating consequence of the code of silence is that it prevents the vast majority of honest officers from doing what they inwardly want to do: help keep their Department corruption free. It is not surprising that the honest cop wants corrupt cops off the job. The consequences of corruption for honest cops are grave: it taints their reputations, destroys their morale and most important, jeopardises their very safety.*

Former Commissioner Owen Leitch saw Spike differently. He told me he believed Spike Daniels murdered Shirley Finn. "Think about it. He hated prostitutes, and he was in charge of firearms at the time."

It came from left field, and it was an allegation that, at first, startled me.

I considered this theory carefully, and while it was not out of the question, it didn't match the profile of the crime. However, if Leitch did think Daniels was responsible, it would explain why he pressured Spike to leave and why he bugged his phone. In 2004, when I interviewed Owen Leitch, I thought his belief might be an error of judgment.

Unlike the mounting evidence against Johnson, there are no clues I am aware of and nothing Leitch revealed to me that supported his claim. In Johnson's case, a witness saw him near the scene on the night of the murder, another witness said Shirley had phoned concerned about her meeting with him that night, and a third witness was threatened with hand grenades after naming him and O'Connor.

Bold and outspoken, Owen Leitch was a controversial, conservative and very political commissioner. In November 1975, while the Norris charade was being played out in the small Registrar's court at the back of the Supreme Court, Premier Sir Charles Court moved to ban political meetings in Forrest Place. The Whitlam dismissal was igniting tensions across the country and may have prompted his action. Forrest Place in Perth's CBD had long been the 'soap box' for political discourse and demonstration in Western Australia. Owen Leitch wrote to various organisations endorsing the decision, attracting nationwide condemnation. Legislation requiring the Commissioner's approval for public meetings was passed in 1977. Leitch's right wing, authoritarian style sat very comfortably with the Premier.

"It was no secret he admired Sir Charles Court as Premier. It was no secret he distrusted 'the reds'. And he wasn't afraid to go public implicating anybody with Left leanings as loony, unlawful, or worse, as a menace to society. His commission was above everything else authoritarian. His style was belligerent, tough and controversial. There hadn't been a commissioner like him—and not one since has been prepared to take on a thinly-disguised political guardianship of a government, via clever use of the law, against those who threatened to defy or disturb the conservative vision for WA," wrote author Jolly Read in his book on the Western Australian communist, Jack Marks.

Mr Leitch said he favoured the Liberal government, as they were less inclined to interfere with operational matters and undermine the separation of powers.

Earlier in his career, Leitch was an investigator and arresting officer in some notable cases. In 1950, he'd crawled into a roof cavity to capture Raymond Armanasco, who'd slaughtered his wife and five of their six children. There were other notable cases; but the case for which he was most remembered was the 1959 murder of heiress, Jillian Brewer.

Owen Leitch arrested 18-year-old deaf mute Darryl Beamish for the crime. Leitch told the court Beamish confessed four times, twice through a sign language interpreter, once in a written statement, and again by a note scrawled in the exercise yard of the police lock-up. Beamish said the confessions were obtained through threats and intimidation and were untrue. Daryl Beamish was convicted of the willful murder of Jillian

Brewer and sentenced to death by hanging for the murder. The death sentence was commuted to life imprisonment of which he served fifteen years.

Serial killer Eric Edgar Cooke confessed to killing Brewer in 1963. In 2005, Darryl Beamish's conviction was overturned. In 2011, fifty years after his conviction, Beamish was awarded a $425,000 exgratia payout for his wrongful conviction. However, in awarding the payment, the Western Australian Attorney General said, *there was a lack of conclusive evidence to suggest that there was serious misconduct by the prosecutors or police in the original conviction.*

As for the retired Commissioner's view on suspects in the Finn case, "Bernie's a suspect, Ray [O'Connor] is a suspect, Spike's a suspect, but I'm not," he said to me in 2004.

Owen Leitch died in 2006. Ten years after his death, a new witness came forward saying Owen Leitch threatened Shirley just two days before the murder. Finn had come to Jacqueline's house concerned about the threat.

I never had the opportunity to put that allegation to Owen Leitch.

Spike Daniels was a tortured soul. After blowing the whistle on police, he was ostracised and, whether it was real or imagined, he lived and died in fear of his life. The people he most grew to fear were amongst the men he once counted as good friends and colleagues.

Retired Assistant Commissioner Les Ayton believes Spike Daniels saw what others chose to ignore: "Spike saw it as organised crime, and looking back, organised crime was well entrenched in Perth, and had its fingers in the police force, and got stronger and stronger and stronger."

"Could he see what others couldn't?" I asked. "Would you call him a visionary?"

"I think they are words. Visionary is not the word...Pragmatist. He saw a wrong and tried to fix it up. He was really reacting to try and right a wrong. I don't think he really thought about it until he got these complaints. He must have known what the prehistory of the police force in his era was...until such time as he got these complaints...and tried to do something about it. He didn't have a vision that I know about. These things happened. He tried to fix it up. Nothing happened when he went to the Vice Squad and the Commissioner, so he tried to do something himself. To me, that is not visionary, that's a decent person trying to right a wrong. He died knowing he'd given it his best shot plus some. He tried his hardest to get the attention of the public and anyone else [for] what he understood to be the level of corruption in the force. You couldn't take that away from him." Mr Ayton told me in an interview in 2002.

Consumed by the injustice of his treatment, Spike Daniels spent his last few years writing his memoirs, *With Equal Poise*, which he hoped would be published after his death. Friends said newspaper reports and conversations would bring back a flood of feelings for Spike or new connections that he hoped might one day vindicate his stance. After a sleepless night, he would ring friends in the early hours of the morning with his latest theory or fact. The obsession never left him. Spike Daniels died in 1992 disgraced and humiliated. His memoirs were never published. Deputy Commissioner Les Ayton was the only commissioned police officer to attend his funeral.

In 2003, a Royal Commission was held into whether there was any substantial corruption in the police force in Western Australia. This revealed that some policemen were helping themselves to hundreds and thousands of dollars worth of drugs and dirty money, taking payoffs and covering up crime. In the midst of the inquiry, former Deputy Commissioner Les Ayton told me, "He [Spike] was a voice saying the system needs changing, but no-one was listening. They're still not listening."

My application to view the transcripts of evidence from the Royal Commission, under Freedom of Information in 2003, was refused. The Department of Premier and Cabinet said the transcripts contain extremely sensitive records and are restricted for seventy-five years. They can be viewed in 2051.

A second application for a small portion of the transcripts was also refused. An appeal to the Information Commissioner upheld the ban.

Archie Marshall is still bitter at his treatment by the Royal Commission. He still believes the call he received on 5 September alleging a woman had been pushed off a boat was genuine. He said his business suffered, his reputation was ruined, and his marriage broke down. He believes he did the right thing by raising the allegations with the authorities; although he believes they failed to investigate these properly. He said, "In the wake of the Royal Commission, I was left with a feeling that there was no honesty and fairness and no support for decent people."

Asked whether he regrets taking up Spike's cause, Archie Marshall replied, "Standing up for what you believe is always worth taking on."

Archie Marshall lodged a complaint with the Crime and Corruption Commission in 2004. They declined to investigate as the Royal Commission was then 28 years old, none of the police officers or other public officers mentioned was still serving, and many of the original witnesses would now be difficult to contact, and their evidence could be unreliable.

19

Politics and Money

Justice and power must be brought together, so that whatever is just may be powerful, and whatever is powerful may be just.

— Blaise Pascal

Back to the laundering—the money kind.

Marshall and Daniels alerted the Norris Royal Commission about a madam moving large sums of money illegally. Attempts to prosecute didn't happen because the body responsible for prosecuting. The Crown Solicitors Office, was compromised. A Crown Counsel in the Crown Solicitors Office was married to the madam.

They didn't know it then, but the scheme was part of an elaborate tax evasion and money-laundering scheme that would finally be exposed at the Costigan Royal Commission years later.

Crown Counsel at the Crown Solicitor's Office, Abraham Bercove, was married in 1975 to Marlene Bercove who ran Nikki's Escort Parlour at Scarborough Beach in Perth's northern suburbs.

The Norris Royal Commission into prostitution ignored this allegation, but the Costigan Royal Commission into the Painters and Dockers Union, held in another state in 1980, investigated.

The Liberal Federal Government hoped the inquiry headed by QC Frank Costigan would expose the dirty underbelly of the Union movement after a series of gangland murders on the wharves in Melbourne, but instead the trail led straight back to corporate Australia.

The top end of town was washing enormous sums of money hoping to avoid tax. To do so, they mixed their money with the black market to send it offshore.

In his final report, Frank Costigan talked of the first moment he realised the magnitude of what he was dealing with: *A witness was giving evidence in relation to the activities of a company said to be engaged in ship repairing. Subsequent investigations showed that not one dollar ever had been earned in that activity.* (The witness was sent to collect some documents and provide these to the Court.) Costigan continued, *...prior to this morning I had not seen signs of money exceeding five thousand dollars or thereabouts. Imagine my surprise to find in the files a cheque for one million, five hundred thousand dollars. Two or three minutes later I found an application by an associate company to the Reserve Bank to bring into this country from Lebanon, four million, five hundred thousand dollars. It didn't really seem to fit in with ship repairing. I decided to look more carefully at this associated company. It had a bank account in a distant suburb in another state. The bank vouchers were subpoenaed. I found that in the three months, some two hundred and fifty million dollars passed through that account. It was one of a dozen such accounts throughout Australia.*

Costigan was very interested in the Bercoves. Bottom of the Harbour tax schemes were said to deprive the government of around a billion dollars. The process involved stripping a company of its assets and accumulated profits, prior to its tax being due, leaving it unable to pay tax.

The Australian Tax Office (ATO) detected the Bottom of the Harbour scheme in 1973 and wanted to put a stop to it. Their senior investigations officer put together a case in WA, then sought the opinion of Crown Counsel through the WA Crown Solicitor's Office. By the end of 1974, a senior Queens Counsel strongly advised that the scheme's promoter should be charged with conspiracy to defraud the Commonwealth. The opinion was based upon documentary evidence and upon facts that were easily proved.

The WA Crown Solicitor's Office had been advised of the scheme, and the ATO had provided the evidence. The ATO expressed great frustration and concern at the failing of the WA Crown Solicitor's Office to take action when the evidence was clearly there.

Marlene Bercove's husband, Abraham, was a Crown Counsel tasked with prosecuting tax cheats on behalf of Australian taxpayers. The Costigan Royal Commission revealed Marlene was secretary-cum-receiver to some one hundred Bottom of the Harbour companies. After Costigan, Abraham Bercove was stood down.

With the delay in prosecution, confidence grew amongst the scheme's promoters that the law could be broken with impunity. The failure of the Crown Solicitor's Office in WA to carry out its primary duty of upholding the law permitted the law to be disregarded and brought into contempt. At the time the tax office identified the scheme in WA, only twenty-seven companies had been stripped of their pre-tax profits, but by 1980 the figure was 1,412.

The Costigan Royal Commission found that the Bottom of the Harbour scheme flourished due to failures of the Western Australian Crown Law Department. Thousands of millions of dollars in tax revenue were lost from the public purse involving some 7,000 companies who exploited the illegal scheme.

Federal Attorney General Peter Durack, Senator Noel Crichton Brown, Defence Minister Ian Viner, WA Premier Ray O' Connor and WA Liberal MP Alan Rocher were named in Parliament in 1982 as being involved in tax avoidance or protecting friends.

Labor MHR for Fremantle, Mr Dawkins, said in Parliament in 1982 that a number of high-level politicians were involved in tax avoidance schemes. *"Perth has become known and notorious for being a place for tax-dodging criminal activities and crookery in high places."*

The leader of the Opposition, Bill Hayden, said in Federal Parliament in 1982 that the WA Liberal Party's administration was *"absolutely corrupted"*.

Raffles hotelier and major organised crime figure Abe Saffron helped set up money channels where crime funds could be paid upwards, to politicians and political parties with guaranteed anonymity. Corrupt police were the well-rewarded foot soldiers.

It is not known how far up the line corrupt payments went in Western Australia in the seventies, but there is some evidence to suggest it went to the very top.

Commercial lawyer Jim Kenneison offered to give evidence at the Norris Royal Commission. Earlier he'd made allegations that Premier Charles Court had moved corrupt money offshore through a Hong Kong bank account in 1971. A journalist overhead Kenneison in private conversation. The lawyer had said he could provide bank account details. Kenneison's claim appeared in the newspaper and Parliamentary Hansard, in what became known as the Homeric House Dossiers. Charles Court sued the newspaper and the journalist for defamation and won.

Mr Kenneison had his documents (including the relevant account details) seized after he was accused of acting for two parties in divorce proceedings. He believes he was targeted for his allegations of corruption against Charles Court. In 1974, he was disbarred over the divorce matter.

"They grabbed every bit of paper they could lay their hands on. They had me at the Barristers' Board on all sorts of charges, and while I was there they were raiding my offices," said Mr Kenneison.

As Jim Kenneison was in Hong Kong when the Royal Commission started, his wife delivered a letter by hand to Ron Davies of the Crown Law Department. Kenneison offered to give evidence about legal corruption and about how Shirley Finn had used Kenneison & Co business trust accounts to move money offshore.

A day after the approach to Mr Davies, WA Police flew to Hong Kong with an extradition order. Mr Kenneison was charged with stealing money from a client's trust account. A charge he denied then and continued to deny till the day he died.

The Crown Law Department in Perth was unconcerned about the hundreds of thousands of dollars being laundered through illegal Bottom of the Harbor schemes despite Commonwealth urgings to prosecute. However, the Department could afford the full weight of international law to retrieve Mr Kenneison and hold him behind bars, alleging a few thousand dollars were unaccounted for.

Allies of Mr Kenneison wrote to the Minister of Police, Ray O'Connor, urging him to intervene: *In keeping with the allegations by Mr Kenneison that he has been singled out in the state, intimidated and persecuted by certain members of the legal profession he sought to have dealt with for alleged corruption under the terms of a Royal Commission Inquiry and who further are alleged by him to have used the Legal Practitioners Act to prevent him from assisting members of the public caught up in cases formerly conducted by either illegal or unprofessional conduct. We the undersigned allege a conspiracy in the procedures relating to his return from Hong Kong to this State.*

They saw the conspiracy as a preconceived plan to deprive Mr Kenneison of his rights under the law of this state and to keep him in custody at the pleasure of those involved.

Mr Kenneison said it took two years for the state to concoct the charge and believed it had worked to sufficiently discredit him, so that even had he been called to testify at the Royal Commission, his evidence would have been seriously undermined.

The amount Kenneison was accused of taking from the trust account varied enormously in the course of his trial. He maintained that the debit entry was matched by a credit entry in another account. In the end, Mr Kenneison was convicted for stealing $8,000 from a client's account he held in trust.

He was sentenced to five years jail and served three.

The Anglican Dean of St George's Cathedral, Vernon Cornish, a former court reporter sat through the entire trial. He considered the verdict a grave injustice, saying after the trial, *"This man has paid his clients to be his clients and been accused of stealing his own money."*

Jim Kenneison was removed from play, but thirty years later he was still angry about all that had transpired when he took on Charlie Court and members of the legal fraternity in Perth, and about all that followed.

He was teaching law at a city TAFE when I first met up with him in 2004.

Life must have appeared very different for a young Mr Kenneison when he passed Law at UWA with honours, becoming the Commonwealth Crown Prosecutor in Darwin in the early sixties, and then Senior Counsel to the Attorney General in South Australia when Don Dunstan was Premier.

He specialised in corporate fraud, "In Corporate crime, you are dealing with pillars of society who have gotten away with murder. For personal reasons, I came back to Perth."

Jim Kenneison started up his own law firm. The brilliant young commercial lawyer stretched the law to the limit to ensure his clients maximised their returns. By 1969, Kenneison & Co had about forty-four staff, specialising in subverting Australia's tough foreign exchange and banking laws. Word spread about Mr Kenneison's speciality, and his client base grew. Foreign banks, wanting to get in on WA's mining action, and some of the wealthiest businessmen in the country were among his clients. "Vast amounts of money went through my trust account, and credits were given overseas. This generated the capital that was needed overseas for the Canadian banks."

Moving money was his speciality. Mr Kenneison explained he didn't ask where the money came from; he didn't want to know. "As far as I'm concerned, it was not my role to be a judge of morals or principals. What I was doing was legal. It was within the law."

Mr Kenneison said Shirley Finn was one of his clients, and that she was moving large sums of money for other people—including politicians and big business. "Now Shirley Finn was looking after the affairs of a lot of key politicians in WA," he said. "It wasn't her money. It was politicians' money and other people's money. Very key people. People at the very top. Sexually and businesswise, she was a very astute woman. Very intelligent indeed and she had an ability to see forward. She was very focussed on what she was doing. She didn't get sidetracked. I met her many times. She wanted to get money overseas. She usually moved it to Singapore, Hong Kong and Shanghai Bank and some of that went on to Credit Suisse. She would bring in suitcases of cash. The money went through my accounts. The tax department would not have found it."

Shirley was due to appear before the Tax Department, two days after her death, over the disputed Hong Kong transfer. Kenneison knew nothing of Shirley's tax problems over the Hong Kong Syndicate transfer but he did say he was acting for her at the time the funds appeared in her account in 1971. These funds were connected to the same tax debt she had sought help with from her father, saying she needed money to pay an MP. Kenneison was unsure whether the funds mentioned in the Homeric House Dossiers were the same as those (labelled Hong Kong Syndicate) that appeared in Shirley Finn's account in Perth in 1971. Shirley was moving a lot of money for a lot of people. He had no recollection of an account she may have set up called Hong Kong Syndicate.

He is clearer on the details of the event that lead to his naming in Parliament by Charles Court in 1972. According to Mr Kenneison, the claim in the Dossiers that Premier Charles Court had moved corrupt money offshore in 1971 through a Hong Kong bank account, stemmed from an incident in his office. He said that Finn and a man by the name of Jo Jones used to bring in large sums of cash for transfer overseas, to subvert foreign exchange laws. Kenneison said businesses sought out his financial service, as he had worked out a way to get around the foreign exchange laws using an accounting system of debits and credits.

He said Jones had transferred a large amount of money to an account in Singapore. After those funds didn't show up at the other end, Kenneison said all hell broke loose in his office. "These men came in and threatened me with hell and damnation, saying that I better find the money or heads would roll. Down to the bank we go. The bank swears black and blue that the money is gone."

He says the men who came to his office became increasingly agitated. "They told me it was Charles Court's money. They said I better find it, and they told me why. This was the money that was being laundered. They're dirty payments. When it came out—and Charles Court knew I knew about it—that's when the knives were out. I was as popular as a pork chop in a synagogue. Later that day, the bank found out what had happened. It went to one branch on Orchard Road instead of the one on the other side. It did go to Hong Kong and Shanghai Bank Singapore, but it went to the wrong branch. The money was later recovered."

Kenneison said he never meant for the conversation to end up in print. However, he was overheard by a journalist when discussing the situation at a function. The allegation was published in the *Nation Review*, one of a range of claims made by various people about the Premier that became known as the Homeric House Dossiers.

Sir Charles Court began suing those behind the papers. In Parliament, he described the claims in the Dossiers as *an elaborate mixture of truths, half-truths, lies and reported statements, surrounded with extravagant phrases, loosely connected. Among the allegations reported in the paper, and* *replied to, in Parliament: A Mr Robert Franzen informed me in February 1972 that he was in a position to obtain the numbers of bank accounts which Mr Court holds in both Hong Kong and Singapore. Mr Franzen told me that in excess of $250,000 was held by Mr Court in banks in each of those cities. I do not know whether Mr Franzen did so inform the author, but it is a lie. There are no such accounts, nor have there ever been such accounts.*

Court then went on to counter the allegations in the Dossiers where lawyer Jim Kenneison is revealed as one of the sources. *"The author (of the Dossiers) says, 'Mr Kenneison told me that Mr Court had shifted substantial sums of money out of Australia to Hong Kong.' I do not know whether Mr Kenneison said this, but it is a lie."*

When Jim Kenneison saw his name in the paper, he knew it meant trouble. He tried not to get involved. His sister Wendy warned him, "I told him, you are treading on dangerous ground. They are powerful people. They will have you."

At this point, in 1972, Mr Kenneison was at the top of his game, a leading commercial lawyer with a thriving practice. He had nothing to gain by criticising such a powerful politician, and much to lose.

Sir Charles Court sued the journalist behind the claims. The freelancer with no money to defend himself acknowledged the claims were without foundation. He was ordered to pay costs. Court then sued *Nation Review* and won that action too.

Despite all that ensued at that time, Mr Kenneison stood by his allegation until his death in 2013.

In 1972, when the Dossiers emerged in the newspaper, a leadership tussle was underway in the Liberal Party. Sir David Brand, Western Australia's longest serving Premier, collapsed at a function in 1970. His health ailing, he continued as Premier, losing the election the following year to the ALP's John Tonkin. It was the end of a long reign of power for the Liberal Party, who weren't used to opposition.

Charles Court was the obvious replacement. As Minister for the North West and Industrial Development in the government of Sir David Brand, Charles Court is largely credited with transforming Western Australia from a provincial backwater to an economic powerhouse. He negotiated deals to exploit the state's enormous mineral wealth, and he assisted many projects to get off the ground. Court negotiated the Hamersley, Robe and Mount Newman iron ore projects, vehemently opposing both major parties in Federal Parliament for their attempts to impose controls on Japanese buying of the ore.

But not everyone was happy with Court's autocratic style.

"Brand was a quiet, placid sort of person, and Charlie was domineering," Ray O'Connor recalled. "They thought he was arrogant. I was approached to get rid of Charlie and put me in as leader. I was always loyal to the Liberal Party. Some wanted to get rid of Charlie. I wasn't happy about it."

The day of the vote, in May 1972, Ray O'Connor met with a few allies for lunch at O'Connor's Restaurant on Hay Street. They asked O'Connor to challenge Sir Charles for the leadership.

"It was on the morning on the day of the vote. They said I had the numbers and could lead the party. It was out of the blue," Mr O'Connor said.

Clive Griffiths presided over the Legislative Council in WA for twenty years. He was at the meeting at O'Connor's restaurant in 1972. "Ray didn't even know he was going to be the candidate selected for the challenge." He said no-one doubted Court would get the job and the only reason for the challenge was to let Sir Charles know he was there by the grace of the party and not as an automatic right.

Mr Kenneison said Court had been prepared for the challenge and delivered a document to Ray O'Connor before the vote. Kenneison was with Ray O'Connor that night and saw the document. "Ray did not have absolute majority. Ray knew about this money matter and asked me to come and see him. It was about midnight, and I travelled from Kalamunda to Mt Lawley. He showed me a letter that had been given to him that implicated him in various acts of immorality. He wanted to know if it's genuine. Court had got a private investigator sniffing around Ray. Ray couldn't help himself. He was a womaniser. If Ray did not withdraw from the ballot, Court was going to distribute this to the media."

Mr Kenneison believed he was summoned because of the information he had on Sir Charles' bank accounts, which O'Connor would use as insurance against any political fallout from the challenge. "I told him I could give him the number[s] of the bank accounts that Court held in Hong Kong."

In Parliament, David Brand made his speech and nominated Sir Charles Court as leader. Another member nominated Ray O'Connor after having checked with Ray that he wanted to stand. Ray stood up and to the shock of everyone who had been present at the lunchtime meeting at O'Connor's restaurant, said he declined the nomination. "The reason I didn't nominate is because I didn't have enough time," he told me in 2004.

He would later tell those that offered their support that his wife had presented allegations of impropriety to him and he was trying to save his marriage. The couple separated the following year.

If Mr Kenneison's account is accurate, then both Sir Charles Court and Ray O'Connor were blackmailing each other, and their ability to administer government impartially, with the issues that were about to arise, was severely compromised.

Ray O'Connor said of the preselection, "I was approached to oppose Sir Charles, but I refused to do it because I thought I wasn't ready." This is contrary to what he had told others at the restaurant, where he had indicated he was willing to accept the role.

Allegations of a blackmail attempt in the lead-up to the preselection made it into the newspapers. Mr O'Connor said he couldn't recall if a blackmail attempt had happened, but when Battye Library historian Stuart Reid interviewed him, in 1996, his memory appeared to be a little clearer.

"It was a cooked up document. As you see, if you read the article involved there it said it was an effort to blackmail me and was obviously false. The chap who made the allegation later came forward and signed a declaration to the fact that it was false. He claimed to me at the time that someone had a gun at his head and forced him to sign the document. But anyhow, the thing is it wasn't true," Ray O'Connor told Reid.

Reid asked Ray O'Connor if any action was taken over the blackmail, the alleged threat, and O'Connor's claim a gun had been held at somebody's head. *"I did something about it; I brought the fellow in and he* signed the declaration that it was all false. I didn't sit there and do nothing."

"What were the nature of the allegations?" Reid asked.

"I can't recollect it fully," O'Connor replied, "but the allegation appeared to be that I'd mixed with some wrong sort of people."

In her biography of Sir Charles, *I Love This Place*, Ronda Jamieson wrote about the leadership tussle, though his opponent is not mentioned. She said Court had the full support of Sir David Brand. *It was therefore doubly surprising and disappointing to Court when some members of the State Liberal Party, including secretary Fred Lathby, criticised him for being, among other things, too hardline in the search for industry to be a successful premier and campaigned strongly against him.*

Sir Charles was furious there was to be an election. By his account, *"things turned nasty"*. Jamieson does not at any stage mention who the challenger is, nor why the challenge was suddenly dropped, just that *In the end, the succession went smoothly and on Court's terms; there was no election.*

Now in Western Australia, Sir Charles Court is as close as you get to royalty. Criticising him in 1970s Perth was tantamount to career suicide.

I requested an interview with Sir Charles Court in 2003. He asked questions be faxed through in advance before he would agree. Among the questions I asked were: What happened the day of the Liberal Party preselection in 1972? Why did you stand down in 1982?

He refused an interview.

In 1972, Charles Court assumed the leadership of the Liberal Party.

The Hong Kong bank accounts allegation was a source of great angst to Sir Charles. As Richard Court wrote in his father's biography, *I remember the time well as it particularly hurt my mother. My mother passed away without ever receiving an apology re the false allegations about secret bank accounts in Hong Kong.*

The Liberal Government swept to power in Western Australia in 1974 with its pro-development, anti-Canberra stance. Sir Charles Court became Premier. He was an autocrat, largely regarded as a one-man band. He was pro-mining, pro-business, pro-whaling, pro-logging, and vehemently opposed to unions.

Ray O'Connor became Minister for Police and Minister for Works. If the blackmail allegations are true, then some water must have passed under the bridge as the Premier appointed O'Connor to these senior roles.

O'Connor had separated from his wife Beverley shortly after the preselection incident and later remarried Vesna Stampalia.

Working out of offices in Dumas House, staff members said they would make excuses for the absent Minister every Friday afternoon. "Mrs Brown and Mrs Green would turn up every Friday—both Italian looking. They'd go in. Ray would pick up the phone. Next thing [a notable businessman] was in there. They'd go into the lounge. Doors locked. Next minute, you'd hear laughter and glasses...then quiet and then laughing... and the two girls would walk out and then Ray and [named businessman] would disappear for the afternoon."

Another staff member, Mick Healey, also remembered the regular Friday visits from girls he believed were prostitutes.

Mick Healey says he was working as acting private secretary to Ray O'Connor at Dumas House in Havelock Street near Parliament House in 1975. He says O'Connor held a late meeting on the Friday night two days before Shirley died. He is certain about the date as he always considered the timing was not coincidental.

"He told me I could go home early, but I stayed on."

He says he saw Bernie Johnson go into the meeting.

Healey recognised three well-known Western Australian businessmen who were at the meeting with Ray O'Connor and Bernie Johnson. Healey knew Bernie Johnson, as he lived around the corner from him, and was able to describe him to me. He said it was the only time he had ever seen Bernie Johnson in the office with O'Connor.

Mick Healey does not know what was discussed, and neither Johnson nor O'Connor recall such a meeting taking place.

Stella Strong named Bernie Johnson and Ray O'Connor as two people who had approached her to set up brothels in Western Australia. Both Johnson and O'Connor were named in the Norris Royal Commission as being involved in setting up brothels—albeit hearsay. Boxer George Stewart told politician Matt Stephens that these two men were behind

Shirley's death, though hand-grenades on his front lawn deterred him from saying more. Shirley's driver is adamant she regularly drove Ray and Shirley places together, and Goldfinger named Ray O'Connor as the man who ordered the hit. Ginger said Bert Tudori organised the murder.

Mr O'Connor strongly denied these claims. However, combined with Shirley's father's evidence of his daughter needing a politician to deal with her tax debt, and the more recent evidence of Leigh Varis (who says she drove Ray O'Connor and Shirley around), Mr O'Connor should have been investigated as a suspect. Regardless, Detective Read, who headed the murder investigation, said O'Connor was not on the list of suspects.

If the WA Police Force has since conducted a thorough investigation into O'Connor's movements and actions in the lead up to the Finn murder, they are not disclosing that information. I have serious doubts that such an investigation has ever taken place.

After losing the 1983 election to Brian Burke, Ray O'Connor went into business with Laurie Connell and lawyer Leon Musca, who were both in business with Bernie Johnson through Kim Wah, a seafood export/import business. In 1989, O'Connor would be granted the Order of Australia for services to government and politics in Western Australia. After the 1992 'WA Inc' Royal Commission had scrutinised some of his business dealings through Ray O'Connor Consultancy, he was charged and found guilty of stealing a $25,000 donation to the Liberal Party, then jailed for eighteen months. After leaving jail, he sold real estate.

I twice looked him in the face and asked him if he had killed Shirley Finn. He denied it, of course, and claimed he had never even met her. I read nothing in his face to show he was lying.

He died in 2013, aged eighty-six.

20

Ring of Blue

Friendships forged in squads of old
Are held with trust like bars of gold
That solid band a ring of blue
An unwritten code to each be true.
When trouble strikes the line is held
Between each man a stable weld
From time to time a link gives way
But the gap is closed within a day.

— Deputy Commissioner Les Ayton (retired), 1980

Some of the retired detectives I spoke to still thought containment of prostitution the best model to prevent criminal enterprises from getting out of control. However, where the containment stopped and started is now not so clear. SP bookmaking, illegal gambling, sly-grogging, drug dealing, and armed robberies have all allegedly been contained in the past, though never officially, with some operators getting the greenlight from police while others were shut out and repeatedly arrested.

Detective Bernie Johnson and gambling lord Bert Tudori claimed this system of containment, which afforded control to favoured operators, helped keep drugs out of Northbridge and WA. Put simply they were wrong. The drug trade with its associated industry of money laundering, standover tactics, loan sharking and corruption flourished under Johnson's watch.

As in other areas of crime, detectives investigating drug distribution had an almost symbiotic relationship with the people they were investigating. To gather intelligence meant mixing with dealers and users, and sometimes lines were crossed. Undercover officers in the Drug Squad were often forced to deal in drugs to catch the crooks. Friendships were forged and, all too often, policemen on a pittance witnessed those above street level making extraordinary profits and getting away with their crimes.

Bernie Johnson's best mate was Detective Ron Whitmore. He was named in the Costigan Royal Commission with Bernie and had helped his friend bust Shirley Finn back in 1969. I invited him to explain his version of events, but he declined.

He was head of the Drug Squad in 1976 when explosive allegations hit the headlines. A drug probe was launched after more than a dozen people lodged affidavits alleging police regularly participated in the sale and distribution of drugs.

The *Sunday Independent*, a Perth newspaper owned by iron ore magnate Lang Hancock, published allegations from affidavits in their possession, which claimed the Drug Squad was in control of the drug trade. Among the claims:

- Detectives had framed pushers and users and then used them to distribute drugs;
- Chosen pushers, acting as informants, would dob in others, keeping out competition. The drugs seized from competitors trying to get in on the action would be returned to police-selected dealers who then released them back on the streets;
- Seller informants were offered lighter sentences—usually probation or a fine instead of jail, by understating the quantities of drugs with which they were caught. The drugs were then returned for distribution; and
- Police and informants collaborated over court evidence.

The most serious of the allegations was that a Drug Squad detective had conspired with another man to murder an informant-dealer, Brian Hahn. The 23-year-old died of a heroin overdose on 4 February 1975. Some dealers said it was because of the death of Hahn that they had decided to speak out.

Journalists Maree Van Steyn and Charles Amery wrote in the Independent: *It's a scene of corruption and big profits with the drug user as a pathetic pawn in a deadly game.*

When the newspaper aired the allegations against the Drug Squad in 1976, another six complainants came forward with further information. Those making complaints against police signed affidavits and lodged them with solicitors. Among the fresh allegations were claims a well-known dealer-informant was dealing with a person or persons at Parliament House, and that police payments to dealers were in the form of drugs, including heroin.

The detectives named in the new statements were the same detectives named in the original statements, with the new declarants saying they did not know the original declarants.

According to a subsequent newspaper report, the new declarations also suggested links between car dealing and drug dealing and claimed that drug users, when their outside supply dried up, approached detectives at Drug Squad headquarters for supplies.

One of the declarants said he worked as an informant-seller for two squad detectives. He itemised four drops with a particular detective who he said had supplied him with hashish from Asia. *"There was gold stamps and oriental writing on the hashish."* Other declarants later stated they were harassed by police after making their statements.

A woman claimed her drug-dealing flatmate had regular appointments at Parliament House. She said the flatmate worked as a dealer-informant for a Drug Squad detective. The police frequently raided their house, but carelessly concealed drugs were never found. The only people ever busted were visitors to the house. *"There was always a lot of dope in the house—in the curtain rods, hidden in the roof and furniture. Blood-stained syringes were also in the sink. But nobody in the house was busted—only visitors to the house. We always seemed to know when a raid was coming,"* she stated.

The sworn affidavits were presented to Police Minister Ray O'Connor. The Premiers Department issued a response from the Police Minister. *A number of declarations and statements were handed to Mr O'Connor and* two lists of names supplied. Mr O'Connor said the first list contained eleven names of persons who were supposedly able and willing to give evidence. Ten of the eleven are convicted persons; five of them charged with, or convicted of drug trafficking offences. Mr O'Connor said all eleven had been interviewed. Three had stated they had no complaints to make.

The second list of ten names was similarly dismissed. Nine of these persons had convictions: eight of them had been convicted of drug offences—some for trafficking.

The statement from the Premier's Department went on to say that Senior Assistant Commissioner Reg Carr would be looking into the possibility of a criminal conspiracy being committed.

The *Daily News* headline on 6 September 1976 the day after the *Sunday Independent* call for an inquiry read, *Plot to Break Police?* It reported that police were investigating the possibility of a conspiracy against the Drug Squad. *Members of the CIB Drug Squad were expected to issue writs by the end of the week against some people who had made allegations against them.*

A gun draws too much attention. Litigation is a far more successful tool to silence a critic. Most people can't even afford to get to court with a lawyer. Bring a criminal charge against someone and you can ruin his or her credibility for life.

The *Sunday Independent* called on the services of US polygraph expert Shelton Brown to test the veracity of the most damning claims from one of the dealers. The test was said to have 95 per cent accuracy. The man repeated his allegations and the test results indicated he was telling the truth.

The newspaper called for a public inquiry.

Instead of investigating the allegations, seven of the complainants were charged with criminal defamation. Warrants were issued to obtain the affidavits allowing Drug Squad detectives to make unprecedented raids on solicitor's offices, seizing confidential documents.

The WA Law Society sought legal opinion because of grave concerns over the issuing of the warrants. *"The confidentiality of lawyers' files is an integral part of our system of justice. To undermine such confidentiality is to undermine public trust in the system and thereby the system itself,"* a spokesman from the Law Society told the Sunday Independent.

The men, who had claimed they were let off lightly for agreeing to play the game, felt the full force of the law after going public. A 24-year-old man, who alleged police had murdered a dealer and were involved in sexual deviancy and drug dealing, was held in custody on the defamation charge. He was convicted for cannabis dealing and jailed for five years. Another complainant, a 29-year-old company director, was given seven years for heroin dealing. At the time, both these sentences were the heaviest jail terms ever imposed on drug dealers in WA in the history of the state.

It reminded me of something Kalgoorlie madam Stella Strong said. "There's no point in speaking out about it [police and political corruption] because, in the end, the criminal always gets crushed."

The following year, Drug Squad head, Detective Ron Whitmore said there had been an enormous growth in heroin distribution in the state.

"Since 1972, it has grown to such a point that we now come into contact with it daily—hearing of it, acting on it, dealing with it," he told *The West Australian.* The five-fold increase in drug abuse during the early seventies marked the beginning of a drug epidemic that remains with us to this day.

The world's foremost expert on the history and politics of drug use, Professor Alfred McCoy, said the cannabis suppliers were local, and heroin suppliers moved in from overseas during this time. Both needed five key ingredients for developing the trade:

- A reliable source of supply;
- A potential group of consumers;
- A tradition of political tolerance for some organised crime;
- Police corruption; and
- An informal alliance between the drug syndicates and some influential leaders of established political parties, senior public servants and skilled professionals.

The system existing in WA to protect illegal gambling and prostitution ensured the five key elements were in place for the exponential growth of the drug trade in the seventies and eighties.

Two Drug Squad detectives, who raided lawyers' offices in the wake of the 1976 'conspiracy', found themselves at the centre of the Greenhead drug scandal five years later.

Kerry Tangney, another key member of Johnson's consorting team in the lead-up to the death of Shirley Finn, replaced Whitmore as head of the Drug Squad in the late seventies.

Judge Norris thought very highly of Kerry Tangney, who was said to be one of the brightest young members of Johnson's consorting team. In his final report to the prostitution Royal Commission back in 1976, Norris stated: *I am completely satisfied with the operations and the integrity of all personnel serving on the Consorting Squad, to name but one, Detective Tangney, who I feel has been subjected to more character exposure than the rest. I am more than satisfied with his integrity and honesty of purpose and these thoughts permeate the entire Consorting Squad.*

Detective Kerry Tangney and three other members of the Drug Squad were charged with conspiring to obtain cannabis with intent to sell or supply in 1981, after four drug dealers alleged the officers had stolen more than eighty kilograms of marijuana. The dealers had been charged with cultivating nine kilograms of marijuana at Greenhead, a fishing village about 250 kilometres north of Perth. When brought before the court, the growers expressed surprise they were only charged with possession of nine kilograms. They told the court the actual amount seized by police was ninety kilograms.

The four police officers also faced charges that they conspired to pervert the course of justice.

The accused denied all charges. The trial was WA's longest District Court Criminal trial at that time. Tangney spent 56 days in the police lock-up.

In 1981, Detective Bernie Johnson took charge of Internal Affairs, a unit set up to investigate complaints of corruption.

The relationship between Tangney and Johnson must have soured since they had travelled to Sydney to arrest notorious hitman Christopher Flannery back in 1974. Facing charges of conspiracy to sell drugs, Tangney claimed Johnson had set him up. He presented evidence on tape alleging Bernie Johnson was involved in a conspiracy of his own. Johnson denied meeting with Tangney soon after the investigation, and when an audio recording was admitted to an inquiry as evidence, it was ruled inaudible and therefore not admissible.

The four detectives were acquitted, but Commissioner Porter dismissed them four days before Christmas 1981. Tangney and another officer charged over the Greenhead drug crop came out swinging. The two sacked detectives called for an urgent public judicial inquiry into the police force.

In January 1982, Marshall Wilson at *The Western Mail* reported the two men had alleged widespread corruption in the Force, including massive cash payments to police by brothel madams and illegal casino operators. They alleged that mafia-style operations controlled prostitution and illegal casinos, and that a senior Western Australian police officer organised graft payments and distributed the proceeds to officers.

Detective Tangney alleged all the illegal gambling operations in Perth could be linked to one man, saying, *"They call him 'The Godfather' and [it's] said his tentacles stretch to most of the illegal casinos operating in the city. The Italian with widespread business interests keeps a low profile and lives an apparently frugal existence."* He was talking about Vincent Rispoli, whose criminal operations had been greatly expanded through his son-in-law, Bert Tudori, and through Bert's brother, Lawrence Tudori.

Mr Tangney spoke of payoffs before Christmas from an illegal gambling representative at the Duchess Room of the Windsor in South Perth. This person passed out small white envelopes containing a Christmas card and a roll of money to Senior CIB officers. *"I saw it with my own eyes,"* he told Marshall Wilson of the *Western Mail* in a tape-recorded interview. *"That was the Christmas bonus. There's another party at Easter."*

Kerry Tangney said sums of between $3,000 and $5,000 were given to detectives each month for favourable treatment under the containment policy. (It was alleged the Tudoris and Rispolis were in charge of prostitution and gambling, and these gifts were a reward to police for turning a blind-eye to all their illegal activities.)

Tangney told Marshall Wilson that the place where Shirley Finn had been found was a well-known spot where Vice Squad detectives regularly met with their closest informants.

He went on to say, *"Does it not strike one as being something of a coincidence for Shirley Finn to have been shot in the head at a spot which was a recognised meeting place for detectives and their informants? I have no proof about the link, but it has always been common talk."*

Kerry Tangney had committed the greatest sin one could commit at that time in the WA Police Force. He had spoken out against fellow detectives and, as Spike Daniels had learnt, this betrayal would come at a great price.

Tangney was the only detective not to receive legal aid for his defence against drug conspiracy charges; he claimed he would have to sell nearly all his assets to pay his legal costs, estimated to be between \$40,000 and \$50,000. Tangney told reporter Marshall Wilson that, prior to the Greenhead incident, he had been given a home alarm after a Perth-based drug dealer had negotiated his killing by a hitman. The evidence was on an illegal phone tap. After Tangney went public about corruption in the Force, the alarm was removed.

Suspended without pay, after charges were laid over the Greenhead seizure, Tangney's public airings of police dirty laundry ended when the government offered him back pay. The conditions of the government offer included signing an agreement not to make any more claims or demands. He has not spoken publicly about his allegations since.

None of the police officers charged over the Greenhead incident were convicted. After leaving the Force, Kerry Tangney bought a service station in the Scarborough/Karrinyup area of WA, later purchasing trendy Subiaco eatery Funtastico. Then, according to a report in *The West Australian*, Tangney launched into the Sydney market in spectacular style, buying a 500-seat eatery overlooking Sydney Harbour just before the 2000 Olympics.

Tangney has rebuilt his life and left behind the tangled web of corruption that permeated the WA Police Force in the seventies. He has no desire to revisit the past and would not contribute any information to this book. "I've left that behind. I went through hell. I've got nothing to say," he said when I approached him at Subiaco restaurant Funtastico in 2003, and I don't blame him.

December 1981 was a bad year for the WA Police Force, not only were the four Drug Squad detectives sacked, another detective was forced to resign after allegations he'd demanded money from prostitutes. Like his colleagues, Tony Wick had impressed Judge Norris with his evidence back in 1976. Judge Norris stated: *I thought him truthful, and the allegation against him improbable.*

A further two police officers resigned the same month, after allegedly being caught on tape by prostitutes who—tired of paying bribes—had set them up.

Opposition leader Brian Burke (later Premier of WA) said that people who had spoken out about alleged corruption were the target of special attention. *"There appears to have been a concerted effort in recent weeks to put some people out of business while other well-known brothels are apparently allowed to continue operating after a single token prosecution of some of the people involved,"* he told *Daily News'* Frazer Guild. *"It is hard to escape the conclusion that people who have blown the whistle on what is allegedly going on have been treated more harshly than others."*

In Charles Court's final term, the Liberal Party ranks were split into two groups, those who supported Sir Charles and those who supported O'Connor—legalised gambling the dominant issue separating the groups. Mr O'Connor was pushing for legalised gambling; Sir Charles was firmly against it. The Tudori brothers were confident they would get the casino licence if O'Connor won the leadership and was able to get a bill through.

When Sir Charles Court bowed out as leader in 1982, without ever really explaining why, he was aged in his seventies

When Raymond James O'Connor took the helm as the 22nd Premier of Western Australia on the 25 January 1982, the corruption scandal was still brewing around him. Seven detectives had resigned the month before, and the Premier was forced to call an inquiry. The government appointed State Ombudsman Oliver F. Dixon to provide advice on a course of action.

Dixon examined allegations raised by the *Western Mail*. These included casino payoffs, madams making cash payments to officers, and an accusation that Detective Inspector Johnson was known as the 'King of Vice' and was somehow involved in the death of Shirley Finn.

When Ombudsman Oliver Dixon called in reporter Marshall Wilson's tape recordings with Kerry Tangney, the editor of the *Western Mail*, Sir Larry Lamb, confirmed the tapes had existed but were now missing. Tangney's allegations had disappeared.

It took Dixon less than two months to table his report in Parliament. The conclusion was delayed as Inspector Bernie Johnson was away overseas at the time, sailing, as he had done in the lead-up to the Norris Royal Commission.

The outcome was predictable: the conduct of present members of the WA Police Force was above suspicion; internal affairs and management were handling allegations of police impropriety well; and the government and police didn't require any further inquiries other than those the Commissioner was already making.

Dixon described Tangney's allegation that police met informants at the spot Shirley Finn was murdered as "ludicrous". *One almost has a mental picture of police cars lining up waiting for their turn to meet their own informants at the prescribed spot.*

He did acknowledge the limitations of the inquiry. *It is almost impossible for an outsider to expose corruption at a high level because such men would be astute enough to prevent any effective investigation.*

As Norris had before him, he exonerated Bernie Johnson, saying that his numerous assets were the result of wise investments. He attacked the media reports, branding them *a triumph of sensationalism over accuracy.*

The *Western Mail* hit back alleging a smokescreen. They refuted the Dixon claims, taking them on, point by point. By contrast, the conservative daily, *The West Australian*, ran the headlines *Police above suspicion* and *No Police Cover-up*. It paid to tow the line. *The West Australian* survived the big business buyouts of the eighties, with Alan Bond and the WA Government coming on line as major shareholders in what became the state's only daily paper.

Dr Harvey Tarvydas (brother of Perth fashion designer Ruth) treated the detective who was named as Seven in the Dixon report. Detective Seven was one of the policemen who resigned after inquiries into allegations of protection payments by prostitutes. All officers were cleared by the Dixon inquiry.

Dr Tarvydas believed the death of Detective Seven was suspicious. Detective Seven had come into his practice for a consultation, suffering from stress and wanting to offload before the scandal erupted. The GP said he still remembers the conversation. Seven was very distressed, and Dr Tarvydas recalled him saying, "You get stuck! They make you do things." At another consultation, Detective Seven asked him, "Do you have a way of being safe from the horrors of these people?"

After resigning, Seven and another detective, who left in the lead-up to the Dixon inquiry, acquired sufficient cash to buy up a few hotels up north, but according to his doctor the cash was running out.

The week before Seven died, "He came to me a number of times over a few days and he was looking absolutely frightened. He was in a panic and told me I might never see him again."

Within days of that discussion, on 24 October 1987, Seven was found dead at home on his kitchen floor with no obvious signs of death. He was aged thirty-nine. The Coroner was unable to find a cause.

Dr Tarvydas showed me a letter from the Coroner seeking information on any suspicious circumstances surrounding the death. However, the doctor didn't have enough confidence in any of Western Australia's investigating bodies, operating at that time, to raise his concerns with the Coroner. He was afraid of what might happen to him if he did.

Detective Seven's body was cremated. Cause of death unknown.

21

Protecting Reputations

It is almost impossible for an outsider to expose corruption at a high level because such men would be astute enough to prevent any effective investigation.

— Oliver Dixon, 1983

Detective Read handed over the Finn murder file to the coroner on 19 March 1976 stating: *Despite a comprehensive and extensive investigation, the identity of the person or persons responsible for the death of Mrs Finn, remains a mystery. I see no immediate prospects in the way of fresh information or new evidence, and it is with a great deal of reluctance that I submit these papers to you for the information of the City Coroner.*

It took police just ten months to give up on finding the killer. Three decades on, he reflected on the motive for the murder. "We never ever found out why or what was the motive for the murder. She was under pressure from the taxation. She had money, her house, the 'SS' on the pool. She was one of those people that said, 'This is me, this is my success.' To strip her of that would have killed her. She liked to impress people. To be stripped of her wealth was too much."

Read concedes the person who murdered Shirley had a lot to lose, and that protection of another's reputation was the strongest probable motive. However, he denies outright that police were amongst the people whose reputation needed protection.

As the police have never acknowledged Shirley was paying protection money, and the officer or officers she was said to be paying were never identified, this avenue of investigation was not fully pursued—if at all.

Several newspaper reports and a 1982 investigation by Ombudsman Oliver Dixon named Bernie Johnson as a widely-rumoured suspect. Bill Read said, "At no time was Bernie Johnson in the hot seat. He was never a suspect. There was no motive for a start; there was no indication that he or any other police officer was involved." Read also stated there was no evidence that Shirley was paying for protection.

Aside from two witnesses who spoke to Spike Daniels, claiming Shirley had told them she paid police, and those detailed in the Norris Royal Commission, Shirley's accountant (from 1971 to 1974, prior to Edward Dymock) told Howard Sattler of *The Sunday Times* in 1982 that Shirley paid protection money to operate. *$1,000 Graft a week to Police*, the headline read.

"She told me she paid about $1,000 a week—about $50,000 a year," the accountant was quoted as saying. He said he was amazed he had not been questioned during investigations into her death, and that officers on the case had not examined her business files.

Allegations of police involvement in her death remain unsubstantiated, Sattler wrote.

Royal Commissions later exposed that corrupt payments to police were—more often than not—squandered on alcohol and gambling to ensure they didn't leave a paper trial. Only when such acts were caught on camera, years later, did the majority of Australians accept that some police were corruptly profiting from crime.

Detective Read confronted the accountant after the article was published. The accountant denied saying Shirley was paying $1,000 a week in graft. *"I did intimate to Howard Sattler that the figure was in the vicinity of $500 a week. When I questioned her, 'What are your expenses in operating this kind of business?' she mentioned these bribes to police."*

Shirley didn't name any police officer to her accountant. *"She led me to believe that the amount was in the vicinity of $500 paid now and again. I just cannot clarify whether it was weekly or periodically, but the figure she mentioned was $500,"* he explained in a statement to police, obtained under FOI.

But madam Stella Strong explained how the system worked, and police protection didn't come cheap. She claimed she paid corrupt officers $100 per girl per week; two girls, $200; ten girls, $1,000. She also claimed that she had paid WA detectives in the very place that Shirley Finn was killed.

The police didn't interview Stella Strong, perhaps because she was living in Kalgoorlie and back then she knew the price of speaking out. Stella told me the detective she paid was Bernie Johnson—a claim that he denies.

In 1982, Ombudsman Oliver Dixon was asked to get to the bottom of Bernie Johnson's assets, which included nine properties and two boats. Dixon reported that Johnson *lived in a house of a standard beyond that expected to be owned by a policeman, owned properties of a value inconsistent with his salary, and owned a yacht of considerable value.* The report noted that allegedly Johnson was known as 'The King of Vice' and in some way connected with the Shirley Finn murder. Dixon's investigation concluded that there was no evidence to support the claims.

Dixon said in his findings: *No investigation can ever prove beyond any possible doubt a man is honest. To reach such a conclusion would involve the searching of every registry of titles, every register of shareholders and every bank account in the world. Even if such an impossible task be undertaken, it could not be conclusive as one could never be sure of the names in which investments were made. In the absence of very specific allegations, one must ultimately rely on what the person under investigation chooses to disclose.* Dixon noted that Johnson made some prudent share and property investments and offered a "satisfactory explanation" of his assets.

The tables turned in the late 1980s. Retired Assistant Commissioner Les Ayton headed Internal Affairs, and Johnson, who had led internal affairs when it began in 1979, was under investigation. He didn't accept Dixon's findings. "We confirmed much of what Dixon found and more, but I always thought there was much more. What we found [of Johnson's wealth] was considerable. It was well over a million bucks. We had information then, and I still believe now that there was a lot more wealth than we could find," he told me in 2003.

He said Johnson wielded an inordinate amount of power in the force, despite never achieving senior rank. "I don't think it's any secret that BJ was one of the people we were looking at. I think it's fair to say that we were able to establish some links with specific people in the crime world that you wouldn't expect to have and certainly not of the nature that you would expect to occur. There was something definitely not right about some of the associations. Sometimes coppers have got to associate with crims, and they do it for the right reasons and in the right way and sometimes get criticised for it. You can't capture that type of crap unless you engage it, but the sort of associations we were seeing [with Johnson] were not those types of associations, and we were highly suspicious of those."

Johnson told me inside knowledge was necessary to catch crooks. As for his real estate properties, gold mine, yacht and cash, Mr Johnson claims he invested well.

Johnson was one of seven senior officers whose names were touted for one of the top jobs in the WA Police Force—head of the CIB—in 1985. The job went to Peter Skehan. After spending most of his career in the CIB, Johnson was transferred to a senior uniform position at the Fremantle regional office in 1987.

He retired unexpectedly in 1990 of his own volition, telling a newspaper reporter: "I was enjoying myself so much on [annual] leave, I thought I'd do it fulltime."

Controversy marred his career, but no investigation has found any clear evidence of wrongdoing. He has never been charged with any crime.

Bernie Johnson had been in business with crooked financier Laurie Connell since the 1980s. He was a co-director with Connell in Kim Wah—a seafood importing business—while still a member of the police force. Kim Ng (Biu Kuren Ng), the man who blew the lid on Sydney's Chinatown drug racket in the sixties and who was listed in NSW Parliament in 1987 as being a principal illegal casino operator, was also a co-director.

Ng fled west around the same time as madams Dorrie Flatman and Stella Strong set up shop in Perth. He reported the presence of senior police at an illegal casino in Sydney's Chinatown in 1967 and said, as a result, he'd been assaulted and loaded up with opium. David Hickie wrote about Ng's strong police links in his groundbreaking book on NSW corruption, *Prince and the Premier*. *Ng had for many years enjoyed associations with members of the force and had been admitted as a social member of the Police Club in Sussex Street, where he came to know by name, sight and rank some very senior officers.*

Police Internal Affairs investigated Kim Wah Seafoods. "We were highly suspicious of that [business] and thought it may be a front for something else," retired Assistant Commissioner Les Ayton said.

As well as being his business partner, Bernie Johnson also worked as a private investigator for Connell while Connell's legal troubles were growing. Charges relating to his involvement in the collapse of Rothwells Bank were deferred when Connell was charged with conspiring to fix the 1983 AHA Bunbury Cup.

Jockey Danny Hobby jumped from a horse, Strike Softly, after Connell paid him a $5,000 bribe. Connell then paid him one million dollars to travel overseas to avoid facing an inquiry. The money eventually dried up, so Hobby rolled over and confessed to police. Horse trainer Bobbie Meyers verified Hobby's story.

Connell was tried and found not guilty of fixing the race but guilty of perverting the course of justice by paying Hobby to leave the country. Connell was sentenced to five years' jail, but was released after serving only one year; Hobby served three years.

The crooked financier was pretty desperate by the time Hobby rolled. Details of a convoluted plot—to deal with jockey Danny Hobby and horse trainer Bob Meyers—later emerged during the perjury trial of bankrupt builder Max 'Rodgers' in 1995. Max had been accused of trying to defraud Laurie Connell and pervert the course of justice.

Max Rodgers was found guilty of attempting to pervert the course of justice by taping conversations and writing letters to discourage jockey Danny Hobby and horse trainer Bob Meyers from testifying against Connell. Max had admitted to being aware he was perverting the course of justice by making the tapes but was unaware of their purpose.

Rodgers was found not guilty of trying to defraud Connell of $450,000 by posing as a police officer who could silence Hobby and Meyers.

Instructing the jury, Judge Brian O'Dea said, *"For you to reach a guilty verdict, you must almost reach the conclusion that they [Rodgers and Connell] were acting together to pervert the course of justice."*

No legal action was taken against Connell over the incident.

Laurie Connell told the District Court that Max, posing as Drug Squad Detective Don Hancock, offered to organise the death of Meyers and the disappearance of Hobby for a fee of $450,000. When Laurie Connell's evidence was called into question at the trial, his paid investigator, retired detective Bernie Johnson, was there to back him up.

In court, Max admitted to having written the letter, opened by Connell's wife, which read, *Laurie, I need to speak to you urgently, can you please call me during business hours. It is very important to speak to you. Regards, D. Hancock.*

Don Hancock was the crooked detective who allegedly set up the Mickelberg brothers over the Perth Mint gold heist. Hancock was later murdered by bikies in 2001. His reputation as a hard man was legendary.

Connell says he rang the phone number attached to the letter from 'Hancock' and subsequent phone calls resulted in two meetings with Max, who used the alias 'Rodgers'. Connell said that during the meeting Max had offered to help him by organising for horse trainer Meyers (who was under police protection) to take a fatal drug overdose and by arranging for jockey Hobby to disappear out of the country.

The use of Hancock's name is telling. Hancock was a crooked cop who had never been dealt with by police. Hancock was also a friend and colleague of Johnson's, so no middleman was needed for such a connection.

In 1995, Max told the court that Connell had approached him first. He said after the financier was charged with race fixing in January 1992, Connell again contacted Max, asking if he would lie under oath. Max said he refused but agreed to a second request to tape some conversations on Connell's behalf. He said he did not concern himself with what Connell intended to do with the tapes; he just needed the $50,000. Max Rodgers was bankrupt at the time.

Retired detective Bernie Johnson testified he hid in the boot of Connell's Mercedes, so he could overhear the conversation, which he said involved Max attempting to extort money from Laurie Connell. Johnson backed up his employer's story.

The judge didn't believe Connell or Johnson, whose convoluted stories matched.

Max's version of events was weighed against Connell's story, and Max's story was considered more credible. The appeal judge told the court: *Alternative explanations for the dealings that appear actually to have taken place between Connell and [Rodgers] are extraordinary and yet one of them apparently is true. In my opinion, there is not much to choose between the two in explanation. On the one hand [Rodgers] says he was enlisted by Connell, on the promise of payment of a large sum of money, to write notes to Connell in another name and to create a bogus tape recording or tape recordings, for such use, not fully understood by [Rodgers], as Connell might wish to make of them. On the other hand, the Crown suggests that he was attempting to perpetrate an extortion upon Connell and in the course of so doing was pretending to be a mythical drug squad detective whose services had been offered to Connell by another senior police officer.*

On behalf of the Crown it is submitted that it is so unlikely as to be absurd that Connell would telephone a virtual stranger and ask the latter to commit perjury. But against that it might be thought very unlikely that Max, a businessman widely known in racing circles, would imagine he could deceive Connell, also apparently widely known in those circles, that he was a drug squad detective; and do it so convincingly as to succeed in extorting money from Connell.

Of course, it obviously is the case that each account has an element of irrationality and unreality about it, but as the events which actually did happen are to be explained by one or other account, and as the rejection of Max's account would involve accepting an alternative account hardly more likely than the former, I am not prepared to conclude that the jury, acting reasonably, would reject Max's account out of hand. It seems to me that a reasonable jury might prefer Max's account.

Bernie Johnson supported Connell's story and if it was dubious then so was Johnson's evidence. Don Hancock's name was well known in Western Australia as one of the state's dirtiest cops. He was a close friend of Bernie Johnson's and had worked on the Finn murder case with him.

Max Rodgers was adamant Connell and Johnson had lied. He said when police asked why an experienced detective of Johnson's ilk might lie, he explained to them Johnson had threatened him once before. He explained how he had seen Johnson outside the Pagoda Restaurant about 200 metres away from the spot where Shirley Finn was murdered, at the same time on the same night that the murder took place.

From the early 1970s, Laurie Connell was said to be fixing races and getting away with it. When a bookmaker complained to police that a well-known Perth radio identity was delaying the broadcast of races while Laurie laid bets already knowing the outcome, police took no action against Connell, but the WA Turf Club banned him from the track for two years. The Turf Club complained to police about their failure to take action against Connell. Two police officers were implicated in this alleged fraud, known as the Kalgoorlie Sting.

At the Perth Cup in 1987, Connell's horse Rocker Racer won by nine lengths. It was almost certainly loaded with etorphine (elephant juice), though mysteriously a swab was never taken. As Connell collected half a million dollars in winnings, ordering champagne all round, the horse was dying in a scene later described as one of racing's most *hauntingly horrid images*.

Connell loved to splash money around, particularly other people's. He was on the verge of bankruptcy when he acquired a Brisbane clothing business, Rothwells, in the 1970s and set about turning it into a merchant bank.

Returning to Perth a few years later a millionaire, 'the lender of last resort' built up close friendships with politicians, donating vast sums to the Liberal and Labor parties' coffers; though only minimal amounts were recorded in the books. He brokered and secured lucrative government deals, receiving enormous commissions.

At his peak, Connell had the spending habits of a heavyweight Arab oil sheikh or a corrupt African dictator, syphoning his country's wealth off into Swiss bank accounts. There was the Cotswolds manor in the UK, the beach house near Busselton, and the bloodstock studs in Western Australia and New Zealand. Australia's biggest racehorse owner owned more than four hundred racehorses and a private racetrack. He had a silver collection valued at three million dollars, a fine collection of Australian paintings; and the family jewellery included a diamond necklace valued at $1.2 million.

He was planning Australia's most luxurious home when Rothwells sank. Seven houses were purchased and then demolished for Connell's mansion. It was to have a 25-metre swimming pool with a retractable roof, courtyards and gardens, a tennis court, a squash court and garage space for the Rolls Royce and seven other cars. The servants' quarters were going to be larger than an average house.

The West Australian Government pumped in $144 million dollars of taxpayers' money in their attempts save Rothwells. Two days after the announcement of a special investigator to examine the merchant bank's collapse, Laurie Connell was removed from an aircraft about to leave Perth for London. National Companies and Securities Commission investigator Ikulin Ratneser told the Supreme Court: *"We have evidence to suggest that in the past few weeks $2.5 to $3 million of property was shipped to the UK for sale in the UK."*

Connell declared he was broke and defended himself in a long-running fraud trial over the loss of more than $300 million through Rothwells 'bank'.

Laurie Connell died in 1996, before the trial into the missing millions from Rothwells had finished. He was 49. The investigation into Rothwells estimated Connell spirited away some $500 million from Rothwells, ranking the theft as one of the largest in Australian history. The fate of the fortune that disappeared out of Rothwells' books over six years, mostly into Connell's pockets, remains the greatest unsolved mystery of the crashes of the 1980s.

As Trevor Sykes wrote in *The Bold Riders: From the viewpoint of the wider public interest, it is regrettable that there was never any satisfactory public accounting of the hundreds of millions that were lost in Connell's private empire.*

The collusion of the WA Government with private business between 1983 and 1991 led to the 'WA Inc' Royal Commission, which found the government had wasted more than $800 million dollars of public money bailing out private interests.

During the 1996 Royal Commission into allegations of corrupt conduct at Wanneroo Council, Johnson's name again came up. He was identified in Parliament as one of four police officers involved in negotiations to buy Western Beryllium Resources from Allan Harriman and Lester John Martin before the pair were convicted over a $1.3 million heroin importation. Harriman told detectives investigating the Council that the four policemen offered him $500,000 for 52 per cent of the gold-mining business in 1987. Harriman rejected the deal, telling his business partner Martin: *"Don't get involved with crooked cops because if they get caught they will leave us holding the baby. Don't get caught with crooked cops. They'll hang you out to dry,"* Parliament heard.

Harriman told police the four detectives wanted a legitimate avenue to launder big amounts of money. He also claimed that it was only after knocking them back that he was investigated for drug trafficking.

Johnson also copped a mention in the Kennedy Royal Commission in 2003.

When I interviewed him, he was writing a book about his life. "Don't know what I'll call it. Maybe, *Takes a thief to catch a thief,*" he told me.

At his retirement speech in 2008, Ron Cannon told the assembled lawyers and judges who had gathered to pay him tribute, "I do know who killed Shirley Finn."

I contacted Mr Cannon after that speech, but he was not prepared to reveal names. Back in 2004, as Finn's lawyer, Ron Cannon had offered these theories on her murder. "I don't think her death had anything to do with her tax problem," he told me. "She never wanted to pay tax; she just wanted to keep spending."

As to why she was killed, Mr Cannon said, "She was always talking about writing a book and dropping people in it. She thought she had more power than what she had."

While Mr Cannon said he didn't believe there was political involvement in the murder, he did say, "The politicians, they were all fakers, they all pretended they could do something for her." He said it quietly, and I only heard it when I replayed the tape. He has refused to name names.

Ron Cannon was said to be present when Mr Spini signed a caveat against Shirley Finn's Mill Point Road Property. The caveat was a form of security to ensure Mr Spini got his money back. He had lent it to Shirley Finn after an approach from her father. Shirley's father insisted she had said the loan was to pay off an MP to deal with her tax problem.

It's feasible that Ron Cannon knew who the MP was, as he helped organise the security for the loan. Did Shirley discuss with him where she was going when she attended his offices to sign off on the security in 1974?

After the murder, back in 1975, Ron Cannon dismissed Jo Shewring's story. He responded in *The West Australian* saying the urgent loan was probably for him. He (Cannon) had gone to Sydney, not Canberra, to see the top taxation lawyer in Australia. The Sydney lawyer had advised Mrs Finn she should repay her tax debt at once. The story given to her father had probably been confused.

Mr Cannon said he went alone.

Ron Cannon swore that it was he who had travelled to Sydney (in August) to consult with a tax expert. *As a result of instructions, I made arrangements with a Sydney firm of solicitors, White Murray and Carew to see Mr Cullinan a barrister specialising in taxation matters and proceeded in August 1974 to Sydney where I consulted with Mr Cullinan.*

However, Mr Cannon did not travel to Sydney in August to consult with the tax expert on Shirley Finn's behalf. Mr Cannon's trip to consult with the tax expert was in March—not August—well before Shirley took out her urgent loan.

That money was used for an alternative trip.

The CIB confirmed that Shirley had flown to Sydney between 14 August 1974 and 9 September 1974 when she repaid the loan by Mr Spini (her father's friend). This trip was clearly not the same trip as that mentioned by Mr Cannon. Possibly he made a mistake in timing, or, at worst, this was a deliberate lie—perjury. His affidavit, published in the newspaper back in 1975, succeeded in casting doubt on Jo Shewring's story.

In 2010, I asked Mr Cannon to explain. *I can't answer the question 'what the loan was for' and whether it was central for the investigation. I was not an investigator of her death. The Police decide what to investigate, not me.*

Mr Cannon said police had never questioned him over the case.

We communicated via email. I reminded Cannon the loan was secured in his office and Mr Spini had said Cannon was present. He replied, *Despite your promptings, I cannot retrieve any memories of the second loan of $5,000.00 in August 1974 and repaid 1 month later, the loan* *being secured by a caveat over a property, described by you as situated in Mill Point Road.*

I understand the difficult circumstances confronting you and your research, and that you are prompted by a genuine desire to achieve some sort of justice for the deceased and her family, in view of the failure of the Police to make an arrest.

I have never been questioned or known of the details of the Cold Case Reviews and I am completely unaware as is the rest of the public of the line of enquiries being pursued by the Police.

Other than giving you these comments and anecdotes I believe I cannot assist you any further.

If you look at the recent case involving Philip Cleary, he lost $630,000 damages in the Victorian Supreme Court, about two months ago. He was sued for defamation as was his publisher Allen & Unwin. It was reported in the internet under the heading "Phil Cleary and James Ramage". It was the biggest damages for defamation in legal history. He had defamed a lawyer by suggesting improper conduct. I suppose they only sue because the publisher had money as it is a waste of time suing if a person is insolvent and uninsured.

I prefer a peaceful life. I am not a crusader. I thus do not want to spend any further time on this matter.

I have been happy to assist you because I know the difficulties confronting you but I am not interested in what version other people have given you. We all have our own interest to protect. A friendly warning—don't trust some of your informants.

I wish you good luck to your book and I look forward to reading it.

Mr Cannon did not travel to Sydney in August after Shirley Finn sought her urgent loan. He should not have written an affidavit to say that he had. Police should have picked up this anomaly at the time.

Don Sutherland saw two men moving hastily down the left-hand side of the Narrows Bridge underpass, and his description always intrigued me. I suspected I knew the identity of the tall man—6ft 2inches or about 188cm, slim build, dark complexion—but who was the man with sandy, goldy-coloured hair, a fair complexion and a sports jacket who looked like a cop?

Who, among the suspects, looked like that and would be capable of murder? Chicka Reeves, the eastern states hitman who'd come to town, was short and walked with a limp. He didn't fit the profile. I conducted a virtual line-up of the suspects and couldn't work out who the second man might be. No-one seemed to fit the profile.

In 2016, retired NSW cop, Roger Rogerson, was in the news again, jailed for life after he was caught on CCTV luring a young university student, Jamie Gao, into a storage unit with the promise Gao could make big money on a drug deal. Instead, Gao received two bullets to the chest. Roger Rogerson and another retired police officer, Glen McNamara, shot Gao and then disposed of his body.

As details of Rogerson's crime emerged, another witness came forward on the Finn murder—a former detective who had worked with Johnson at the time of the Finn Murder. He did not want to be identified, but said that just days after the Finn murder, Bernie Johnson had introduced him to Roger Rogerson and Abe Saffron at the Raffles Hotel. My informant did not know why Rogerson was in town at that time.

Another witness, a former working girl, says Shirley Finn was at the Raffles Hotel with Roger Rogerson, Abe Saffron, an Asian man "with a puggy face", and Bernie Johnson on Saturday 21 June 1975, the night before Shirley was killed.

Rogerson fitted the description of the second man seen moving away from the Dodge and was more than capable of carrying out such a brazen crime. In June 2016, *The West Australian* reported that detectives from WA's cold case squad quizzed Rogerson about the Finn murder, but he admitted nothing.

Rogerson was sentenced to life in prison in September 2016. Judge Geoffrey Bellew said, "*The joint criminal enterprise to which each offender was a party was extensive in its planning, brutal in its execution and callous in its aftermath.*"

His lawyers have indicated he will appeal his sentence.

22

Bridget's Fight

Crime takes but a moment but justice an eternity.
— Ellen O'Grady

In 2015, I took Bridget back to the Riverview Street house she had left as a young girl on the edge of womanhood. It was 40 years since she'd last stepped inside the gate of her old South Perth home. The owner kindly allowed us access—one of many small kindnesses on our journey. The home still stands as it was: a manicured garden, an elegant, simple home in a beautiful tree-lined street in one of Perth's better riverside suburbs. The pond and rose garden were sweetly scented. A smile swept across Bridget's face as she stepped inside.

The leadlight windows captured the light; a brass chandelier hung from an ornate vaulted ceiling. There were the carved wooden architraves and the window seats; the dining room where she'd eaten a roast dinner with her first love and future father of her three children; the bar and the pool where she'd enjoyed a barbeque with her mum; the upstairs bedroom she'd snuck out of to be with her boyfriend Kim. Much of the home was just as she remembered it. Bridget was wearing a dress with a flared skirt that she fanned out, as her mother had once done in the ball gown she so loved. Later Bridget told me that walking back into her old home was one of the happiest days of her life.

After the murder, Bridget lived with her father for a while and attended Kent Street High. Her mother's public death made her a target of ridicule. She rebelled and was expelled, ending up in Bridgewater, a home for neglected children. She, too, became a teenage mother.

Shirley's parents (Bridget's grandparents) went to their daughter's wedding, and to her funeral. They never told Shirley's siblings that the woman sometimes dubbed the 'Queen of Vice', whose controversial execution regularly made the headlines, was their sister. To them she was an unknown woman from a different world. While they protected Shirley's brother and sister, their grandchildren were left exposed. No-one wanted to be associated with the troubled children of a murdered madam.

When I first met Bridget she was timid, fearful and untrusting. She told me little. She was still living with Kim, in a simple house in the Perth hills. At that first meeting, the story from her childhood of telling her teacher that her parents owned a lolly shop was the story that stood out most for me. Over the years, she shared her mother's reports, her welfare papers and her heartache. I gradually crossed the line from being professionally detached to becoming her friend.

Bridget has held down jobs and never been in serious trouble with the law. "I never wanted to give the cops a penny. I've not even ever had a speeding ticket." She explained it was her children who kept her going. Like her mother, Bridget gave birth to three children, two boys and a girl.

There are two women in my life I value above all others, and they are women I could never imagine doing without. They are my mother and my daughter, and Bridget has lost both. Bridget's mother and her daughter are buried side-by-side at Karrakatta. Her daughter was just fifteen when she was killed in a car accident.

Nothing can bring back Bridget's daughter, nor her mother. These are pains that never leave her. Still, she desperately hopes that one day the people responsible for her mother's death will be found and brought to justice.

"It consumes my life. I think about it all the time and it gets worse as my life goes on. I find myself visiting my mother's grave. It's the one thing I want before I die," she said, "to know who killed my mother."

Bridget's two sons give her enormous joy and support.

In 2005, I had spoken to more than twenty-five witnesses, including Stella Strong, Leigh Varis, Jo Shewring, Archie Marshall, and Ron Cannon. I had read through hundreds of documents, and paid for title and company searches, and believed I had enough information to push for an inquiry. I presented my information to the family. Bridget and Steven applied to the coroner for an inquest into the death of their mother. I believed that, combined with police investigative powers, a conviction might be possible. I offered to work with police for an outcome. Police could get the canteen diary, number plates, DNA, subpoena the writings of Detective Bernie Johnson and Arthur Simms, who had both written books; pull apart the Mill Point Road title; and investigate Ray O'Connor, Bernie Johnson and Ron Cannon. We hoped they would take the challenge on. When Bridget asked how the review was going, she was told it was being looked at. After a year, we stopped asking.

I was working and had a young family. There was only so much time I could dedicate to finding justice for Bridget and her family. The story had given me much grief and had taken a great deal of my time and energy.

Two years after her application, the Coroner advised Bridget—via a letter she didn't receive—that there was no new substantive information warranting an inquest. We disagree. Had action been taken at that time, there would have been some chance of justice.

On Facebook, in 2012, Bridget put out a cry for justice. She'd been to her mother's grave again and made another promise to her, hoping that justice might one day prevail. Her brother, Shane, had passed away, and before he died he asked her to fight on. I rang Bridget, saying, "If you can overcome your shyness, and put your noggin up on television, I'll do my best to get things happening—at the very least, someone independent to look at the case." Bridget had never spoken to the media. She is painfully shy and hates public speaking.

She overcame her fear and, in 2012, did her first media interview on Channel 9. Coupled with the media coverage, she made a formal request for the files relating to her mother's murder to be handed over to an independent authority for scrutiny. She considered it a grave injustice that the files remained with the alleged perpetrators. That media report would be the first of many to come. The first time she was interviewed live on radio, she was gripped with fear and couldn't speak. The host wrapped the interview up quickly. She is still terrified, but she is also very determined. With the media pressure, the WA Police announced a cold case review of the Shirley Finn murder. They told us it would take months, as it's a complicated case. They took four years.

In 2013, Bridget launched a Facebook page, *Who Murdered Shirley Finn*. People who knew Bridget and her mother connected with her; some offered kindness and support; some came with new information.

With a conviction unlikely due to the age of the case, we needed the support of the WA Police and the Crime and Corruption Commission to get an inquiry happening. We did not feel their motivation would be strong.

In 2014, the father of Bridget's children, Kim Chambers—who had attended a barbeque at Bridget's home the night before her mother was executed, and who lived as Bridget's defacto for much of her life—was murdered while on holidays in the Philippines.

Bridget wrote to Bernie Johnson that year:

I am writing to you to appeal to the young police officer you once were. Remember when you started out in the job and the first time you came across a grieving family that you wanted to help find justice. Remember the passion you felt and how much you wanted a result. Remember when you believed in justice.

I gather you are not well, but I am hoping you will find it in yourself to make a huge difference to the life of another weighted down by the slow grinding search for answers about what happened to my mother. Imagine your own daughter at 13 years of age, the age I was when I lost my mother. I have never been in trouble with the law.

I am asking you to please meet with me and tell me what happened the night my mother died.

I need to know, and I feel certain that you have the answers.

She never received a reply.

Then in 2016, she received the news she had been longing for. Forty-one years after the murder of her mother, Bridget was granted an inquest. She rang me in tears. Despite our bull-headed efforts, we hadn't really believed it would ever happen.

"It was the anniversary of my daughter's death. I was already emotional. I just cried and cried. It took ages to sink in," she told me.

When the euphoria wore off, we began assembling evidence, realising the monumental task that lay ahead and the limitations of what could be achieved after such a long passage of time.

Bridget is optimistic she will receive some answers. "I'm hoping to find out who murdered my mother, who else was involved; and if they can't give me that, at least an admission that there's been corruption."

23

Shooting at Shadows

More than one ordered the hit. Big people. I think
they killed the son too. He was in jail for nothing.

— Rocco 'Ginger' Antonetti

Shane Finn was engaging and intelligent—not what I expected when the bald headed, tattooed man (on parole for murder) sat down with me for coffee at the Battye Library back in 2004. Shane Finn had spent most of his forty-four years in an institution, the latest being a sixteen-year stint for the murder of Christopher 'Stitch' Harris in 1988.

Ginger Antonetti, from Ginger's Two-Up School, implied Shane had been set up. I had since spoken to Karry Smith, the senior public servant who investigated Shane's case on behalf of the government, who held the same view.

Shane couldn't really remember the night it happened, but the trial transcripts said the case was straightforward, and Shane had confessed.

Harris had criticised Finn's mum. Shane had flown into a rage, stabbing Harris in the chest. Shane said he remembered nothing of the night including his confession. He accepted he did it but is frustrated he can't remember more of the night.

Shane had completed his sentence and was supposed to have attended a parole meeting the day we met, but chose to miss it. The failure to attend meant he would be heading back to prison. He didn't mind; he was more comfortable in jail than out.

Shane was in Hillston Boys Home when his mother died. He didn't take the news of her murder well. He says he was injected with Valium and sedated for two weeks after the crime.

In the weeks leading up to her murder, Shirley had threatened if he returned home she would kill him. Shane had a history of anti-social behaviour, with violence between his parents a factor.

He learnt early that his mum carried huge amounts of cash. He found a rectangular cosmetic case packed full of fat wads of $10 and $20 bills, and soon learnt the combination of his mum's safes. They were always choc-a-block with wads of cash. There were folders of shares and property titles too, but Shane wasn't interested in those—just the cash. He and his mum fought over the theft and he was sent back to a boys' home. Shane and Steve both remembered the domestic violence that frequented their upbringing, with both parents throwing punches.

After Shirley's murder, people who had loved knowing Shirley and attending her famous parties were now ashamed to be associated with her in anyway. Shirley Finn became the brunt of jokes on the radio, adding to the kids' shame and hurt.

The boys went to live with Des for a while, but his new wife, who had children of her own, found the troubled teens difficult. The boys were left to fend for themselves, turning to their mother's partner, Rose, for help. When Bridget ran away and was put in Bridgewater, Shane hatched plans to free her.

"The people we can't deal with at all is each other. We blame each other for a lot of stuff. After—we were ostracised. Bridget and Steve were both expelled from Kent Street. I got refused entry. She [Bridget] ended up in Bridgewater. Being in Bridgewater, something died for her. I tried kidnapping her a couple of times, but then I got done for stealing the car to come and get her.

"At that point, I truly lost any respect for the society I lived in. I don't believe that I have the same pain as Bridget and Steven. We're worlds away in the way we think. I think the reason I alienated myself from them is I couldn't understand the pain I saw in them. I stayed stoned or pissed most of the time." Shane's arms were tattooed with the names of his brother *Steve* and sister *Bridget* and with the word *mum*.

"Rose did what she could, but was in no state to give the kids any meaningful help. Each time Rose has vented her spleen, shit happens. She's been chased out of the state twice, coz I went with her because she took over the mother's role," Shane Finn said.

"I gravitated to her world. Where she went, I went. When she gets pressure applied to her, she turns junky. She is still at war with Bernie Johnson. He's the one who delivered the news to Rose. 'You wouldn't believe this,' she said. 'He smiled at me…he fuckin' smiled at me.'"

Shane said the police tried to help him out with a trade. "They gave me the lock picking kit. They said, 'Learn a trade.' They gave me lock picks from scientific branch. The message was, 'Learn a trade, Shane'. Gave me lock picks, a gun and manual."

"So they wanted to 'greenlight' you to become an armed robber?" I asked.

"Yeah! If I played the game, I was laughing; problem is, I didn't play the game."

He claims that he was asked by police officers to deal with a rogue detective they felt was behind the murder of his mother, and told that they (the police officers) would gladly hand him the gun. Shane said he was told by police officers they were ashamed of what they believed the detective had done. In 1988, he says, word got out that Shane would avenge his mother's death; whether they were just words of an angry frustrated young man will never be known, as before long he was jailed for murder.

Former Attorney General Peter Foss reviewed the Shane Finn case. His Chief-of-Staff, Karry Smith, sought medical and scientific opinions in the eastern states on whether Shane could have inflicted the wound, given his broken collarbone, and the angle of the blade and the depth of the wound. She told me the advice she received deemed that Shane Finn could not have murdered Harris.

Shane had consumed a lethal cocktail of drugs and alcohol on the night Christopher 'Stitch' Harris was stabbed in the chest. He took Rohypnol, "so [he] didn't have to face the day", Valium, Serapax, Doloxenes; and then, between three of them, they drank a 4-litre cask of wine, two bottles of rum and vodka. He couldn't recall any of the events. He was out of it.

At his trial, the third man in the flat claimed he had seen Finn, with a knife in his hands, standing over Harris, shouting out something like, "Do you want to say that about my mother now, you bastard?"

Finn claimed he had been too drunk on the night to form any intent to kill and that he had acted in the heat of passion because he had been provoked by insults to the memory of his murdered mother. He signed the confession. He believes he did the crime. Shane Finn was convicted by a Supreme Court jury of wilful murder and jailed for life.

During his release from jail in June 2004, I raised with him the information from Karry Smith that former Attorney General Peter Foss had reviewed his case as a possible wrongful conviction. Shane didn't want to go there. He had no desire to have his conviction overturned. He has had his share of anger and pain and could not cope with any more. The murder gave him some status that he never really had before. In jail he felt more comfortable; he belonged. 'Murderer' became part of who he was. 'Tough guy', 'angry', 'sociopath', 'heinous criminal'—he'll tell you all the labels himself.

"I would take great umbrage that I may not have done something that I just spent sixteen years of my life paying for. I would rather own it than to have someone say you didn't do that and there's a strong suggestion I didn't.

"No! I own that. I don't give a rat's fucking arsehole. I own it. I'm already going back to jail. Fuck that. I don't want to start getting upset with people and carrying on like a pork chop. No. I own that. No-one's taking that away from me. Fuck that."

While there was no love lost between Shane and his mother, he still wants her killers caught. "I dragged shop keepers over the counter because I couldn't stand people saying things like, 'She's just a fucking whore'. I'm not a sociopath or psychopath, just never spent enough time in society. Being a prisoner and wearing green, it's automatically assumed I'm a liar, so I take great pride in telling the truth because I'm expected to be a liar. That's my quality," Shane said.

At Casuarina maximum security prison, Finn studied art history and visual design. An outstanding artist, he has twice won the Vice-Chancellor's Award for his paintings.

"I was told my painting showed I was obsessed with my mother's death. I explained to them, it was a painting in response to the media's glamorisation, denigration, or dehumanisation of her death," Shane said.

His paintings are bright in shades of pink and purple, multi-layered and smeared with innuendo. His mother is portrayed in the centre as the Queen of Hearts from a playing card—a reference to her oft-used title, the 'Queen of Vice'—with a censor's stamp, a gas mask, scissors, and all sorts of metaphorical objects layered over and around her in a swirl of bright colours. The painting was not what I expected from the man sitting opposite me.

Shane and Steve had been living with Shirley until about two weeks before their mother's murder. Shane had worked out the combination to his mum's safe and taken $20. *"Mum was always generous regarding money for us kids, but four or five months before she died she became real stingy,"* Steve told police, shortly after his mother's death. Shirley lost her temper and kicked Steve out of home. He moved in with friends.

Steve told me he still wishes he was home that day. "I would have at least liked to have made up with her. Knowing that we didn't make amends and we departed on that note. I like to remember my mum standing beside me on good terms."

The father of two worked as a plant fitter in Rockingham, an industrial coastal centre south of Perth, when I met him in 2003. He is gaunt and smokes heavily, but has survived the hard road along which his life has travelled.

He was sixteen when his mother died. He found it hard to accept his mother was a madam and a lesbian because her children's lives had been protected from her business. After her death, the whole sordid affair was constantly in the adolescent's face. When other kids suggested Steve's mother was a madam, he denied it. It was hard enough dealing with her death without coping with the embarrassing rumours and details of her illegal activities and private life.

Radio disc jockeys made jokes about his mother's life and death. He didn't find them funny. His grief is still apparent, made worse by the fact he's never had answers about what happened to his mother.

"We had so many fun times. I could sit down at the end of her bed, she would be sleeping in until 3 o'clock in the afternoon and we could just reel off jokes to each other." He showed me a photo of himself as a toddler laughing. His mother is holding a garden hose, splashing his feet with water. "This is how I want to remember her."

Shane Finn died of cancer in 2011. In the years before his death he turned his life around. He told his sister before he died that he hoped his mother's killer might yet be found and brought to justice.

Steven Finn died in 2016, shortly after the announcement an inquest would be held into his mother's death. Both Bridget's brothers died young, aged in their fifties. Bridget is the only one of her siblings left to carry on the fight.

Not the Final Chapter

Those who do not remember the past are doomed to repeat it.
— George Santayana

I have enormous respect for police and do not underestimate the magnitude of the tasks they deal with every day. They confront human frailties and emotion at their most raw. They unravel lies, fend off aggression, soothe victims and their families when faced with the worst news of their lives, enforce a civil code to smooth the nation's functioning; and they are society's guardians in our hour of need.

Within two years of beginning this story, I realised the case was beyond me—it appeared to be a multi-layered conspiracy that ate away at the heart of our justice system, compromising good police officers and well-intentioned bystanders. In short, the bullies had won.

Men like Spike Daniels, Jim Kenneison and Archie Marshall were left broken on the scrap heap of life. They hadn't stood a chance. Witnesses, who inadvertently saw something they shouldn't have, were still plagued with sleepless nights, fear and guilt—unable to rely on our justice system sufficiently to allow them to share what they knew.

Three broken children, with no chance at justice, were seemingly too beaten to fight. If I have won one battle, it is to see Bridget grow in strength and confidence.

I wanted police to show me where I was wrong: how the WA Police and the WA government would never let this happen in Australia; how our justice system was better than this; and, if the stories I was hearing were true, I hoped for outrage and a quest to find answers and to hold the corrupt accountable. It was a very lonely fight. No one seemed to listen or care. I imagine Spike Daniels felt the same. Archie Marshall is 86-years-old, holding on and waiting for his day in court.

I felt I had let Bridget down and promised to support her fight for justice for her mother. We planned a slow trickling media campaign reminding those that were sitting back resting and believing they had got away with it, that their actions had consequences. Bridget, her brothers, good police officers, civil libertarians, witnesses, and justice were all still hurting.

My children grew up; I changed jobs. My life moved on— a series of deaths—the people on my pages were slipping away. Stella Strong, Des Finn, Owen Leitch, Dorrie Flatman, Ron Cannon, Jim Kenneison and Ray O'Connor—I held a strange relationship with each of them. Then there were Steven and Shane Finn, not much older than me—gone too young, crushed by the weight of their lives. I became the keeper of their stories and news of their deaths reminded me of my buried pages. Some evidence has been lost forever: those who wouldn't speak, or couldn't, or who I didn't get around to speaking with, and who are now not here. Consorting Squad detective Arthur Simms is a suspect. He wanted to speak. He wrote a tell-all book to ease his conscience and then drank himself to death. When I contacted his family, I discovered they were so horrified by the contents of his manuscript they burned the book— secrets up in smoke.

Our long fight was rewarded with the inquest planned in 2017. We do not know what new stories it may uncover. In the last two years alone, we have learned so much from new witnesses who've come forward: Brian, the police officer in the canteen who saw Shirley in the days before she died; Jacqueline who saw Shirley at her home and overheard the threat Finn had received; and Vicky, who went fishing with her friends and saw a rifle pulled from the river. Who knows what other pieces of the puzzle may yet come together?

While much evidence is missing and there are varying versions of events, the available accounts indicate corruption, at every level, and complicity within the government departments that administer justice in Western Australia. From the Crown Law Department, through the Perth City Council and the WA Police Force to Parliament House—even the media was said to be on the payroll of the crooks.

When those that make laws break them, then government itself is endangered. For better or worse this governing body and its servants are society's teachers, by example.

Two systems of law operated in the state of Western Australia. The marginalised, having no recourse to justice, were the greatest victims of corruption. Powerful forces could manipulate the legal system and make the administration of justice difficult for even the most honest and determined judge or lawyer. The powerful, the rich, and the friends of the inner circle could get away with murder, so long as they and their associates didn't speak out. If anyone did tell the truth, their smallest crimes and misdemeanours were ruthlessly pursued, exposed and—where possible—prosecuted.

The failure to fully scrutinise those who set up, organised and were allegedly corrupted through the prostitution trade in the seventies, along with the loss or removal of key evidence and threats to witnesses, has never been addressed by the police force or any anti-corruption bodies in the state.

The crime has left an indelible stain on the reputation of the WA Police Force and the politicians who oversaw them. When no-one was charged with the murder of Shirley Finn, the belief grew that powers beyond the law could commit the most grievous of crimes without redress.

So isolated was Western Australian that a third-world justice system operated with little accountability. Bullying and the exploitation of women was rife. Moguls were born on government cronyism and corruption, patronage was given to men with no scruples; while those on the outside looked on and watched the thievery and skullduggery, unwilling or unable to expose it.

The need for a WA Inc Royal Commission into corruption, illegal conduct, improper conduct and bribery in government in the eighties was a predictable outcome of government policies and practices developed in the sixties and seventies. That politics and crime were so closely linked for several decades remains one of the state's dirtiest secrets—Western Australia truly was the Wild Wild West.

History, evidence and the people who played a part in Shirley Finn's murder are slipping away. I hope for Bridget's sake that the final chapter of this story may one day be written.

Acknowledgments

My agent, George Karlov, is the most tenacious, determined and supportive agent any author could hope for. Your belief that this story should be told, and your support over many years have kept me going when I felt like giving up. Thank you.

To the brave people who stood up to corruption, like Spike Daniels, Avon Lovell, Frank Scott and Archie Marshall: the work you did in the tough days when shining a light was a dangerous business is why so much of this story can now be told. I didn't know Spike, but Archie handed me volumes of material from the era. Archie has fought the long fight and still does.

To those that spoke to me despite being afraid to do so, I appreciate your bravery.

To journalists, such as Torrance Mendez at *The West Australian,* who did the hard yards along the way, thank you for your help.

To Steve Howell at the Battye Library who was able to provide answers to my obscure questions and verify many historical facts. You are a remarkable researcher and a wonderful asset to the state.

To my father, John Wills, and journalist, Deborah Kennedy, thank you for your help in editing the manuscript early on in my journey.

David Conners, a one-man band publishing operation in Brisbane, took on this story when no one else would. Without him, it never would have seen the light of day. He died soon after the first rough draft of the book came out.

From there it gathered momentum, significant new witnesses, more information, and the team at Fontaine were tasked to make sense of the multiple strands and did so with extraordinary professionalism. Their eye for detail breathed new life into the story, streamlining this complicated tale into a more digestible form—invaluable.

My patient husband Jeff put up with sleepless nights and endless interruptions while continuing to encourage me along the way. Because he's interested enough to chat about my work, we found Vicky, who was fishing with friends when they pulled a rifle from the Swan River forty years ago. It may well have been our murder weapon.

And to all my family, friends and colleagues, thank you for listening to my frustrations, despair, hope and endless yarns as I've tried to unravel many twisted tales tracked down in the hope of finding the truth.

Thank you in advance to those who might be inspired by this story to do what is right and come forward with facts and evidence that have remained hidden, and that might help bring closure for all involved.

To the many people who have already contributed their stories, or added to the stories of people who played a part, thank you.

But mostly my thanks go to Bridget and her family. She has become a great friend whom I admire. She has been thrown far more than most people could ever cope with, but she's still fighting. Thank you for your support.

References

INTERVIEWS

Recorded Audio

Jacqueline – Witness. Shirley Finn came to her house in the days leading to the murder.

Archie Marshall – Civil libertarian.

Assistant Commissioner Les Ayton (retired) – Former head of Internal Affairs.

Bert Tudori – Former deputy lord mayor, proprietor of The Zanzibar and Il Trovatore, contained gambling operator.

Bouncer (anon) – Worked with George Stewart and Shirley, and provided security for Shirley.

Brian – Police officer (retired).

Bridget Finn – Shirley's daughter.

Charles James Kenneison – Disbarred barrister who moved money offshore, allegedly for Finn and politicians.

Des Finn – Shirley's ex-husband.

Detective Inspector William (Bill) Read (retired) – Senior investigator on the original investigation.

Dorothea (Dorrie) Flatman – Madam operating under police containment.

Frank Scott – Police whistleblower.

Geoff McMurray – Police officer (retired).

George Stewart – Close friend and confidante of Shirley Finn, former staff member.

George Webber – Shirley's ex-boyfriend. Recorded by Bridget.

General Agency Company (anon).

'Ginger' Rocco Antonetti – Proprietor of Ginger's Two-Up School, contained gambling operator.

Glenn Properjohn – Friend of Shirley Finn, and her dressmaker.

Harvey Tarvydas – GP. Shortly before the death of a patient ('Detective Seven', no known cause of death), that patient told Dr Tarvydas he was going to be killed.

Inspector Bernard Bromilow Johnson (retired) – Head of Consorting Squad in the lead up to Finn murder, allegedly sanctioned Shirley Finn to operate.

James Devereaux – Property owner at William Street brothel, when debt defaulted upon Shirley's death he reclaimed the brothel property.

John Mearns – Witness who reported licence plates of vehicles at murder scene to police.

Kim Flatman – Husband of brothel madam Dorrie Flatman.

Leigh Varis – Driver for Shirley Finn.

Matt Stephens, MLA Nationals (retired) – Received confidential information from George Stewart.

Pat Holmes – Daughter of Violet Walker – A suspicious skeleton washed up on Cottesloe Beach and was discussed in 1975 Royal Commission. In 2004, the skeleton was exhumed with permission of Pat and found to be her mother.

Paul Murray – Journalist, broadcaster and former editor of *The West Australian*.

Ray O'Connor – Former Premier and Police Minister.

Ron Cannon – Barrister and solicitor.

Scherry – Exotic dancer and friend of Shirley Finn.

Shane Finn – Shirley's son.

Stella Strong – Madam operating under police containment.

Steven Finn – Shirley's son.

Tom and Shirley Dercksen – Former Dutch Consul and his wife who rescued Shirley after she was kidnapped near Cervantes.

By Email

David Williams – Author, *This Little Piggy*.

Noted (Interviews with author)

Bill Hassell MLA (retired).

Karry Smith – Working for politician Peter Foss.

Clive Cullinan – Tax consultant.

Clive Griffiths MLA (retired).

Commissioner George Owen Leitch (retired).

'Dave' – Witness who heard shots and saw a police car on the night of the murder.

Detective A. J. Wick (retired).

Detective Arthur Simms (retired).

Don Joshua – Crew member of the Iron Yampi.

Don Sutherland – Witness who drove past the crime scene on the night of the murder.

Edward Spini – Loan title.

Federal Police officer – anon.

Goldfinger – anon.

Hon. Robert French – Chief Justice of the High Court.

'Joe' – Witness who saw a police officer get into Shirley Finn's Dodge from a police van.

John Scott – Friend of Charles 'Chicka' Reeves.

Linda Watson.

Margaret Stewart.

Ron Todman.

Vicky – Fishing with her brother and his friend when they pulled a rifle from the river.

Transcripts of Interviews with Archie Marshall and Spike Daniels.

Des Finn (also tape recorded).

Dot Walsh.

Dulcie (Mary) Scrimgeour.

Interview with Shirley Finn's father, Jo Shewring (also tape recorded).

Pandora Young (also tape recorded).

The following refused interview:

Kerry Tangney.

Sir Charles Court.

WA Police Force.

N.B.: Some sources requested anonymity. This was granted with careful consideration.

BOOKS AND CDS

Bingley, A. N. *On The Game*, Optima Press, WA 1992.

Bottom, B. *Shadow of Shame*, Sun Books 1998.

Bottom, B. *Connections II*, Sun Books 1997.

Brown, M. (ed). *Australian Crime*, The Book Co International 1993.

Brown, M. *Rorting: The Great Australian Crime*, Lansdowne, Australia 1998.

Byrne, G. *Built on a Hilltop – A History of the Sisters of the Good Shepherd in Western Australia 1902-2002*, Sisters of the Good Shepherd, Leederville 2002.

Court, Charles. *Charles Court – The Early Years*, edited by Geoffrey Blainey and Ronda Jamieson, Fremantle Arts Centre Press 1995.

Conole, P. *Protect and Serve. A History of Policing in Western Australia*, WA Police Service 2002.

Cornish, P. *Western Australia in the 20th Century*, Fremantle Arts Centre Press 1999.

Cuter, Jack. *With Malice Aforethought*, St Georges Books 1982.

Dale, J. Huckstepp. *A Dangerous Life*, Allen & Unwin 2000.

Daniels, H. E. *With Equal Poise*, unpublished memoir.

Dawn, C. *Pros And Cons: A Working Girls Guide To The Worlds Oldest Profession*, Pros and Cons, Australia 1998.

De Maria, William. *Deadly Disclosures: Whistleblowing and the Ethical Meltdown Of Australia*, Wakefield Press, SA 1999.

Dempster, Quentin. *Honest Cops*, ABC Enterprises 1992.

Encel, Vivien and Sharpe, Alan. *25 True Australian Crimes*, Kingsclear Books, NSW 1997.

Gregory, J. *City of Light*, City of Perth 2003.

Goldsmith, A., Israel, M., Daly, K. *Crime and Justice: An Australian Textbook in Criminology*, Lawbook Co., NSW 2003.

Hickie, David. *The Prince and the Premier*, Angus & Robertson, NSW 1985.

Jamieson, Ronda. *Charles Court: I Love This Place*, St Georges Books, WA 2011.

Lovell, A. *The Mickelberg Stitch*, Creative Research, Perth 1985.

Lovell, A. *Split Image*, Creative Research, Perth 1990.

McCoy, A. W. *Drug Traffic Narcotics and Organised Crime in Australia*, Harper and Row, Sydney 1980.

O'Brien, P. and Webb, M. *The Executive State, WA Inc and the Consitution*, Constitutional Press 1991.

Perkins, R., Prestage G., Sharp, R., and Lovejoy, F. *Sex Work and Sex Workers in Australia*, UNSW Press 1994.

Prasser, S., Wear, R. and Nethercote, J. (eds). *Corruption and Reform: The Fitzgerald Vision*, University of Qld Press 1990.

Purdue, Brian. *Indictable Offences in Western Australia where a conviction was recorded 1830-1984*, CD Rom.

Read, J. *Marksy: The Life of Jack Marks*, Read Media, South Fremantle, WA 1998.

Reeves, Tony. *Mr Big: Lennie McPherson and his life of Crime*, Allen & Unwin, Sydney 2005.

Reid, G. D. *The Premiers of WA 1890-1982*, University of Western Australia 1982.

Saffron, A. *Gentle Satan: My Life with Abe Saffron*, Penguin Australia 2009.

Sexton, M. *Uncertain Justice: Inside Australia's Legal System*, New Holland 2000.

Walker, Leedham. *The Good Old Days*, Access Press 2000.

Sacks, M. A. (ed). *The Way 79 Who is Who: Synoptic Biographies of Western Australians*, Crawley Publishers, WA 1980.

Smith, Cate. *The Starting Stalls*, WhichCraft Pub, Leederville 1993.

Williams, D. *This Little Piggy Stayed Home*: Barlow, Chambers and the Mafia, Panorama Books 1989.

Whitton, E. *Can of Worms: A Citizen's Reference Book to Crime and the Administration of Justice*, Fairfax Library, Sydney 1986.

ARTICLES AND THESES

Adams, S. and Frances, R. 'Lifting the veil: the representation of sex work in Australian museums and galleries', *Labour History*, no. 85, November 2003, pp.47-64.

Cohen, J. 'Biography of a Kalgoorlie Madam', *Australian Style*, No 7 1994, p.62-65.

Davidson, R. 'Prostitution in Perth and Fremantle and on the Eastern Goldfields 1895-1939', (thesis) 1980.

Johnson, K. and Puchy, A. 'Unsolved murders, Madam Butterfly', *Who Magazine*, 11 December 1995.

Mendez, T. 'Reporting Police and Crime: The Death of a Protected Witness', Australian Centre for Independent Journalism, George Munster Forum 2001. (http://acij.uts.edu.au/forums/2001gmforum2a.html)

Nielsen, R. 'The Politics of Long-Term Corruption Reform: A Combined Social Movement and Action-Learning Approach', *Business Ethics Quarterly*, Volume 10 Issue 1, 2000, pp.305-317.

O'Connor, R.J. '*Interview with Raymond James O'Connor, politician*', interviewed by Stuart Reid, Battye Library 1996.

The West Australian

Sex Charges Bring Gaol, 7 July 73.

Conspiracy Trial Couple Acquitted, 11 August 1973.

Daniels seeks Vice Probe, 7 August 1974.

Police to report on brothels, 9 August 1974.

Accused: I didn't admit robbery, 1 November 1974.

Flannery found not guilty, 7 November 1974.

O'Connor pledges his job, 5 September 1975.

Two Liberals quit at Wembley, 6 September 1975.

Government orders vice probe, 30 September 1975.

Consultant stole $4,500, (re Bernie Carpenter, [1980-undated copy]).

Tangney to stay silent on police, 21 January 1982.

Raid on agent's office, 3 February 1982.

Police above suspicion, says report and No Police cover-up, 31 March 1982.

Bond for man who financed Brothel, June 16 1982.

Murray, P. Madam owes $171,000 in tax, 11 August 1982.

Verboon, K. Detective; My assets must go, 17 December 1982.

Mann, A. Clubs Bar doors to Gamblers, 3 January 1983.

Appeal Fails, 10 February 1988.

Miller W. How Peters traps police Dogs, 16 November 1989. (Reporter a Victorian Policeman policeman for 13 years later trapped Peters with tap, then joined AFP)

Cash, R. State of Crime. WA drugs trio busted by a bug, 13 May 1989.

Solly, R. Escort woman goes out screaming, 25 October 1990.

Solly, R. Vice woman held in police-troop raid, 25 October 1990.

Royal commission echoed 30 years ago, 25 November 1990.

Solly, R. Glamour in the slammer, Robert Taylor, 28 November 1990.

Cash, R. Business lured tycoon, ex-police, con-victim, 20 March 1991.

Chatty, J. Found guilty in race-fix case, 23 February 1995.

Gibson, R. QC: O'Connor stole $25,000 donation, 2 November 1993.

Mendez, T. Police say file is intact, 15 September 1994.

Mendez, T. Police killed Finn: witness 17 September 1994.

Chatty, J. Connell reveals offer to get rid of witnesses, 21 February 1995.

Lang, M. Down, a rocky road to ruin, 18 February 1995.

Barrass, T. Police 'wanted laundry', 9 November 1995.

Cash, R. Links in the Golden Chain, 20 December 1995.

Bell, S. Policeman's wife owns eight brothels, 12 July 1996.

Townsend, J. Child vice report Shock, 23 May 1998.

No money for Net Porn Sting, 28 May 1998.

Adshead, G. Bert and the bikie; Why is Perth's Deputy Lord Mayor having coffee with a top Coffin Cheater? 29 November 2003.

Gibson, R. Gem probe cop 'beyond bribe', Friday 8 August 2003.

Banks, A. Tudori, bikie met at PCC over nightclub, 2 December 2003.

Longley, G. Bert's den was a safe bet, 6 December 2003.

Adshead, G, WA detectives question former cops, 23-24 May 2015.

Taylor, G. Ex-cop named in new claim on Finn death, 20-21 Februray 2016.

The Sunday Independent

Amery, C. & Van Steyn, M.Top Secret Drug Probe, 5 September 1976.

Drug 'Liars' in Test, 12 September 1976.

More Drug Allegations; six others speak out, 12 September 1976.

The Detectives: Police Act against Squad's Accusers, 17 September 1976.

Lawyers Move Against 'Grave' Police Actions, 17 October 1976.

Inside Perth's Illegal Casinos, 24 October 1976.

Thousands Lost on the Tables, 24 October 1976

Gambling Charade, 31 October 1976.

Gold Running linked to WA, 21 November 1976.

Madam offers house to charity, 14 February 1982.

The Daily News

Plot to Break Police, 6 September 1976.

Drug Allegations; Plot to Break Police Daily News, 6 September 1976.

New Police Blast, 15 September 1976.

Police sold me pot - witness, 27 October 1981.

More Police 'Deals' Claim, 28 October 1981.

Those who tell are targets, 11 February 1982.

D'Orazio M. Dixon Backs Phone Taps, 31 March 1982.

Police okayed brothel, 15 June 1982.

The Western Mail

Mayman, J. The Big-Time Criminals Have Arrived, 19 September 1981.

Night that Rasputin lost $22,500, 28 November 1981.

Police Quit after Claims of Pay-offs, 24-27 December 1981.

The Mysterious murder of a flamboyant madam, 16 January 1982.

Tangney talks of pay-offs at South Perth Christmas party, 16 January 1982.

Wilson, M. Axed cops call for big 'graft' probe, 16-17 January 1982.

Wilson, M. Perth prostitutes name MP's, 23 January 1982.

Madam owes $171, 000 in tax, 6 February 1982.

Wilson, M. Pair to snub Dixon Probe, 13 February 1982.

Another Cop Quits (undated following Dixon report).

Dixon gets tape of threat, 6 March 1982.

Smokescreen, 3-4 April 1982.

National Times

Graham, D. If you want a brothel ask a policeman, 2 January 1986.

The Sunday Times

Robinson, B. Police Minister orders WA Mafia Inquiry, 16 July 1972.

Big Gambling Ring Smashed, Based In WA Say Police, 25 October 1972.

Argo, P. Huge Gold Thefts in WA Linked to Drugs, 3 August 1975.

Argo, P. Dust-to Dust end to heady era of riches Sunday Times, 8 August 1975.

Pratt, B. Murdered Madam's Private World, 29 August 1975.

Argo, P. Police raid smashes gang of white slavers, WA girl on her way home, 23 July 1978.

Sattler, H. $1000 graft a week to police, 31 January 1982.

Jacobson, I. Dealings Done for Ginger, 31 December 1995.

Taylor N. Why the heat is on WA's police force, June 1996.

The Sydney Sun Herald

Report of speech from Independent MP Dennis Stevenson, ACT Legislative Assembly, 28 April 1991.

Alan Gill. Bad girls do the best sheets, 24 April 2003.

GOVERNMENT PUBLICATIONS

Austrac – Money laundering and Financial Industry Regulators, Serious Criminal Activities, Bill Coad, 9 March 2001. http://www.austrac.gov.au/publications/other_documents/moneylaundering/45.html.

Commonwealth – New South Wales Joint Task Force on drug trafficking, 1982 AGPS Canberra.

Community Panel on Prostitution, Submission by the West Australian Branch of the Australian Association of Social Workers, May 1990.

Disciplinary Appeal Board re Abraham Bercove, 21 February 1983.

Evans, J.L. *The Proceeds of Crime: Problems of Investigation and Prosecution*, International Centre for Criminal Law Reform and Criminal Justice Policy at the University of British Columbia.

Leaked police file on Kalgoorlie Sting, 1975.

National Crime Authority – *Annual Reports 1984-1990*, AGPS Canberra.

Office of the Information Commissioner (WA) – *Tickner and Police*, 1994 File Ref: 94110.

Organised Crime – papers presented by Mr Douglas Meagher QC to the 53rd ANZAAS Congress, Perth Western Australia, 16 to 20 May 1983.

Organised Criminal Activity A Report by the Parliamentary Joint Committee on the National Crime Authority, November1995 http://www.aph.gov.au/senate/committee/nca_ctte/ncapedo/ncapedo1.html.

Parliament of the Commonwealth of Australia, *Asian Organised Crime in Australia*, a Discussion Paper by the Parliamentary Joint Committee on the National Crime Authority, February 1995.

Police Report by Detective IC W. H. Read. *Inquiry into the murder of Shirley June Finn*, 7 April 1976.

R. L. Hailstone *Ethical Decision Making in the Public Sector*, Criminal Justice Commission, 28 August 1997.

APA Citation
Australian Royal Commission of Inquiry into Drugs, Gilmour, G. H., Lenihan, D. M., Linford, R., & Williams, E. S. 1. (1980). Australian Royal Commission of Inquiry into Drugs: Report. Canberra: A.G.P.S..

MLA Citation
Australian Royal Commission of Inquiry into Drugs, et al. Australian Royal Commission of Inquiry Into Drugs: Report. Canberra: A.G.P.S., 1980.

Report of the Royal Commission into Gambling, Mr P. R. Adams QC, Chairman, 1974.

Review of the Western Australia Police Witness Protection Program Report by Len Roberts-Smith RFD QC Vol 1 & Vol 2, 30 June 2000.

Royal Commission into Matters surrounding the Administration of the Law Relating to Prostitution. The Hon. J.G. Norris – Commissioner, Mr W. J Shepherd – Secretary, Counsel assisting – D. O'Dea. 1975.

Royal Commission into whether there has been any corrupt or criminal behaviour by and Western Australian Police Officer, Geoffrey Kennedy QC Government of Western Australia 2004.

Royal Commission of Inquiry into Drug Trafficking. Justice D. G. Stewart AGPS Canberra 1983.

Royal Commission on Newspaper Articles regarding the Totalisator Agency Board by Major General Sir Douglas Anthony Kendrew by James Herbert Forrest, 2 November 1967.

Royal Commission on the activities of the Federated Ship Painters and Dockers Union. F. X. Costigan QC. Interim Report 1982 and Final Report 1984 AGPS Canberra.

Select Committee on the Western Australian Police Service Hon. Derrick Tomlinson MLC Parliament of Western Australia, June 1996.

Shirley Finn – Western Australia Police Force Correspondence between Tax Office and S. Finn and Witness depositions, obtained under FOI.

State Records – CIB Perth file 75/50882 Re: Human female skeletal and other remains found at Cottesloe Beach, 7 September 1975.

The Northbridge History Project; Department of Premier and Cabinet, 2007.

The Supplementary Report of O. F. Dixon on, The action taken by the police regarding allegations of graft and corruption within the police force and What further action is necessary regarding such allegations, 1982.

Thomas A. Lawson. Justice on the Edge. http://www.ditpublishing.com/justice/index. html, 21 January 2001.

Violet Walker – missing person file – WA Police 1975 obtained under FOI.

Want to make a bet?: gambling and crime in Australasia, Australasian Centre for Policing Research – by Rebekah Doley, 2000.

Wayward Governance: Illegality and its Control in the Public Sector, Australian Institute of Criminology, 13 November 2002. http://www.aic.gov.au/publications/lcj/ wayward/ch9.html

Western Australian Parliamentary Hansard

OTHER GOVERNMENT SOURCES

ASIC – Company Searches.

Births, Deaths and Marriages.

LANDGATE – land title searches.

Metropolitan Cemeteries Board – http://www.mcb.wa.gov.au/nameSearch.html

National Archives Australia – Immigration papers (Zdena Hockova), Service Records, Court Cases.

Supreme Court File transcripts. (Murder trial of prostitute Lisa – 1974, trial of Max (Rodgers) perjury).

TELEVISION/RADIO/WEB/THEATRE

Perkins R. Street Prostitution and its Manipulation by Law, Uni. of NSW.

Smith, C. Starting Stalls, 2003.

STW9 A Current Affair. Bernie Johnson Speaks, November 2008 Paula Hudson.

STW9 A Current Affair. Mr Rentakill – The WA connection, Louise Momber.

The Poseidon Adventure and the Stock Market – Trevor Sykes and Frank Crook ABC online "memories", 1969.

www.aic.gov.au/publications/proceedings/16/ Perkins.pdf.

PAPERS HELD BY THE FINN FAMILY

Child Welfare Department re: Shirley (Finn) 1955-1966. (N.B. – the government later refused Bridget access to these papers).

Shirley June Shewring- school reports

The Estate documents from the Public Trustee.

Who's Who?

THE COPS

Ayton, Les – WA Deputy Commissioner of Police and head of Internal Affairs (retired). Chased Detective Johnson for many years without result.

Brian – The 40-year career cop who saw Finn in the police canteen in the days leading up to her murder. Buried the secret for 40 years due to threats to him and his family.

Daniels, Harold Edwin 'Spike' – Police Superintendent – whistleblower. Crushed for speaking out. Died disgraced and humiliated in 1992.

Detective Seven – Resigned after inquiries into allegations of protection payments from prostitutes in the 1980s. He died in suspicious circumstances.

Hancock, Don – Detective – 'The Grey Fox'. Murdered by a bomb placed under his car in Perth in 2001. Was a member of the Finn murder investigation team. Framed the Mickelberg brothers for the theft of gold bars from the Perth Mint in 1982.

Johnson, Bernard Bromilow – Detective – (retired) head of Consorting Squad at time of Finn murder, allegedly ran gambling and prostitution protection racket. Nicknamed the King of Vice.

Kiernan, Max – WA Detective – (retired) in charge of prostitution control with Wick, Tangney and Johnson in the lead up to the Finn murder. The 2002 Kennedy Royal Commission into police corruption heard allegations that Kiernan received a corrupt payment to shut down an inquiry into the theft of diamonds from the Argyle Diamond Mine.

Leitch, Owen – Commissioner of Police in 1975. Fast tracked to the top two months after the Finn murder.

Lewandowski, Anthony – Detective – his conscience got the better of him and he confessed to fabricating evidence against Peter Mickelberg who was wrongfully convicted over the Perth Mint Swindle in 1982. Committed suicide.

Rogerson, Roger – The serial killer cop convicted of the murder of James Gao in 2016. The NSW detective was said to be in Perth at the time of the Finn murder with suspect and friend, Detective Bernie Johnson.

Scott, Frank – Police whistleblower.

Simms, Arthur – Detective and suspect in the Finn murder. He wanted to talk and wrote a manuscript, but the manuscript was burned.

Skeffington, John – Detective Skeffington, Johnson and Whitmore gave Dorrie Flatman the green light to run her trade monopoly in Perth and helped shut down her opposition. After leaving the force he became a business partner with Detective Bernie Johnson and Kim Ng in Kim Wah Seafood importers.

Tangney, Kerry – Detective in charge of prostitution control at time of Finn murder. He alleged police were involved in the Finn murder after he was dismissed from the force in the wake of a drug scandal.

Whitmore, Ron – Detective. Consorting officer working in prostitution control. Whitmore and Johnson arrested Shirley Finn ahead of her entry into the containment system.

Wick, Tony – Detective in charge of prostitution control in the lead up to the Finn murder. He resigned in 1982 in the wake of corruption scandal alleging he and colleague Detective Seven collected payments from Perth prostitutes.

THE GIRLS

Bercove, Marlene – Ran escort agency, arrived from Sydney around the same time as Dorrie Flatman. Marlene was married to Abraham Bercove – Crown Law Solicitor. She was secretary cum receiver for some 100 'Bottom of the Harbour' companies while her husband's job was to prosecute tax evasion in WA.

Dean, Rosalie (a.k.a. Black) – Shirley's partner, Rose. Grew up rough in Victoria before finding shelter with Shirley Finn.

Brifman, Shirley – Prostitute and madam who blew the whistle on corrupt cops in Queensland and NSW. The crown case against some of the police officers fell apart when she was found dead in 1972 of a barbiturate overdose in a Queensland safe house. No inquest was held.

Davies, Janet – Arrived from Sydney with Dorrie after the Sydney brothel wars in the sixties. Still running January's brothel in 2004, next door to former Il Trovatore gambling club.

De Bray, Josie – Roe Street madam. Had all her property confiscated during the Second World War. The Federal government became landlord. Roe Street was shut down in 1959.

Lisa (alias) – Flatman prostitute who killed her husband after enduring years of domestic violence. Spoke to Superintendent Daniels and told him big money had changed hands to drop prostitution charges. She then changed her story at the Norris Royal Commission.

Finn, Shirley – Madam. Murdered because she knew too much.

Flatman, Dorrie – The top dog in the WA sex industry in the seventies. Ran seven brothels in Sydney and then took over the brothel trade in Perth in the late sixties. To her deathbed, she denied paying police.

Harding, Gladys – Former Roe St madam. Shut out when Dorrie and Shirley took over the trade.

Helen – Ran Bettina's Brothel for Dorrie Flatman. Showed former madam, Gladys Harding, three envelopes and said one was to pay police.

Irene – Kalgoorlie brothel madam. Her husband, Joe Borg, headed up the brothel trade in Sydney's notorious

Doors district until he was killed in a car bombing in 1968. Irene headed west with many of Borg's associates and set up in Kalgoorlie.

Pandora – Madam who tried to operate but couldn't get police approval. Told police whistleblower Spike Daniels she was subjected to violence and mafia threats and forced to leave.

Scherry (alias) – Topless go-go dancer who worked at the Oasis Nightclub with Shirley Finn.

Scrimgeour, Dulcie (Mary) – Former Roe St madam. Shut out when Dorrie and Shirley took over the trade. Bought a 'contained' brothel after Shirley's death.

Strong, Stella – Ran brothels in Sydney before heading west in the late sixties. Police protected madam in Perth with Shirley Finn and Dorrie Flatman, before fleeing to Kalgoorlie after a series of fire-bombings.

Varis, Leigh – Former Kalgoorlie councillor, driver for Shirley Finn. Said she regularly drove the Police Minister, and later Premier Ray O'Connor, around with Shirley Finn.

Walsh, Dot – Former Roe St madam. Shut out when Dorrie and Shirley took over the trade.

Watson, Linda – Former madam. Blew the whistle on police protection money and then started an exit house for girls who wanted to escape prostitution.

ROGUE'S GALLERY

Antonetti, Rocco 'Ginger' – Gambling identity, ran Ginger's 'Two-Up' School in Northbridge under the containment system. Knew Shirley and knew the system. Said not only was Finn murdered, but her son was set up for a murder he didn't commit.

Borg, Joe – Blown up in the Sydney brothel wars of the late sixties. His wife and some of his girls fled to Perth where they continued to work in the contained brothel industry

Butterly, Archibald – charged with Christopher 'Rentakill' Flannery and Robyn Holt over David Jones Robbery in Perth in 1975 when a security guard was shot. Holt and Butterly were convicted, but Flannery was acquitted. Butterly was later convicted with WA bikie Coffin Cheater, Eddie Withnell, over violent armed robbery in 1977.

Connell, Laurie – Race fixer, conman, merchant banker, fraudster. One of Australia's biggest corporate crooks, behind the collapse of Rothwells' merchant bank with estimated losses of 600 million dollars. Used government mates for the bailout in what became known as WA Inc. Died Feb 1996.

Flannery, Christopher – Hitman, known as 'Mr Rent-A-Kill'. Carried out the dirty work for corrupt NSW cop, Roger Rogerson, and others. Arrested by Bernie Johnson and Kerry Tangney over the 1974 David Jones robbery in Perth. Sydney criminal, Neddy Smith, said Flannery paid a bribe to Rogerson to escape conviction. Flannery is missing, presumed dead.

Holt, Robyn – Convicted of armed robbery of David Jones in Perth with Archibald Butterly in 1974. Hitman Christopher Flannery was acquitted of the crime.

Mussari, Paul – Heroin trafficker and drug kingpin who spent most of his adult life behind bars.

Ng, Kim – Business partner of Bernie Johnson and Laurie Connell in seafood company in the 1980s. Exposed Sydney Chinatown drug rackets in the late sixties then fled west. Close relationship with police in Sydney and WA.

Rispoli, Carlo and Enrico – Illegal casino operators with relatives, Bert and Lawrie Tudori. Partners in Il Trovatore. Money lenders.

Rispoli, Vincent – Brother-in-law to Bert and Laurie. Ran Il Trovatore until the casino expanded in the seventies.

Saffron, 'Abe' Abraham – Mr Sin. Nightclub owner and property developer said to head up organised crime in Australia. Ran hotels and nightclubs Australia-wide. In Perth, he owned the Raffles Hotel at Applecross and three other hotels. He corrupted politicians and cops across the country, and 'fixed' any problems they got into.

Tudori, Bert and Lawrence (Laurie) – The protected gambling lords of the day. Also said to be involved in prostitution and to partner with police detective

Bernie Johnson in illegal gambling and gold tenements.

THE POLITICIANS

Askin, Sir Robert – NSW Premier. Allegedly made a deal with nightclub owner and Sydney crime king, Abe Saffron, to organise crime. Was a similar deal made in the West?

Brand, Sir David – WA's longest serving Premier – 1959-1971. In the Brand government, Ray O'Connor was Minister supporting Charles Court.

Burke, Brian – Premier 1983 – His government got into bed with big business and paid the price. Disgraced over the WA Inc scandal. Jailed for fraud in 1994 and sentenced to two years jail; jailed again in 1997 for three years for stealing ALP party funds.

Court, Sir Charles – Premier 1975–1982. Replaced David Brand in 1972 as head of the Liberal Party in WA, defeating ALP Premier John Tonkin in 1975 to become Premier. Premier at the time of the Finn murder

Dowding, Peter – Premier 1988-1990, succeeding Brian Burke. Barrister. During the WA Inc inquiry, he was criticized for continuing to support Rothwells' Merchant Bank at enormous cost to WA taxpayers when it was clear the bank was doomed to fail. In 1975, Dowding represented police whistleblower, Spike Daniels, at the Norris Royal Commission.

O'Connor, Ray – Minister for Police at the time of the Finn murder. Premier 1982-83. Succeeded Sir Charles Court. Convicted of fraud following the WA Inc scandal and jailed in 1995. He was said to have been having a relationship with Shirley Finn in the years leading up to her murder.

Stephens, Matt – National Party MLA in the seventies. Friend and supporter of whistleblower Spike Daniels.

Tonkin, John – ALP Premier WA 1971-74.

THE LAWYERS

Cannon, Ron – Barrister and solicitor. Shirley Finn's lawyer; held Finn's trust account and tidied up the books on her death. The books were never called for evidence.

Kenneison, Charles James – Commercial lawyer. Moved millions of dollars for Shirley Finn. Alleged Sir Charles Court moved money through Hong Kong Bank accounts. Was soon after disbarred and arrested on fraud charges. Has made repeated complaints of corruption to the police and government bodies.

Norris, J. R. – Judge. Headed Royal Commission into the Laws relating to Prostitution, which blatantly ignored evidence of corruption.

French, Robert – Chief Justice of the High Court of Australia. Represented Spike Daniels at the Norris Royal Commission.

THE WITNESSES

The Bouncer – Spoke to Shirley the day she died. Worked as security at Finn & Flatman brothels.

Healey, Mick – Acting Private Secretary to Ray O'Connor, witnessed a meeting between Bernie Johnson and Ray O'Connor and other businesspeople on Friday night before the murder.

Jacqueline – Partner of SP Bookmaker Don Mack. Shirley came to her home two days before she died and was overheard by Jacqueline saying she'd been threatened. Held her secret for 40 years due to fear.

Mearns, John – Passed by the crime scene in a vehicle with his wife on the morning after the murder and saw a green car parked next to Shirley's Dodge. Wrote down the number plate and tried to give it to police. Gave several statements to police that went missing.

Max 'Rodgers' (alias) – Claims he saw Bernie Johnson near the crime scene around 10pm on the night of the murder, mentioned it to Johnson and was bashed as a result. Involved in illegal dealings with Laurie Connell under the alias 'Rodgers'.

Sutherland, Don – Drove passed the crime scene about 11pm and saw two men leaving hastily. Got a good look at them and when he heard about the crime went to police wanting to give detailed descriptions. They didn't want to know. He did give a statement, but when he applied to police to get it, it wasn't there.

'*Joe*' *(alias)* – Saw a white van at the crime scene around 10pm on the night of the murder. Got a good look at the occupant. Repeatedly tried to give the information to police.

'*Dave*' (alias) – parked near the crime scene on the night of the murder. Heard gunshots and saw a white van and a black car. Warned to keep quiet.

THE BUSINESSMEN

Brown, Ron – Wealthy businessman who bought a new yacht, Ebb Tide. When Bernie skipped town after the murder, he sailed off on Ebb tide.

Dymock, Edward – Shirley's accountant.

Evans, Rod – SP bookmaker. John Curtin Foundation – WA Inc – Brian Burke. Friend and associate of Shirley Finn.

Mack, Don – SP Bookmaker and owner of the Oasis Nightclub where Shirley Finn worked.

Jones, Jo – The mysterious foreign banking representative who Kenneison says assisted Shirley Finn in getting money offshore for businesses and politicians.

Stewart, George – Business partner with Shirley Finn at the Royal Show. Shirley had a body painting tent next to his boxing tent. Close friend of Shirley Finn who knew too much. Hand-grenades were put on his lawn as a warning not to speak out.

Webber George – Shirley Finn's partner when she first started in the containment system.

FONTAINE
—PRESS—

Check out more great Australian true crime books:
visit www.fontainepress.com

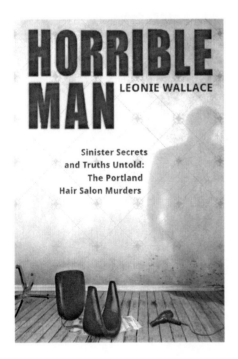

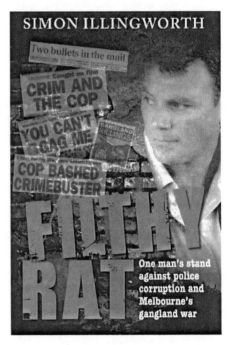

Words, once printed, have a life of their own.

CPSIA information can be obtained
at www.ICGtesting.com
Printed in the USA
LVOW10s1218100517
533994LV00001B/125/P